Here Comes Everybody

Here Comes Everybody

Bodymind and Encounter Culture

William C. Schutz

IRVINGTON PUBLISHERS,INC.
551 FIFTH AVENUE NEW YORK,N.Y. 10017

First Irvington Edition 1982
Copyright © 1971 by William C. Schutz

Library of Congress Cataloging in Publication Data

Schutz, William C.
    Here comes everybody.

    Reprint. Originally published: 1st ed. New York:
Harper & Row, 1971.
    Bibliography: p.
    Includes index.
    1. Group relations training.   I.   Title.
HM132.S383   1982   158'.2   82-7784
ISBN o-8290-0972-8
ISBN 0-8290-0971-X (pbk.)

To Michael Murphy
and the Flying Circus:

Bettsie Carter
Seymour Carter
Linda Cross
Betty Fuller
Anne Heider
John Heider
Stuart Miller
Sukie Miller
Pamela Portugal
Steve Stroud

Contents

Bulletins

The great fact emerges that after that historic date all holographs so far exhumed initialled by Haromphrey bear the sigla H.C.E. and while he was only and long and always good Dook Umphrey for the hunger-lean spalpeens of Lucalizod and Chimbers to his cronies it was equally certainly a pleasant turn of the populace which gave him as sense of those normative letters the nickname Here Comes Everybody. An imposing everybody he always indeed looked, constantly the same as and equal to himself and magnificently well worthy of any and all such universalization, . . .

—James Joyce, *Finnegan's Wake*

Introduction

Caleb is my older son. He's fourteen, and we have a reverse generation gap. I'm too hip for him. He disagrees with many of the things I say. He likes it that many people recognize me, unless they disapprove of me. Then he's embarrassed, and doesn't want them to know we're related.

My severest critic, he nevertheless occasionally puts a principle of mine into practice. Like openness. A black student in his newly integrated school called Caleb "Mac." Finally Caleb got up the courage to tell him he didn't like to be called "Mac." Just as the black didn't like to be called "Boy," Caleb didn't like "Mac." Caleb told him with trepidation. But to his surprise and delight it worked. No more "Mac." And they're beginning to become friends. Caleb told me this with great enthusiasm and great caution. He didn't want me to think he approved generally of my ideas. Just that in this instance honesty did seem to work.

That's what this book is about. Trying a new way of being,

even though it may be a little frightening. Technically, being honest with people and in touch with yourself isn't a new admonition. But we barely do it at all. The dishonesty rampant in this country is poisoning people just as our air and water are being poisoned. It must stop.

"Here comes everybody" is borrowed from Joyce's character H.C.E. in *Finnegan's Wake*. When people are regarded superficially their differences are accentuated—black and white, male and female, aggressive and passive, intellectual and emotional, happy and sad, radical and reactionary. But as we understand each other, differences fade and the oneness of man emerges— the same needs, the same fears, the same struggles, the same desires. Here comes everybody.

The bodymind concept—the unity of all levels of man—and the encounter group offer ways of penetrating deeply, of contacting people at their core, of getting to the parts of everyone that are alike. These methods help people get past the different ways that each copes with his life, to look around and find that everyone is trying to cope with the same problem, just using different methods. Here comes everybody.

The open encounter group is the chief method discussed in this book. It is a specific technique, but its ramifications extend to wherever people are. Encounter is a way of being. It could be the basis for a new culture: the encounter culture. I'm going to go into detail as to how I think such groups operate best, as well as into their underlying philosophy.

Encounter groups are proliferating today. The national media—*Time, Look, Newsweek, Life*—now cover encounter groups. Encounter group leaders appear on television talking to Johnny Carson, Merv Griffin, David Susskind, David Frost, and Dick Cavett. Industry, education, government, and religious institutions are all conducting encounter groups. Free universities abound with them. Rightwingers view them with screeching alarm and pack up their representatives armed with newspaper clippings to tour the countryside and warn the citizenry.

Proponents claim that encounter is the great hope of the civilization, a revolution in psychotherapy, the basis for a new and greater education, a revolution in the relations between couples, the best hope for black-white, student-administration, and international relations. Persons who have gone to encounter workshops do report astonishing life-changing effects on their marriages, careers, and feelings about themselves.

Opponents, who usually attack encounter under the name "sensitivity training," claim encounters meddle into private lives. They call it hate therapy, brainwashing, and claim it reduces people to group-think, obliterating individuality, undermining morality and democracy, and eliminating respect for authority and the absolute values that have made our country great.

What is this phenomenon that can rouse such a storm? I have been conducting encounter groups for about thirteen years and I believe strongly in them and in the principles that underly them. I'd like to describe my view of encounter as clearly as possible because of the great relevance of this phenomenon to the social problems and to eternal personal verities. This book can also be of value to psychotherapists, for it presents many alternatives to traditional methods and a somewhat atypical idea of the role of the therapist. To best realize this value, it should be supplemented by my earlier book, *Joy.*

Recent objections to the dominant American culture have been grouped under the term "counterculture." This term embodies many justifiable and timely criticisms of the present social structure, but it is weak on alternatives. I view the encounter culture as offering a real alternative. This alternative is a process rather than a specific set of solutions to problems. Encountering requires open relating, self-awareness, and total unity of the self. This basis for human relationships can replace the present hypocritical stance as a necessary step before more civilized, meaningful, and rational solutions to social problems can be attained.

The type of interaction basic to an encounter culture actually occurs in what I call the *open encounter*. The meaning of "encounter" is derived from its meaning in the phrase "encounter group," but it is used here without the word "group" to indicate that encounter is an everyday way of relating not restricted to a special type of group.

The encounter group derived from the T-group (T for training) originated by the National Training Laboratories in 1947. The T-group originally concentrated primarily on group process, that is, on phases of group development, group roles, leadership patterns, and the decision-making process.

About five years later, the T-group began to pay more attention to individual dynamics. The term "sensitivity training" was adopted to describe this development, which began in California, as well as to describe the original T-groups. The term "encounter group," or "basic encounter group" as used by Carl Rogers, has become associated more with the primarily personally oriented T-group, that is, one that focuses on the individual. The "open encounter group" uses the format of an encounter group, aims at personal growth and realization of human potential, and admits a wide range of other types of activities into the experience if they give promise of enhancing the aims of the group.

"Open" has several meanings. For one, the encounter is open to all sorts of methods. It borrows from any approach that seems promising and incorporates that approach into the encounter framework. This incorporation has already occurred with dramatic methods, fantasy, hypnosis, nonverbal, meditation, mysticism, massage, sensory awareness, and a wide variety of methods involving the body and energy. "Open" also implies that the method is always changing and evolving. The groups we run today are run very differently from last year's and next year's groups. "Open" also underlines the basic ingredient of the technique, openness and honesty. This is the necessary foundation on which the rest is built, and without which there cannot be open encounter.

"Open encounter" refers not only to the specific situation of an encounter group, but also to a way of being with people outside any deliberate setting. I regard it as the ultimate application of the encounter group: normal social relations that have the openness and honesty, the spontaneity and affection, the directness and clarity that can be attained now in encounter groups.

This book begins with some theoretical ideas. I'm suspicious of theory. Too often it's used to legitimate personal needs. If a therapist is uncomfortable looking people in the eye, he can evolve a theory that requires placing the patient out of eye range. If a therapist feels clumsy initiating action toward people, he can construct a theory that requires the therapist only to respond. If the therapist is easily bored, he can devise a theory that elicits screaming, yelling, crying, fighting. This unsubtle characterization of Freudian, Rogerian, and my own approaches illustrates the possibilities of a theorist's personality affecting his theory. Lack of awareness of this relationship can be a drawback. I'm going to try to stay aware, and as I write, I'm going to encounter the book, and I'll record some of my feelings. Right now I'm concerned about making pontifical statements that are, in fact, based on the humble origins of my own weaknesses. I don't mean that a theory is wrong because it has a humble origin, simply that the reader should examine it carefully. Maybe the theory is more true for me, personally, than for most people. Or there may be exceptions to it that I'm not aware of. When I'm aware of a relevant personal need, I'll mention it, and you can be the judge. I'll start now.

My family's life was based on evasion. People rarely talked

straight. Everything was aimed at presenting an appearance. My own ability to be open and honest is something I've developed since I've become an adult, and I'm still not great at it. Possibly I go overboard on the importance of openness because it's so hard for me to be open. I always had the feeling that important things were happening around our house about which no one told me. "Children should be seen and not heard." So I force my groups to be open, to tell me everything. Don't hide anything from me! And I love gossip. I love to know everything that's going on. Perhaps if this weren't such a concern for him, another therapist would be more balanced in this area.

The progress that I have made toward being open spoils me for people who aren't as open. And I often suspect that one reason for running groups as I do is to help create people whom I like better. This is difficult to say—arrogant, pompous—but it's important to say even if it seems unsavory if I'm to be open with you in a way that is helpful.

One other personal need strikes me as I read over what I've written. I went to some lengths to give my approach a distinctive name. I want the credit for it, and the unique name helps. Perhaps I've tried too hard to make my approach different for that reason. Maybe it isn't really that different. After all, many psychotherapies and group approaches stress honesty. Why is mine different? Well, I do it more . . . oh . . . we'll see.

As I wrote much of this material, I was overcome periodically by feelings of incompetence: feelings that many people know more than I do about what I'm writing, that I was simply borrowing techniques from other people and putting them together. And I worried about giving other people enough credit for what I learned from them, for I sometimes have a tendency to stop someone who's telling me a good idea because I want to have had it. Further, in my desire to be unique and better, I sometimes deprecate other approaches more than I would like to. Having now written it, I think it will be less of a problem, but please keep these things in mind as you read.

This book is about encounter as a way of being as exemplified by the open encounter group, a group oriented toward release and development of the human potential of its members. The open encounter group is an expansion of a psychotherapy group. It has profound implications for education, it is relevant to the development of creativity, it can help people who live and/or work together get along more happily and productively, it is an effective way of dealing with social conflict, and it could serve as a model for all human relations in or out of an encounter group.

Open encounter is based on the belief that man is a unified being and functions on many levels at once: physical, emotional, intellectual, interpersonal, social, and spiritual. These levels are intimately interrelated, and actions on any one level are inevitably accompanied by actions on all others. Further, the laws that hold for man as a unified organism also apply to a group and larger social units. The principles used to understand individuals and groups are, in essence, the same.

There is a life flow in man on all of these levels, an energy that flows through cycles of motivation, preparation, performance, and consummation. When these energy cycles are interrupted, physical blocks lead to physical illness, emotional blocks to mental illness, intellectual blocks to underachieving, social blocks to incompatibility, war, and violence, and spiritual blocks postpone a realization of the total man. Removal of blocks is the therapeutic task; development of the energy cycles is the task of education and living fully.

One's self-concept is the set of presumptions under which he acts. It is his self-perception on all levels: physical, emotional, intellectual, interpersonal, social, and spiritual. If he has a weak and restricted self-concept he will not act up to his full capacity. As his self-concept is expanded and enhanced, more of a man will be utilized and his life flow will be invigorated.

The life flow functions best in the presence of openness. Blocks can be removed when an individual is open to himself and to others. Achieving self-awareness and being open and honest with others allows the energy to flow freely. Self-deception and dishonesty block energy and take it out of the life flow. The open encounter unblocks energy and allows it to be used for more productive purposes.

Man's self-concept is enhanced when he takes responsibility for himself. If he feels that he is responsible, competent, important, and lovable, he will be more likely to express those parts of himself.

I have stated the philosophy of open encounter in some spiritual terms—life flow, energy cycle—because I feel the spiritual element is central, although I don't understand it well. This philosophy could also be put in terms of trying to find and free the god that is within each man. The tenet of individual responsibility is actually a plea to relate to each man's strength or goodness rather than to his sickness. The spiritual ideas are all very new for me but I feel that as this work continues they will become more central and clearer just as the relation of body, mind, and group is now becoming clearer.

Here Comes Everybody

A CONCEPTION OF MAN AND HUMAN RELATING

The Body

Understanding the body is central to the philosophy of open encounter. Man is indeed a unity; and the body, the mind, the feelings, interpersonal behavior, and the spirit are all manifestations of one essence. Every thought, gesture, muscle tension, feeling, stomach gurgle, nose scratch, fart, hummed tune, slip of the tongue, illness—everything is significant and meaningful and related to the now. It is possible to know and understand oneself on all these levels, and the more one knows the more he is free to determine his own life.

If I know what my body tells me, I know my deepest feelings and I can choose what to do. If I know how to control the chemical balance in my body, I can put myself in any state I wish, ecstasy, vigilance, or whatever. Given a complete knowledge of myself, I can determine my life; lacking that mastery, I am controlled in ways that are often undesirable, unproductive, worrisome, and confusing.

1

As an example, here's an exercise. It will be more meaningful if you do it now, before reading on. (I learned this from Dorothy Nolte.) Shut your eyes and imagine that you want very strongly to be somewhere else, but I am forcing you to remain right where you are. Do that for about a minute before reading on.

Now consider where you feel this feeling in your body. Some people feel it in the face, others in the jaws, arms, chest, or legs. I usually feel it most strongly as a pull in my throat. One day I was sitting in a friend's room talking with two people. Suddenly my throat began feeling tight. Remembering this exercise, I started wondering whether or not I wanted to be somewhere else. Of course. I became aware that I wasn't enjoying the conversation; I wanted to do some shopping, but felt obligated to my friend to remain and talk. As long as I wasn't dealing with this conflict consciously, my body had to deal with it. Part of my body was stationary, complying with what I thought was my friend's wish, while another part, my throat, was straining to get away, responding to my personal desire. Once I became aware of the conflict, I could make a conscious decision to stay or go. I decided that my feeling for my friend was greater than my desire to go shopping so I stayed. My throat tension disappeared. I had changed the level of conflict from my body to my consciousness and resolved it there. My body therefore did not have to absorb the conflict; it did not have to prepare itself to move in two conflicting directions.

I decided to try to extend this insight to a sore throat I was getting at the same time. Almost all my colds, I recalled, started as sore throats and then spread into my head. Perhaps that means that they begin when, without awareness, I want to be elsewhere very strongly for a protracted period, the soreness being the result of prolonged irritation due to the constant tension. At the time I wondered about this I was in New York, away from my home in Big Sur. As I thought about it the conflict became clear. I wanted to return to Big Sur but I also felt that there were things I wanted to accomplish in New York. Again I brought the conflict to my awareness and made the conscious decision to stay two or three more days in New York before going home. Although a throat as painful as the one I had almost always in the past had led to a cold, with that decision my throat cleared up, and by the time I arrived home I was completely well.

I'm now in the process of trying to identify the meaning of other bodily areas. What does it mean when my chest gets tight, or my stomach sour (maybe a threat to masculinity), or my stomach gets knotted (sometimes I'm withholding something important, sometimes threat of rejection), or a headache, or a lower back pain. I'm sure they are all signs of some unresolved conflict that is not in my awareness and that must therefore be expressed by my body. There is probably some specificity of meaning, but just how much I don't know yet. I'm also fairly convinced that the meanings are rather specific to each person's body, although there are also some statistically frequent causes for particular body parts.

When you did the exercise at the beginning of this section, it is very likely that you felt the experience of being trapped not in the throat as I did but in some other part of your body. Certain emotions do have a strong tendency to appear in specific parts of the body, like fear and anger in the stomach, or masculinity threats in the neck and shoulders. Each person may find his own unique pattern aided by the statistical generalities.

I remember a woman whose feet looked as if she had always worn shoes three sizes too small. Her toes were jammed up against her feet with the joints high in the air, so that there was relatively little foot surface touching the ground. Her emotional problem was that she didn't feel stable, didn't have "both feet on the ground," was "a pushover," couldn't "stand her ground." Her husband constantly did things that hurt her but she couldn't "take a stand," or "stand up to him." These are all phrases that she used spontaneously when discussing her situation. She was undergoing a method of deep massage—or, more accurately, fascial organization—called Rolfing, in which the Rolfer manipulates the body to get it back toward a normal position. As he worked on her foot the toes began to slide forward. The whole foot began to come down and distribute the body weight more evenly. As the days passed the foot slid down further and further toward its normal position. The following day she went on a fantasy trip that revolved entirely about her feeling of stability and groundedness. She also confronted her husband from her new-found center of strength. Physically, she reported feeling parts of the bottom of her foot she had never felt before and spent days barefoot, reveling in the feeling of touching the ground with her whole foot.

The distorted foot had been felt emotionally as a lack of personal stability. Physical correction of the foot aided the resolution of the stability problem at the conscious level. Obviously many other things had to happen concurrently in order for the effect to occur, but the physical change was central to her altered state.

The assumption of the unity of man allows for the possibility of several techniques now available to help individuals become aware of themselves more fully in order to achieve important therapeutic gains and to learn how to enjoy themselves more fully. The technique of Rolfing, a method of structural integration for the body devised by Ida Rolf, provides a physical basis for this exploration. The various intrapsychic methods, especially fantasy and gestalt therapy, offer techniques for uncovering psychic elements. Combining both of these in an encounter framework results in a way of combining the body, the intrapsychic, and the interpersonal in a very powerful way.

In all of these approaches, the distinction between the therapeutic and educative—between eliminating the negative and accentuating the positive—is of great importance. I feel that in my work I have developed the therapeutic methods very deeply, but have been weak on methods for accentuating and developing the positive. I'll try to correct that here, though I may be less than successful, because I'm not that familiar personally with methods for achieving joy. The therapeutic aspects consist of locating blocks, tensions, and conflicts, and of finding ways to break through them. The educative aspect consists of gaining control over your own being and doing whatever you want to do.

In order to understand the relation between body and mind in detail, I want to describe one particular technique of body work, Rolfing, and its connection with feelings and thoughts. This technique is based on a very careful approach to the physical body, and in addition to its intrinsic physical worth, it offers a language for understanding the relation of the body to the other levels of human functioning.

This description of Rolfing is my own. It does not do violence to Ida Rolf's ideas (she has looked it over), but she does not necessarily agree with parts of it, especially the elaborations into the psychological realm.

Rolfing is based on a conception of the nature of human tissue, especially muscle and fascia. The consistency of human tissue is assumed to be more elastic and plastic than is usually believed. It's difficult to think of an analogous substance. When a muscle is used in its normal way it contracts and relaxes, and as it does it is strengthened. The normal muscle can contract or relax as required. When there is some trauma to the tissue, such as a sudden wrench through an accident, excessive tensing through emotional events, or through the need to remain tense from a body imbalance requiring compensation, then with time the elastic quality is reduced. A muscle becomes tense as a way of stopping feeling; it is the physical equivalent of a psychological defense. The muscle, after a sufficient number or severity of these episodes, becomes chronically tense and loses its flexible responsiveness. Pressure on it then becomes painful because it has no way to go along with and absorb the pressure, much as a person who holds his hand rigid when catching a ball thrown hard will feel a sting, while if he can let his hand float back as he catches it there is no pain.

Excluding for the moment permanently altered tissue as happens in surgery, there are four states of the tissue. These states are fundamental to all concepts of human growth, including therapy and education. The first state is one in which the tissue is perfectly normal and healthy, and strong pressure is absorbed without pain. The person can relax or contract his tissue at will. This type of tissue has undergone no trauma and holds no blocks. It can transmit energy in a normal fashion. It is as if the tissue is saying, "I will relax on request."

A second state of tissue involves tension, but if outside physical pressure is applied to it, and the person is asked to put his consciousness at that point of contact of the pressure, he is able to will the muscle to relax and absorb the pressure without pain. This is tissue that has undergone a minor trauma; the muscle has tightened to prevent a recurrence of the trauma, but the tightening is sufficiently minor so that the support, trust, and help of an outside person is sufficient to allow a willful release of the tension. The tissue is saying, "I will relax if you reassure and support me."

The third state of tissue is one in which the psychological and physical levels interact. If the tense muscle is holding back feeling from an experience too frightening to be reassured simply by outside support, then a combination of psychological support and outside physical pressure on the tense muscle may be sufficient to relieve the tension. The tension is protecting against fear or anger or tears or whatever, and if the tension is penetrated physically so that it no longer holds back these feelings, the feelings surface. The wall behind which a person is hiding is broken down, revealing him in the cowering position.

Then successful therapeutic work with that feeling can help him to work through the fear and no longer need the barrier, that is, no longer need to hold his muscles tense. The tissue is saying, "I will relax if you will support me and also help by forcing me to relax."

The fourth state of the tissue occurs when the muscle is tense and will not relax even under supportive conditions. This tissue is still in sufficient trauma that more than support or pressure is required for the person to give up the defensive tension. Whatever is being protected by the tightening requires other work, probably psychotherapeutic, to make the situation safe enough for the person to let go and make himself vulnerable. The tissue is saying simply, "I won't relax."

This situation with body tissue is parallel to psychological repression and suppression. The theory of repression holds that certain memories, because of their threatening content, are held out of consciousness through either an unconscious process (repression) or a deliberate effort (suppression). Further, these processes lead to many apparently unrelated acts as ways of dealing with the repressed material, such as paranoid reactions. One way of understanding the relation of repression and suppression is to speak of the conditions under which the person can recall the hidden material. In suppression a person may deliberately not want people to know of an act because of embarrassment. Usually a supportive person offering the prospect of understanding, or an offer of such great value as to be worth going through the embarrassment, will be sufficient to regain the hidden material.

However, this type of inducement is usually not sufficient for repressed material. This material was often imprinted in early childhood and has become so deeply imbedded that therapeutic work is necessary to eliminate the barriers to bringing this material to consciousness.

The similarity of the body tissue states to the psychological situations is striking. In both cases the body or psyche exhibits a continuum of aberrations requiring a series of techniques varying in strength and variety to resolve. The suggestion then seems plain that these are in fact not two phenomena at all but the same one viewed on two different levels. A repressed thought or feeling manifests itself as a chronic muscle tension (or a similar physical phenomenon) at some appropriate place in the body. The degree of repression is manifested physically as the intractability to pressure and to the return to a normal physical position.

Another way of understanding this phenomenon is through the concept of conflict. The tense muscle may be looked at as a result of a bodily conflict, one part of the person wanting to use the muscle, and another part wanting to prevent its use. The result is that the muscle prepares for action and is then stopped, being held in the preparatory condition of an unfinished energy cycle. This may happen, for example, when a child wants to run away from home. His legs prepare to run, but he is also afraid of being alone and on his own, so he inhibits the completion of the act of running. If this happens enough, the leg muscles can become chronically contracted, the tension literally "embodying" the conflict.

Physically, the fascial envelope, a thin layer over the muscle, will lose its elasticity through lack of exercise, so that when a muscle has become stuck in a tense position, the subsequent relaxing of the muscle is difficult and painful. It is as if someone crawled into a leather sleeping bag and out of fear curled up tightly in the middle for a long time. Then the leather dried and hardened. Now, even if he lost his fear and wanted to stretch out, it would be very difficult because he would now have to soften the leather.

When events unpleasant enough to be blacked from consciousness occur, the blockage stops part of the life flow of energy. If this type of event recurs often enough, his psyche and his body alter to make the blockage a chronic muscle tension that holds the feeling from awareness. Therapy is an attempt to get the blockage opened to allow the life flow to continue. A common example involves a crying child, particularly a male child. By the age of five he may have the repeated experience that each time he cries his mother says, "Stop that crying." After a while, whenever his chin starts to quiver preparatory to crying, he stops it through fear of displeasing his mother. Psychologically he builds defenses that enable him not to cry so easily. Physically he tenses the muscles of his chin. If he can stop his chin from quivering, perhaps he can stop the whole muscular pattern that leads to tears. His chin muscles get chronically tense. Perhaps that makes his chin look small, pulls down the muscles around his mouth and tightens his neck muscles, making him more susceptible to throat troubles. If twenty years later someone attempts to massage his chin muscles deep enough to loosen them, he may relax the chronic tension and tears will start flowing. It is as if the film of the person's life was stopped at age five and, now, twenty years later, the projector is turned on again and the flow continues. The tears that were held back flow, the memories, thoughts, feelings, sensations all return, and with careful work the incident can be worked through emotionally so there is no longer any need for the chin to remain tense. It can relax and related muscles along with it.

The action of "releasing the tension, both psychic and physical, through verbalizing or acting out an adequate resolution of a repressed traumatic experience with appropriate emotion" is called an *abreaction*. In our terms it means releasing a block and working it through psychologically. The phenomenon of abreaction is important in open encounter.

This phenomenon of becoming more aware of the body can be achieved by other techniques, such as the following. You might try this before you read on. Shut your eyes and ears and put all of your attention into each part of your body, one part at a time, starting at the top: forehead, eyes, mouth, throat, neck, back of neck, shoulders, arms, chest, back, stomach, small of back, butt, genitals, upper legs, back of upper legs, lower legs, back of lower legs, ankles, feet. Then start at the periphery, the skin, and gradually go toward your middle, your core. Some parts will tingle, others will feel almost nothing. Note which parts you can feel when you concentrate on them and which parts are relatively dead or remote.

It is possible to make an awareness map of each person's body through this method. Certain parts of the body are very much a part of the person and other parts are literally disowned or alienated. Observation of the skin texture and temperature often gives another clue to the degree to which a body part has been integrated into the total person. Alienated parts frequently have flesh that is saggy and poorly nourished due to lack of attention and concern. Sometimes a woman's bosom gives the appearance of not being loved; it appears dead, gray, saggy. Or a section of hip is chalky, bunched, and without resilience or vitality. Other parts, by contrast, are well formed, ruddy, elastic, and seemingly full of energy. The neglected parts are often cooler in temperature due to poorer circulation.

Again, the relation between the psyche and the body is striking. The consciousness map is related to personal integration. Dead spots physically indicate a lack of integration of the individual into a whole person. If the genital area is lifeless, sexuality has not been coordinated with the rest of the person. Any time a psychological area is difficult for a person to assimilate, be it sex, aggression, love, anger, intellect, tears, or whatever, there is a corresponding body part in the same condition.

The Self-Concept

Several years ago I was concurrently leading groups of psychotics at a mental hospital and leading groups of highly successful men as an industrial consultant. I observed that the early child-hood dynamics of these two groups were not nearly so different from each other as would be expected. Most psychiatrists have had intensive experience with psychotics, but rarely do they have an opportunity to examine well-functioning people at the same depth and intensity. A dominating mother and weak father, for example, do indeed occur frequently in the schizophrenic's background, but they also appear frequently in the backgrounds of corporation vice presidents, school superintendents, government officials, and nursing supervisors.

What seems more significant than the specific childhood event is its effect on the child's self-concept. A divorce, for instance, can leave a young son feeling that he's inadequate, unwanted, unimportant, and worthless. If he is shunted out of the room when the topic is broached, if he is not told honestly what has happened, if he is allowed to feel—as many children do—that he is responsible for the break-up, if he feels unworthy and deserted by the father, then he can emerge from that situation with a damaged self-concept. It is damaged not only in that he has a diminished feeling about himself, but that his body has responded in a diminished way.

I'm now speculating backward from adult bodies I have seen. Feeling small and childlike can lead to retaining baby fat into adulthood. Often people will be chubby and unwrinkled as if they were afraid to grow any older or more mature. Or their genital development can be impeded, where grown genitalia indicate adult manhood. Frequently a ring of muscle tension down the groin and under the genitals to the anus is found in those who hold tightly to their genital area and don't let it move. These muscle tensions can restrict the flow of blood to the genital area, reduce the nourishment, and not allow the genitals to reach their full size. Or the feeling of having said something wrong can lead to a throat block and difficulty in speaking loud or screaming. If after the divorce the mother put too much responsibility on the child, his shoulders can be

rounded and appear weighted down, not just as a postural de-
fect but as an actual chronic muscle tension pattern.

On the other hand, if the divorce is handled well, the child's
self-concept is enhanced both mentally and physically. If the
child is brought into the divorce situation, has it explained to
him, has his role clarified and the relation he has to each parent
known, has his help or his desires asked so that he can participate, and is even asked to take over the parts of the father's role
that he feels he can handle, then he can be greatly enhanced
as a person. Psychologically he can feel needed, able to cope
with difficult situations, loved, and important. Physically his
structure may be held more erect. A feeling of himself as a
worthy person, capable of allowing people to look at him, can
lead him to pull his head and neck out of his shoulders and hold
his head high, thus tending to lengthen and straighten his spine.
He may also feel stable and securely rooted to reality, which
manifests itself in his standing solidly on the ground with feet
straight ahead and legs directly under his pelvis. This posture,
along with an ability to handle strong feeling, allows for deep,
full breathing that allows feeling to spread throughout the body
and gives a general body tone by oxygenating the blood. Thus
the enhanced self-concept is a more permanent part of the self.

As I write this, I feel that I am straining your credulity with
all of these assertions about physical changes due to emotional
events. These are strange notions and quite different from those
we usually accept. Please try to accept the validity of my statements at this point. I think they will become more understandable and believable as you read on.

Parents and friends attach an unending series of labels to
their children, many of which are believed by the child and
become assimilated as part of his self-concept. Once these de-
scriptions are internalized they block development of that aspect of his person. I can recall being told as a child that I was
forgetful and always losing things. That feeling has remained

with me; in fact, it's true to the present day and is one of the reasons this book isn't better documented by references to the work of other people. When any topic arose in school that required memorization, I simply shut off and didn't really try. I never did learn a foreign language well and hardly ever learned history. And as a psychologist it was only with great effort that I read the work of other people, partly because I was convinced I wouldn't remember it accurately anyway. Fortunately, my self-concept did include confidence in my ability to think clearly, so I did make a successful effort to learn anything involving a logical principle. Although there may be some truth (and I still think there is) in the negative assessment of my memory, I certainly could have tried and learned much more had I gotten the idea early that my memory was a good one, or at least average.

One very important accomplishment of a successful encounter experience is to reraise the issue of any negative self-concept element that was implanted early and never reconsidered. An encounter group member is often asked to do the thing he "knows" he can't do. In this way the atrophied part may be revitalized and the person expanded. This happened to me when I was running the Esalen residential program. I mentioned to the residents that I had never been able to sing in public, and that if after nine months of the program I could do that, the program would have been a success for me. After four days of intense encounter I found myself on my feet singing "The Impossible Dream," "That's My Desire," and a sprightly medley from the 1940s. I do feel that it's much easier now— though still not simple, mind you—to sing and generally do things I used to regard as embarrassing and beyond my ability in front of large groups.

A valuable kind of experience that leads to reexamining old categories is psychedelic drug trips. I hesitate to write about this since possession of the drugs is illegal, but I've had this experience and find it quite valuable to report. Perhaps some day these drugs will be looked at more rationally and these promising lines may be explored. During an LSD trip a friend who had been told as a young girl that she was clumsy and uncoordinated happened to catch an object that was falling off a table. This delighted her. She had never done that before. Suddenly the built-in inhibitions, fear of criticism, fear of making a fool of herself were penetrated by the drug so that she was primarily in touch with her body and her own desire to move. This experience seemed to allow her to discard the notion of her own clumsiness once and for all. Since then she dances more freely and has been playing many sports with amazingly increased ability. She has discovered that she is quite coordinated indeed.

On the physical level these jammed areas of the self-concept can be in any condition of permanence, depending upon how severe the original induction of the trait was and the length of time and frequency with which it was reinforced. In the case of my singing, it appeared that the psychological work in the group, combined with some body work on my throat, jaws, and chest (see Rolfing) was sufficient.

Parental feelings toward a child are conveyed nonverbally even more than verbally. The child who is dismissed from the room when important issues are discussed gets the message that he is unimportant and incompetent. In hundreds of ways— muscle tensions, voice tones, and facial gestures—the adult communicates his feelings toward the child and helps him to build his self-concept.

When my daughter Laurie was about three years old she had stopped wetting her bed. Then one day after a few months she wet it again. Now I know as a psychologist that this often happens and that it's nothing to be alarmed about. So I consoled her and told her it was all right, though I noticed that she still looked unhappy. Then I walked over to the bed and ripped off the sheet violently. She started to weep. As I bent to console her the truth of the situation hit me. She was right. Beneath my understanding exterior there was an angry father screaming quietly, "Why don't you stop wetting? Don't you realize the other kids your age have stopped? How can I be the best parent on the block if you continue this way?" She picked up my feeling very accurately, apparently in the tightness of my consoling voice, and then for certain in the vigor of my sheet ripping.

The nonverbal clues are so clear, especially to children, that I just assume they know how I'm feeling at some significant level. There's no place to hide. The best a parent can do is to be aware of his own feelings toward the child and deal with them directly rather than try to hide them and be found out. In that way the picture of the child that the parent conveys is at least known to the parent himself and he is not transmitting an image of which he is unaware.

The same comments hold true for the child's body image. Parents transmit their feelings about a child physically by the way they touch or avoid touching his body and the instructions they give him about physical contact. If they touch and caress a body part they convey that this is a prized and desirable thing. If it is avoided, ignored, or warned against, the body part is seen as alien, odious, and to be rejected. The most obvious victims of this communication are the genitals and the area around the anus. Many parents pointedly avoid touching those areas, don't look at them, and cover them at every opportunity. During growth the anal and genital areas are increasingly alienated from the rest of the body as the source of shame and punishment. Early toilet training can lead to attempts to cut off activity in these areas, to stop the flow of feeling.

Usually the genital-anal area seems most avoided, followed perhaps by parts of the face like the mouth and perhaps the chest of a female child. As one gets further from these scorned areas, it is more likely that parents, or people in general, will touch them. For boys the chest, shoulder, and upper arm regions are safe to touch and, indeed, in boys' games especially, there is a great deal of arms around shoulders, punching in upper arms, and tousling hair. Occasionally someone will chance a pat on the rump, but it is usually noticed immediately and inevitably commented on, often with a titter. In addition to taboo areas, there seems to be a tendency to locate the person around his head, since that is the part that talks and sees and hears and the part that is spoken to, while the parts distant from the head get relatively less attention. The legs and feet are rarely the focus of much interest, and many people lose contact with these remote members of their bodies. For most people the chest, shoulders, upper arms, and the periphery of the head are most easily identified with the self.

The unconscious parental feelings communicated through touch or lack of touch can lead to feelings of confusion and conflict in a child. Sometimes a "modern" parent will say all the right things but won't touch his child very much. The child's confusion comes from the inconsistency of levels: if they really approve of me so much like they say they do, why won't they touch me? It is significant that the closest adults ever come to touching each other totally is in the love-making situation, where there is an effort toward total acceptance and love of the whole person. But unfortunately we have created a severe dichotomy between the love-making touch and any other kind. Touching is very important in open encounter groups, for it conveys a level of personal acceptance difficult to express in any other way. This suggests that an infant should be encouraged to touch his whole body, including his genitals, and parents should do the same. Massaging the child often is one way of conveying love for each part of his body and helping the child to accept and love it too. Gentle pressure to contact the inner parts of the body would enhance this body acceptance.

Another approach to accepting a child, and thereby helping

him to accept himself, is provided by the Senoi tribe of Malaysia. Its culture is built on reporting dreams, and each morning dreams are reported and elders instruct the dreamers how to improve their dreams. But perhaps the essential part is that the dreams of all, including children, are accepted by the tribe. Thus each person is accepted down to his unconscious. An acceptance this deep must be very strengthening to the self-concept. It avoids the feeling frequent in our culture that we are superficially accepted, but if people knew what we were "really" like, we'd be rejected.

The Interpersonal

Our self-concept is largely derived from our relations with other people. In our dealings we exchange various commodities with these people and must make adjustments. In order to understand this interpersonal level I will use a framework first introduced in my book *FIRO*.

Each person has three basic interpersonal needs that are manifested in behavior and feelings toward other people. But this activity is rooted in a person's feelings about himself, his self-concept. The three basic need areas are posited to be *inclusion, control*, and *affection*.

Inclusion refers to feelings about being important or significant, of having some worth so that people will care. The aspect of the self-concept related to *control* is the feeling of competence, including intelligence, appearance, practicality, and general ability to cope with the world. The area of *affection* revolves around feelings of being lovable, of feeling that if one's personal core is revealed in its entirety it will be seen as a lovely thing.

Inclusion behavior refers to associations between people, being excluded or included, belonging, togetherness. The need to be included manifests itself as wanting to be attended to, and to attract attention and interaction. The college militant is often objecting mostly to the lack of attention paid him, the auto-mated student. Even if he is given negative attention he is partially satisfied.

Being a distinct person—that is, having a particular identity —is an essential aspect of inclusion. An integral part of being recognized and paid attention to is that the individual be distin-guishable from other people. The height of being identifiable is to be understood, since it implies that someone is interested enough to discover a person's unique characteristics.

An issue that arises frequently at the outset of group relations is that of commitment, the decision to become involved in a given relationship. Usually, in the initial testing of a relation-ship, individuals try to present themselves to one another partly to find out what facet of themselves others will be interested in. Frequently a member is silent at first because he is not sure that people are interested in him.

Inclusion is unlike affection in that it does not involve strong emotional attachments to individual persons. It is unlike control in that the preoccupation is with prominence, not dominance. Since inclusion involves the process of formation, it usually oc-curs first in the life of a group. People must decide whether they do or don't want to form a group.

A person who has too little inclusion, the undersocial, tends to be introverted and withdrawn. He consciously wants to maintain this distance between himself and others, and insists that he doesn't want to get enmeshed with people and lose his privacy. Unconsciously, however, he definitely wants others to pay attention to him. His biggest fears are that people will ignore him and would just as soon leave him behind. His uncon-scious attitude may be summarized by, "No one is interested in me, so I'm not going to risk being ignored. I'll stay away from people and get along by myself." He has a strong drive toward self-sufficiency as a technique for existence without others. Behind his withdrawal is the private feeling that others don't understand him. His deepest anxiety, that referring to the self-concept, is that he is worthless. He thinks that if no one ever considered him important enough to receive attention, he must be of no value whatsoever.

The oversocial person tends toward extroversion. He seeks people incessantly and wants them to seek him out. He is also afraid that they will ignore him. His unconscious feelings are the same as those of the withdrawn person, but his overt behavior is the opposite. His unconscious attitude is summarized by, "Although no one is interested in me, I'll make people pay attention to me in any way I can." His inclination is always to seek companionship, for he is the type who can't stand to be alone. All of his activities will be designed to be done in a group.

The interpersonal behavior of the oversocial type of person is designed to focus attention on himself, to make people notice him, to be prominent. The direct method is to be an intensive, exhibitive participator. By simply forcing himself on the group, he forces the group to focus attention on him. A more subtle technique is to try to acquire power (control) or to be well-liked (affection), but it is still for the primary purpose of gaining attention.

To the individual for whom inclusion was resolved in childhood, interaction with people presents no problem. He is comfortable with or without people. He can be a high or low participant in a group without anxiety. He is capable of strong commitment to and involvement with certain groups, but can also withhold commitment if he feels it is appropriate. Unconsciously, he feels that he is a worthwhile, significant person.

On the physical level, inclusion has to do with penetration of the boundaries between the self and the rest of the world, and therefore deals primarily with the periphery of the body, the skin and sense organs, the eyes, ears, nose, and mouth. Attitudes toward these organs may be related to attitudes toward being included with people. If contact with people is a fearsome thing, then the eyes keep people from intruding by not seeing others clearly, and then in order to see them clearly, it is permitted to put up a barrier—a barrier called glasses. When eyes are in the active process of seeing, and don't really want to see, they become dull and seem to retire toward the back of the head. Ears which don't want inclusion hear people who are close as if they were far away. Closeness is not accepted and people are kept at a distance. The mouth and lips become tight and impenetrable. The skin shies away from being touched; it is easily tickled, gets rashes and hives easily so that people will not come near. The muscles of the skin may also become tightened so that feeling is minimized, resulting in a leathery touch feeling.

All of these devices need not be used by one individual. There are probably special circumstances that bring about the preeminence of one over the other. The rock opera *Tommy* describes a boy who sees his mother in bed with another man and becomes blind, who hears them talking and becomes deaf, and who is told never to tell anyone what he saw and heard and becomes mute. In a dramatic form this is probably a good example for the reason for specifying which sense organ is the preferred one for avoiding inclusion.

On a recent trip that involved discussing work with a large number of people, my voice started getting hoarse, which I took to mean that I didn't want to talk any more. But then I noticed my hearing becoming erratic. Of course it was psychological; I simply didn't want to listen to all these people anymore. I began to understand how desirable and possible it would be to become deaf, at least in that situation.

If being included is important, the body may reflect it by having these peripheral organs perform in the opposite way.

The eyes become vigilant, looking for people in order to see them clearly. They try to see people who are far away as actually being closer. Possible outcomes of this are especially good vision and perhaps vertical lines between the eyebrows reflecting the effort put into seeing clearly. You can try this right now by looking at some object, preferably a person, in two ways. First look at him dully, as if your eyes were open but actually way back in your head and seeing as little as possible while appearing to give attention. Then look at the same object and feel your eyes leap out and grab him, taking in every aspect of him. The difference in the two feelings is usually very marked and gives some sense of how voluntary such a common phenomenon as looking can be.

The person with a high need for inclusion will have acute senses of smell and hearing, bringing far things near. The skin is receptive to touch and probably is open and soft. This is the pure inclusion pattern. Very quickly complications arise. The person open to inclusion can be sensitive to rejection and develop a barrier. Or he may allow touch and then be afraid.

An interesting body difference occurred in a class in Rolfing. One man who was learning to be a Rolfer, reacted to the assaults of the teacher Ida Rolf—who uses assault as a teaching method—by immediately responding with a defense, a self-justification, a counterattack, a lengthy explanation. I, on the other hand responded to her attacks with utter coolness and calm, allowing her to continue unabated, sometimes agreeing with her point, possibly joking away some of her steam, while underneath, quietly knowing that I was right.

When it came to Rolfing each of us, a startling difference appeared in the way we responded at the periphery of our bodies, the skin. When my friend was physically penetrated he would scream and holler, ask for time out, complain, cry, and reassess the competence of the Rolf practitioner. I would feel most of those things, too, but be very stoic and allow the practi-

tioner to penetrate quite far. But then he would be discon-
certed by two things. When he took his hand out my skin would
spring back to where it was like rubber, apparently unaffected
by his push. Also, if he pushed deeply enough into the flesh, he
met a barrier that felt like steel. In other words, he and I represented in our bodies almost the identical reactions we made
psychologically, his immediate response, my apparent acceptance but deeper resistance.

Another possibility in exploring the physical correlates of inclusion comes from a comment about sexual intercourse, and
brings up physical function to add to the structural physical
considerations I have been talking about. In the sexual act,
various phases can be distinguished that parallel inclusion, control, and affection. Inclusion problems refer to the initial phases
of the act, the feelings about penetration. A male with problems
of inclusion will probably have erection problems. His conflict
over whether or not to penetrate would be reflected in the
nervous enervation of the penis and its willingness or not to be
ready to enter. A similar situation arises for a woman where
inclusion problems are reflected in the readiness of her vagina
to receive the penis, whether she's loose enough and moist
enough. Also, the pelvic muscles for both that should be relaxed
for maximum pleasure may be tightened if conflict still exists.

Breathing is also primarily an inclusion phenomenon. It's the
way of entering or leaving any situation. If no commitment is
desired the breath is cut off along with a tightening of the
muscles. This cuts down virtually all vital functions. A full commitment of a person's time and energy involves full breathing,
a charged-up body. The Indians and yogis have recognized the
importance of breathing control, pranayama, for centuries. It is
the key to someone's involvement. Routinely, when I'm giving
a lecture or demonstration to a large group, I will begin by
doing some activity that requires them to breathe deeply,
either screaming, pounding, deep breathing, or anything that

gets them pumped up. I find it makes a big difference in the audience's attention and presence.

The same holds for an encounter group. Whenever a member shows a lack of involvement, getting him into some activity requiring deep breathing almost inevitably brings him in. Breathing patterns become ingrained early in life, and a person is usually not aware of his lack of full breathing. Improving the breathing pattern is probably one of the fastest ways to change the feeling of the entire organism. In bioenergetic therapy, the "air or breath is equivalent to the spirit, the pneuma of ancient religions, a symbol of the divine power residing in God, the father figure. Breathing is an aggressive act in that inspiration is an active process. The body sucks in the air. The way one breathes manifests one's feeling about his right to get what he wants from life."

In terms of the body systems, not only are the sense organs and respiration related to inclusion, but so are the digestive and excretory systems, which focus on exchange with the environment and which deal with whether an object will be in or out of the body. These systems express the body's desire to incorporate or reject outside objects. A person with a desire to exclude will reject food and/or excrete readily and, in the extreme, develop vomiting and diarrhea. One who is anxious to include will go in the other direction, namely, overeating and constipation. A well-resolved relation in the inclusion area should result in good digestion and elimination.

If we consider the interaction between a person and his body, the inclusion problem is one of energy. A body excludes itself in the world by being energyless. The difference between living and not living is the difference between having the flows of energy, nerve impulses, blood circulation, breathing, and so on, and not having them. When a body includes itself, it is filled with energy and feeling.

Hence the problem of inclusion is in or out; the interaction centers on encounter, and the physical aspect is that of energy.

Control behavior refers to the decision-making process between people and the areas of power, influence, and authority. The need for control varies along a continuum from the desire for authority over others (and therefore over one's future) to the need to be controlled and have responsibility lifted from oneself.

An argument provides the setting for distinguishing the inclusion-seeker from the control-seeker. The one seeking inclusion or prominence wants very much to be one of the participants in the argument, while the control-seeker wants to be the winner, or, if not the winner, on the same side as the winner. If forced to choose, the prominence-seeker would prefer to be the losing participant, while the dominance-seeker would prefer to be a winning nonparticipant.

Control is also manifested in behavior directed toward people who try to control. Expressions of independence and rebellion exemplify lack of willingness to be controlled, while compliance, submission, and taking orders indicate various degrees of accepting control. There is no necessary relation between an individual's behavior toward controlling others and his behavior toward being controlled. The sergeant may domineer his men, for example, and also accept orders from his lieutenant with pleasure and gratefulness, while the neighborhood bully may dominate his peers and also rebel against his parents.

Control behavior differs from inclusion behavior in that it does not require prominence. The power behind the throne is an excellent example of a role that would fill a high-control need and a low need for inclusion. The joker exemplifies a high-inclusion and low need for control. Control behavior differs from affection behavior in that it has to do with power relations rather than emotional closeness. The frequent difficulties between those who want to get down to business and those who want to get to know one another better illustrate a situation in which control behavior is more important for some and affection behavior for others.

Concern about one's competence, especially in the area of masculinity, leads to overmasculine responses. This is often seen in politics, where concern about one's assertiveness often leads to absurd overreaction to physical threats, especially when a government official has police or soldiers at his disposal.

Control problems usually follow those of inclusion in the development of a group or of an interpersonal relationship. Once the group has formed, it begins to differentiate; different people take or seek different roles, and often power struggles, competition, and influence become central issues. In terms of interaction, these issues are matters of confrontation, to use a term now in vogue.

The extreme person who is too low on control, called an abdicrat, is one who tends toward submission and abdication of power and responsibility in his interpersonal behavior. He gravitates toward a subordinate position where he will not have to take responsibility for making decisions, where someone else takes charge. He consciously wants people to relieve him of his obligations. He does not control others even when he should; for example, he would not take charge even during a fire in a children's schoolhouse in which he was the only adult. He never makes a decision if he can refer it to someone else.

For the individual who has successfully resolved his relations in the control area in childhood, power and control present no problem. He feels comfortable giving or not giving orders, taking or not taking orders, whatever is appropriate to the situation. Unlike the abdicrat and autocrat, he is not preoccupied with fears of his own helplessness, stupidity, and incompetence. He feels that other people respect his competence and will be realistic with respect to trusting him with decision-making.

Speculation on the physical concomitants of control behavior begins with control of the muscles through tightening and through intellectual or nervous system activity. The central nervous system, along with the endocrine system, is generally credited with controlling the anatomy.

Ida Rolf has a fascinating concept of the relation of the core of the body, by which she means the head and spinal column, to the envelope, which includes the two girdles, the pelvic and shoulder girdles with attached appendages, legs and arms. Her idea is that the core represents *being* and the envelope *doing*. Some people develop one and not the other, both, or neither.

For a male, a great deal of control is usually expressed in the formation of the upper arms, shoulders, and neck. Attaining masculinity is frequently related to having hulking, heavily developed shoulders and neck and back muscles. Wrestlers and football linemen typify this formation in the extreme, as the large muscle that goes from the middle of the back up into the neck, the trapezius, is so overdeveloped that it appears that they have no necks.

The feeling of being out of control, and thereby vulnerable, was brought home to me personally when a Rolfer working on my neck freed the trapezius muscle that I had held chronically tight so that my head and neck began to rise up out of my shoulders. As I stood there with my head elevated to a place where it felt both unfamiliar and wonderfully free, I felt frightened. The image that came to mind was of the boy in the circus who sticks his head through the bullseye of a target for people to throw balls at. I felt very exposed, very much in plain sight for everyone to see, with no place to hide. You may capture some of that feeling by standing up straight, putting your chin in and letting your head rise up as if it had a string through the crown, and let your shoulders relax down. When you get as high as you can, look around. When this happened to me I had a clear feeling of why my head had sunk into my shoulders. It was safer, more protected, and less vulnerable.

In general, the pattern of muscle tensions represent the defense pattern of a person. It is the way in which he controls himself so that he can cope with the world. A pattern of no chronic muscle tensions—as opposed to muscle tone—would then represent a nondefensive state, perhaps something like the egolessness of the Eastern mystics.

Intellectual control involves voluntary shaping of the body propensities. Control is exercised over the body's desires by moral codes and in line with parental upbringing so that thought is used to govern action.

In the interaction between a person and his body, the control problem is one of centering. A body undercontrolled is disorganized; a body overcontrolled is rigid. A well-controlled body functions with integration among its parts so that they flow easily and appropriately. Inappropriate movement and coordination result when the body is uncertain of what it is doing. Centering means placing everything in its appropriate place so that one is "hooked-up". Being off center makes all movement slightly disconnected.

In the sexual act, control has to do with the occasion and timing of the orgasms and the direction of movement. Withholding an orgasm is an act of personal control that often has a hostile motive, "you can't satisfy me." Sexual control problems would include difficulty of orgasm, premature ejaculation, and the lack of ability to let go.

Thus the problem of control is top or bottom; the primary interaction is confrontation, and the physical aspect is that of centering.

Affection behavior refers to close personal emotional feelings between two people, especially love and hate in their various degrees. Affection is a dyadic relation, that is, it can occur only between pairs of people at any one time, whereas both inclusion and control relations may occur either in dyads or between one person and a group of persons.

Since affection is based on building emotional ties, it is usually the last phase to emerge in the development of a human relation. In the inclusion phase, people must *encounter* each other and decide to continue their relation; control issues require them to *confront* one another and work out how they will be related. To continue the relation, affection ties must form and people must embrace each other to form a lasting bond, and also to say goodbye.

The person with too little affection, the underpersonal type, tends to avoid close ties with others. He maintains his one-to-one relations on a superficial, distant level and is most comfortable when others do the same with him. He consciously wishes to maintain this emotional distance, and frequently expresses a desire not to get emotionally involved, while unconsciously he seeks a satisfactory affectional relation. His fear is that no one loves him, and in a group situation he is afraid he won't be liked. He has great difficulty in genuinely liking people, and distrusts their feelings toward him.

His attitude could be summarized by, "I find the affection area very painful since I have been rejected, therefore I shall avoid close personal relations in the future." The direct technique of the underpersonal is to avoid emotional closeness or involvement, even to the point of being antagonistic. The subtle technique is to be superficially friendly to everyone. This behavior acts as a safeguard against having to get close to, or become personal with, any one person.

In his self-concept, the underpersonal believes that if people knew him well, they would discover traits that make him unlovable. As opposed to the inclusion anxiety that the self is worthless and empty, and the control anxiety that the self is stupid and irresponsible, the affection anxiety is that the self is nasty and unlovable.

The overpersonal type attempts to become extremely close to others. He definitely wants other to treat him in a very close way. The unconscious feeling on which he operates is, "My first experiences with affection were painful, but perhaps if I try again they will turn out to be better." Being liked is extremely important to him in his attempt to relieve his anxiety about being always rejected and unloved. The direct technique for being liked is an overt attempt to gain approval, be extremely personal, ingratiating, intimate, and confiding. The subtle technique is more manipulative and possessive, to devour friends and subtly punish any attempts by them to establish other friendships.

The basic feelings for the overpersonal are the same as those for the underpersonal. Both responses are extreme, both are motivated by a strong need for affection, both are accompanied by a strong anxiety about ever being loved and basically about being unlovable, and both have considerable hostility behind them stemming from the anticipation of rejection.

For the individual who successfully resolved his affectional relations in childhood, close emotional interaction with another person presents no problem. He is comfortable in such a personal relation as well as in a situation requiring emotional distance. It is important for him to be liked, but if not he can accept the fact that the dislike is the result of the relation between himself and one other person; in other words, the dislike does not mean that he is a totally unlovable person. And he is capable of giving genuine affection.

The primary interaction of the affection area is that of embrace, either literal or symbolic. The expression of appropriate deeper feelings is the major issue, particularly in group situations, where a paradox arises. At the beginning of the group there are many expressions as to how difficult it is to express hostility to people. It often later develops that there is only one thing more difficult—expressing warm, positive feelings.

A difference between inclusion, control, and affection behavior is illustrated by the different feelings a man has in being turned down by a fraternity, failed in a course by a professor, and rejected by his girl. The fraternity excludes him, telling him that as a group they don't have sufficient interest in him. The professor fails him and says, in effect, that he finds him incompetent in his field. His girl rejects him, implying that she doesn't find him lovable.

The affectional aspect of the sexual act is the feeling that follows its completion. This can be anything from a flood of warm, affectionate, loving feelings to a revulsion and thoughts of "what am I doing here?" It depends partly on how well the heart and genitals are connected. The circulatory (heart) and reproductive (genital) systems are most directly related to the area of affection.

In the interaction between a person and his body, the affectional problem is one of *acceptance*. The body may be charged up with energy and coordinated through centering, but the problem of body acceptance remains. An accepted body can allow feeling to flow through it without avoiding any part. Sensation is not blocked. An unaccepted body works against itself, trying to become sickly or dissociated. Thus, the ideal body feels energetic, centered, and acceptable.

With respect to an interpersonal relation, inclusion is concerned primarily with the formation of a relation, whereas control and affection are concerned with relations already formed. Within existent relations, control is the area concerned with who gives orders and makes decisions, whereas affection is concerned with how emotionally close or distant the relation becomes.

In summary, the problem of affection is close or far; the interaction is embrace, and the physical aspect is acceptance.

Honesty and Openness

One of the fundamental concepts of open encounter is honesty and openness, and it is crucially important to the realization of human potential. An understanding of the interconnection of levels helps to clarify the great importance of honesty, for its failure is a failure on all human levels.

The honesty revolution of which encounter groups are a central part is a revolution against the fabric of our society. It has become very much a part of human life to be devious and hypocritical and the youth and black revolts center around this issue. In my view this is a revolt too long in coming. My silent generation was much more prone to believe you can't fight City Hall, and to let it go at that. Corruption and hypocrisy have become so deeply ingrained among us that the actions of the Establishment almost invite violence, or at least extraordinary measures, in reaction. Muckraking books come out periodically, such as *Silent Spring, Unsafe at Any Speed, The Rich and the Super-Rich.* They have their impact, and are then largely forgotten.

Hypocrisy is widely accepted and assumed to be the preferred way to live. Former Secretary of State Dean Rusk was once quoted in *Time:* "I feel that diplomacy requires calm. Diplomacy has worked for hundreds of years to eliminate the accidents of personality from the conduct of State affairs. That's why, for example, we sign a diplomatic note, 'Accept, Excellency, the assurances of my highest consideration,' when in fact, you're telling him to go to Hell."

I find this a revealing statement. First, a person as highly placed as the Secretary of State approves of lying as a characteristic mode of relating. Second, he naïvely assumes that it is possible to eliminate personality from diplomatic negotiations. Third, he assumes that conventional diplomacy has worked for all these years, although one of its primary goals, peace, has virtually never been achieved, and seems to be getting farther away rather than closer.

Public manners are shot through with hypocrisy, emphasizing image and appearance rather than reality. *Time* also quoted

Jacqueline Kennedy Onassis, one of our chief models for human, especially public, behavior: " 'Look as if you've won, John,' urged Jackie when they posed after earning a red ribbon for second place." In other words, present a false appearance regardless of how you feel.

In the *San Francisco Chronicle* a column by Charles McCabe entitled "Honesty, Ugh!" pronounced: "Honesty may be the best policy in most things, but it certainly is not in affairs of the heart. Nor is it, really, in any more or less intimate social interchange." An article in *Redbook* called "Why Wives Lie to Their Husbands," a generally supportive article for lying, rationalizes: "Many of the lies that women reported to me did indeed appear so thoughtful and benign that it hardly seemed right to call them lies at all." Then, to clarify: "After the first years of marriage, truth most often is held to threaten the peace when it concerns money and sex."

The public also expresses righteous indignation at something done privately in the opposite way. In a case in which a nightclub owner was being sued for obscenity and lewdness, the *Chronicle* (November 21, 1969) reported: "Police Chief John McDonald of Redwood City is investigating how several of the dancers and a stag movie which had been presented as evidence at the trial . . . ended up as entertainment before the Redwood City Elks Club the same evening."

What is publicly regarded as ideal behavior can sometimes be a very damaging model. There is, for example, great public value put on stoicism in the face of tragedy. Mrs. Kennedy's response to the President's death is a widely publicized example. Her public image was one of virtually emotionless bravery. From many studies of death it is known that the spouse of a dying person usually has many and mixed feelings. In addition to grief, sadness, and loss, there is usually some degree of relief from the negative parts of the relationship, as well as anger for being left. Mrs. Kennedy's behavior revealed very little emotion of any kind. Further, according to press stories, several incidents around that time showing weakness, anger, conflict, or other ignoble feelings were the subject of much effort on the part of the Kennedys to keep out of William Manchester's book about the former President. The result could well be that when a wife loses her husband and feels some of these common negative feelings, her guilt will be reinforced by the fact that Mrs. Kennedy apparently had none of these feelings.

When working in a mental hospital I saw that the same phenomenon of public hypocrisies or unreal principles had damaged ordinary men. A large number of psychoses seemed to be due to the conflict between the psychological and biological feelings within the individual and the strictures of the church. The awareness of feeling desire for another man's wife, or of wanting to hit a parent, or to be rid of a child was so unacceptable that the person had to despise himself and cut off the parts of himself from each other. The religious scruples did not accept humanness but, rather, condemned it. Every time there is a religious or social value that becomes a norm and is not in accord with human feelings, it creates guilt, shame, and emotional and psychological destruction.

In education, the retreat from openness is expressed as the "legitimacy of the remote." If a child wants to study anything far removed from his immediate feelings and situation, such as the history of the Babylonians, life on Venus, cotton production in Bolivia, or Algernon Swinburne's poetry, he is given much support. But if he should want to gain a greater understanding of his immediate situation—how he feels in the classroom, his relation to the teacher, his competitive feelings with classmates, his feelings of stupidity, or his sexual impulses—they are made very difficult for him to learn about and often lead to feverish activity on the part of some community members to prohibit such learning.

Part of the reason for the resistance to openness in human

relations is the fear of facing one's self, a fear developed through a childhood usually devoted to learning self-deception. The prospect of being open often leads some segments of society to experience real terror. Rightwing attacks on sensitivity training as "brainwashing" and other outraged terms border on panic. When the request for honesty brings such a reaction, the social unacceptability of one of society's most cherished principles, "Honesty is the best policy," becomes clear.

There are, however, many encouraging signs of a turn toward honesty in public and private life. Many black-white encounter groups have been considerably effective. Couples groups are beginning to be based on honesty as the fundamental ingredient. The tremendous revolt of the youth and blacks is, in large part, a revolt against dishonesty and duplicity ("tell it like it is"). Encounter groups (T-groups) have been tried in the State Department and in state governments, albeit with mixed success. And these groups have spread very rapidly in industry, education, and nursing. Some avant-garde educational plans, such as George Leonard's *Education and Ecstasy* and A. S. Neill's *Summerhill,* are based on something akin to open encounter. The tremendous proliferation of growth centers of the Esalen type —from 1 to over 100 in less than three years—is another sign of the deep need being satisfied by this approach. The philosophy of honesty and reality are being felt.

But the cultural norm is clearly more oriented to good manners, tact, sparing other people's feelings, little white lies, "what they don't know won't hurt them," and so on—in short, a much more restricted and selective view of honesty. Perhaps if such a view is so pervasive there are some sound psychological bases for it, and they must be considered before advocating the honest approach toward one's self and others.

I am not fully clear myself about the times and areas where honesty should be compromised. All of my experience to date, both professionally and personally, indicates that everyone can be far more honest than he is; that putting a relationship on a more honest basis makes for a qualitatively richer, more fulfilling life; that being honest makes your body feel better—usually more open, less tight, and better functioning; that honesty opens doors into a new life much like losing virginity allows for new levels of personal intimacy. I know also that excessive honesty can lead to hurt and draggy relationships.

At this point I would advocate that a person achieve as much honesty about and with himself as he can, without any limitation; that in a close relationship there should be a period of total openness and honesty, preferably early, and after experiencing this feeling, the two people should decide together on the basis of mutual agreement where curtailing honesty is desirable; and that in casual relationships, a person should assess how much honesty the situation will take matter-of-factly and then be slightly more honest than that.

In the case of self-honesty, the major problem is learning how to be in touch with your feelings. Virtually all of us are trained not to consider how we feel. When a young boy is told that men don't cry, don't be a sissy, don't be weak, don't have bad thoughts, and so on, he begins to disown negative, weak, lustful, and other thoughts not approved by parents. The result in most cases is an automatic shutting off of unwanted or punished feelings, which soon progresses from not revealing the feelings to others to not being aware of them in one's self. One of the greatest accomplishments of my childhood was to be able to go through a whole dental appointment without yelling. That proved I could take it. In order to take it, I had to diminish the pain. The way a body tries to cut off pain is by tightening the muscles, as when gripping the dental chair, and by restricting breathing. In order not to feel the pain, I had to tighten my jaw and neck muscles and all the muscles in my arms and hands. You can experience this muscle pattern by opening your mouth as if you were in a dental chair, gripping the arms of your chair, and trying to prevent the pain. You can feel all of the muscles that contract. There was such reward for this bravery that I first didn't admit to the pain, then I tried to put it out of my consciousness. I tried to become what they wanted me to become: someone who doesn't feel pain, or at least isn't bothered by it. It wasn't until a good deal later that I could admit that it hurt like hell and I was scared shitless of going to the dentist.

This pattern is a very common one: a child trying to become like others want him to become, gradually fooling himself that he is that way by blocking his feelings from consciousness, but having built into his body both his real feeling and a defense against it. He is functioning at three conflicting levels; the deep body feelings (fear) and the conscious belief (bravery) don't agree, and the defense (tight muscles, denial) is an attempt, usually only partially successful, to match the conscious feelings with the body. This is the beginning of alienation from the self, loss of identity, and loss of centering.

As a boy attempts to alter his feelings in order to be a man, basic physical feelings and conscious self-beliefs get farther from each other and the need to keep them separate becomes greater because he is building an interconnected personality. For example, his next experience might be feeling compassion for weak things, felt in the body as a soft feeling around the heart and a reaching out of the arms. Since the cultural image of manliness is to deny such "feminine" feelings, the heart muscle may tense to stop the warm feelings, and the shoulder muscles may stop the energy flow down the arms by tightening, resulting in large bunched muscles at the shoulders and a thin upper arm where the energy is blocked. Both blockages to prevent feeling "soft," and in the jaw to prevent feeling pain, are connected under the general title "manly," and the motivation for holding either one is increased because a loosening of one threatens the other.

As these muscle tensions multiply, this effect gets much

greater until the person builds up a large network of fantasy about himself with a strong charge of energy to hold onto the fantasy. The body becomes increasingly tight as these tension patterns multiply, and along with the muscle restrictions may come other physical symptoms. The body is pulled out of alignment with excessive pressure put on various organs: the blood vessels become constricted, thus lessening the blood supply and nutrition to various parts of the body; breathing gets constricted, thereby reducing oxygenation of the blood; endocrines and nerve plexes are under unnatural pressure; and generally the body becomes weakened, more susceptible to illness, lacking in energy, and less supple, graceful, and economic in motion.

One feeling about this situation is "I don't know who I am." It takes various forms: "I want to be this kind of person but I don't feel that way"; "I want a good relation with a man but I always spoil it"; "I want to relax but I'm always worried"; "I want to speak up but I'm shy and embarrassed." In other words, thoughts and feelings don't match. The body and the head have become separated and out of contact with each other.

The big problem is how to go from our present state of duplicity to the open, honest, self-aware condition. The problem becomes a familiar one in psychotherapy: how to penetrate defenses and not leave a person too vulnerable, defenseless. The whole encounter group procedure is designed to attain more openness. The procedures described here and in *Joy* are all designed to make this journey through releasing blocks and freeing energy in a way that a person can deal with it as it is occurring.

Since people are different, when they get near a point of self-awareness and openness, they (always including their body) may rebel at a certain point and not want any more. They may be saying that they can function best with their current level of defensiveness and tightness. I've seen two major reasons for this. Some people find the flood of feeling too overwhelming; the elation and depression are too great. Some finely tuned actresses have this problem. Feelings are too sensitive and must be under more control. The other objection comes from those who have invested too much into directing their defensive structure. They feel, and I sometimes agree, that they are functioning adequately now, and that the pain and work involved in penetrating this complex defensive superstructure and rebuilding a personality isn't worth the effort (in addition to which it isn't at all certain in my mind that the new structure will be more satisfactory). I find this especially with older people, but not exclusively. In this case the goal for these people is more limited, concentrating on the relief of more superficial blocks and on the ease of daily living. In both cases, however, I would not take the person's word for it at first, because it is part of most personality defenses to give a premature testimonial: "Thank you very much, you've helped me a great deal. (Now leave me alone)." And this plea often comes at exactly the point where the most important breakthrough is about to occur.

Honesty with the self leads to congruence between thought and feeling, to a feeling of wholeness and integration, contributing to the solution of the identity problem. Once a person is in close touch with his body he can be self-corrective when things are deviant, permitting him to restore his balance. His physical condition is also better known to him and incipient illnesses can be anticipated, analyzed, and usually avoided. Diet becomes more important because the body sends messages about what it needs and what it doesn't like. This sensitivity increases pleasure and perceptions of all types. Food tastes better, colors are more vivid, forms are sharper, tastes tastier, smells smellier. The whole organism is finely tuned and vital energy flows.

For the purpose of discussing honesty in a close relationship, let us refer to the male-female couple, married or not. When I was appearing on television to promote *Joy* and to give some of those ideas a public airing, I was invariably inundated by dissenting panel members or guests when I would state that it was a good idea to be completely honest in marriage. One interviewer wanted me to make an exception of premarital experiences; and generally I came away feeling I had either overlooked something everyone else knew (a feeling I often have), or else I was on to something that could make a great positive difference.

When the movie *Bob and Carol and Ted and Alice* came out, the question of marital honesty was raised for the whole country, indeed, for the world. The picture was based on an idea derived from an Esalen workshop, that honesty between couples is good. I have mixed feelings about the movie. Its portrayal of Esalen was ludicrous, and it never seemed to decide whether it was a parody of the honesty idea or was serious.

Apparently trying total honesty between members of a couple is quite a new idea. I have tried it myself in a couple, and our friends at Esalen—perhaps ten couples—have also been trying it; and it has been used in the couples groups, now totaling about 100 couples. The pursuit of honesty is begun by asking the couples to think of three secrets they have never told their mate and that would be most likely to jeopardize their relationship. During the course of the workshop they tell these secrets. The dominant secret is adultery, but the list also involves homosexual affairs, fantasies, feelings of hostility, and many other things. Later we ask them to reveal three positive secrets, feelings of admiration or appreciation that they haven't told their mate. These are often harder to tell because of the latent competition and jealousy. When the negative secrets are revealed there is a whole sequence of emotional consequences, including outrage, sarcasm, pickiness, sadness, hatred, intellectualizing, and usually, finally, an exploration of the lack in the relationship that led to the action.

Of course, different couples go through this in different ways, but there often are balanced outrages. The husband may reveal adultery only to find that his wife has the same secret. The outcome of this and related experiences is, in the large majority of cases, a refreshing new beginning for the couple, a feeling of being remarried on a totally different basis, a renewal of feelings between the two. This feeling comes mainly from newly released energy. The energy that goes into withholding is released and can go into the loving relation. A person is now more open and available to his partner.

For example, if his secret is "I am no longer sexually attracted to you, and I'm having an affair with my secretary who does turn me on," then there are large areas of life that the couple doesn't share. He must be very careful. His muscle tensions, breathing, and other functions must be at least temporarily constricted when his wife calls the office, when she asks about his work, when she wants to know how things went, when he has to figure out how to sneak off without her knowing, when sex is discussed, when they see a movie with adultery as the theme, and so on. Further, he can no longer be spontaneous with his wife. He must censor everything before it comes out for fear of exposure. More and more areas of their life are avoided, more and more of his energy is tied up in his secret. The result is that he gets tired easily when he gets home, and they have nothing to talk about comfortably. The primary feeling they are aware of is that their relationship is getting dull. If there are more secrets the situation multiplies. If she also has secrets, their energy drain starts mutual reinforcing. Frequent illness often begins at this point, often not diagnosable. This happens in countless marriages and takes a heavy toll psychologically and physically. When a couple breaks through the secrets, the rejuvenation of their relationship through the infusion of this new energy is a delight to see.

One incident early in a relationship of my own is an excellent example of the relation between thoughts, feelings, the body and honesty in intimate relations. In the course of our relationship we dealt with the problem of what we have come to call Topic A, how a couple deals with their sexual desires for other people. We decided early in our relationship that if we really loved each other we would like to enhance the other's freedom, so we would allow outside sexual adventures. She did it first. She came in one night and announced that she had screwed John. I then had my first experience of noncongruence between thought and feeling, head and body. My thought was supportive: that's fine, dear; you've done what we said; I understand and, my, aren't we advanced. My stomach, however, had as large a knot in it as I've ever experienced. It didn't seem to be nearly so calm and understanding as my words were.

After I had weathered this initial storm we settled down to try to work through this incident, to understand it and resolve all the feelings it roused. On Monday morning we began talking and using all the encounter techniques we knew to make sure we got to the bottom of the issue, exploring her latent hostility, my insecurity about masculinity, and so on. That went very well and by evening I felt very good about her; we had worked it through. Then we went to bed together and I started to make love to her, but behold—no erection. I looked down and there was absolutely no hardness or angle of elevation to my penis, just a droop. It was a strange feeling, a feeling that truth was in the body. Much of my belief that my feelings toward her were resolved was bullshit (definition: words unconnected with feelings). So next day we went at it again, dealing with my relation to my mother, her relation to her father, etc. Tuesday night I again felt good, but I looked down—very slight tumescence, very slight angle of elevation, and that's all. On Wednesday, we got into what I wasn't doing for her, how she wasn't satisfactory to me, and so forth; at night slightly harder, slightly more elevated. It was like my penis was the answer in the back of the book. After the day's activities we would look down to see if we had really gotten through all the issues or not. It took until Saturday before I could enter her.

The response of the body to most couples' problems generally, and to infidelity especially, is very definite. Often a woman will be verbally condoning her man's activities but her body will not be responding to him, either by not wanting intercourse, her vagina not getting wet, or by not having orgasms. This is one reason why attention to how the body functions is a good opening into the total relationship. Dishonesty between members of a couple almost always affects the body, even if the head deals with the situation with apparent rationality and acceptance.

What happens next after the couple has agreed to be as honest and open as they are able to be? One girl and I lived this way for several years and I can tell you how we evolved. The first problem was to get to basic honesty, which was tied in with the difficulty of being self-aware mentioned above. We found that no matter how many times we revealed secrets to each other there were still some left. The problem of being in total touch with oneself seems lifelong. Finally, we found that we had gone too far. This constant dredging up of all feelings was making our relationship so oppressive and heavy it wasn't worth it. For example, I thought of other women frequently when I was making love to her. Finally I told her. She was somewhat hurt, but then revealed that she sometimes fantasied Paul Newman and Paul McCartney of the Beatles when we were making love. I was very chagrined; we talked it out, and made use of it by finding out what our fantasied figures offered that we weren't getting from each other. But it became a drag to announce to each other the cast of characters, if any, after each love-making session. So we agreed not to unless one of us particularly wanted to know. We just assumed that it would happen from time to time, that it probably had some advantages, like being a way to deal with attractions to others, that it might mean we weren't entirely satisfactory to each other at that moment, but that it was all right. And it was more fun if we didn't have to discuss it each time. This was the practice that we followed. If some aspect of honesty once explored seemed more oppressive than useful, we would agree together not to say it, but with the understanding that if either of us wanted to know, the other would tell honestly.

These seem to be the important features of honesty in an intimate relationship. Total honesty should be experienced first, because a judgment about what areas the couple wants to keep open and what areas they agree to keep closed cannot be made soundly without their having had the firsthand experience of the full openness. After that the choice of areas can be made jointly. The mutual decision is vital. If one person makes it for the other's own good it is almost certainly defensive and will lead to difficulty. Agreeing that the closed area can always be opened up again is essential and gives confidence that the relationship will not slip back. It also means that you are each other's closest confidants, which helps to solidify the relationship. This solution allows for differences between couples. Some may decide after experiencing total openness that they want to remain that way; others choose openness for different areas, different circumstances, for different lengths of time, perhaps even for one person and not the other (there's no reason why it has to be the same for both people, if they agree that the honesty for one shall be different than for the other). In general, most couples profit from more honesty than they think they can handle, with a resulting increase of energy, spontaneity, and closeness.

The problem of honesty between people who have less than an intimate relationship is even more complex and varied. Probably the major factor is the importance of the relationship. In the case of a nurse and a doctor working closely together on a hospital ward, it is very likely that a good relationship between them will result in more efficiency in their work, and more happiness and good therapy for their patients. On the other hand, the relation between a woman and a one-time salesperson does not usually have that momentous quality. If they are withholding some basic feelings about each other, it probably doesn't make a great deal of difference in their transaction and they probably prefer to expend their psychic and physical energies in some other way than in encountering each other.

The factor that is most overlooked in dishonesty in casual relations is the great effect of the dishonesty on other people and events, an effect that is often not understood. For instance, I once consulted with a nursing school to help them improve their efficiency and personal satisfaction. One thing I noted as I wandered around talking to various members of the nursing department was the large number of complaints by the students about one thing in particular, an overload of coursework and practice. This is not an uncommon complaint anywhere, but it seemed more acute in this situation.

When I brought this up with the faculty they told me about the great proliferation of nursing knowledge, the more stringent requirements, new drugs, new procedures, and so on. Many started their explanations with that venerated phrase "the kids of today," and some—not all—mentioned the increase in psychiatric orientation of today's nurse compared to the old. As I met in an encounter group with the nursing faculty, this last factor became the key to the problem. All the reasons they gave had some merit, but the primary difficulty seemed to be an important split in the faculty over the role of psychiatry in nursing training as opposed to more experience with medical procedures. The differences would flare up occasionally and were known by all in a clandestine way, but the belief that the situation would work out if people were civil meant that the differences were never confronted. If they weren't confronted how were they resolved? Should the students study a great deal of psychiatry or more medical practice? The solution to the interpersonal problem was to require the students to take both, thus the faculty members did not have to face each other. This solution, of course, overloaded the students.

This situation parallels the one in which the individual fails to deal with a conscious conflict (as with my wanting to leave New York) so that the conflict must be dealt with on the body level in the form of illness or tension. In the New York example, part of my body wanted to be there and part didn't, hence the tension. With the nursing faculty, part wanted psychiatric courses and part didn't, so the students had to deal with the conflict.

There is a growing recognition of the centrality of dishonesty in social and political problems, and the complexity of even the concept of dialogue. Dialogue without self-awareness is sophistry. Peace talks and confrontations are all off target unless accompanied by insight into the self, otherwise they result in righteous indignation and mutual accusations. One excellent example was pointed out by Anthony Lewis, the *New York Times* London correspondent:

American students are told they must respect institutions. Their President deplores mindless attacks on all the great institutions which have been created by free civilizations. But the same president orders a massive armed attack in a foreign country without going through the procedures laid down by the Constitution for making war or even asking Congress for less formal support.

The students hear their president express regret that we live in an age of anarchy both abroad and at home. But the president sends American troops into Cambodia without the slightest deference to the processes of international order: Not consulting his allies, not informing other Southeast Asian countries who with his encouragement were organizing a conference on Cambodia, not asking the government whose territory he ordered bombed and invaded. . . .

The general principle is this: If a conflict is not resolved on a higher or more complex level of organization, it will be expressed in its unresolved form on a lower level. An individual's unresolved conflicts will be expressed as a physical ailment on the body level; a small group conflict (faculty) will be expressed as an individual's problem (students); a government official's (Nixon's) conflict must be absorbed by his constituency (citizens). This is the price paid for lack of honesty and openness. This principle is crucial and will be returned to later.

What about privacy? Does the view that openness is a valuable goal eliminate the old-fashioned virtue of privacy? Essentially, yes. First, I want to distinguish aloneness from privacy. Everyone can profit from occasional periods of being alone. By privacy, I mean doing and thinking things that you don't want to tell anyone. The limits to this I've described above, but within these I find that the more I can be completely open about everything I say or do, the more I feel like a totally free man, responsible for myself, and free to let anyone know me. For me, and I suspect for many others, privacy began because of sexual guilt. The only way I could masturbate without being discovered was through privacy. I think that what a couple usually means when they say they want privacy from their children is that they want to screw unmolested and unseen. Other reasons for wanting others to stay away have more to do with aloneness, like a man wanting to read his paper undisturbed. He doesn't usually need to keep what he is doing secret.

Privacy usually means hiding something you are ashamed of. A relative of mine was just fired and the word went out to all family members not to let outsiders know. "Say he quit to go to work for himself. It's nobody's business anyway." We are ashamed, so we invoke privacy. The military exploits its security system outrageously to cover blunders. As a young naval officer I saw all manner of documents labeled Secret that had nothing whatever to do with national security, but that simply covered up a stupid or dishonest activity. Privacy also acts on the body level to tie up energy and tighten up musculature so that others won't find out what you find difficult to deal with in yourself.

Bulletin: *Couples Encounter Group*

May 1984, DES MOINES, IOWA:—One of the new encounter groups for couples uncovered some important phenomena. Following is an abridged transcript of a meeting of four Des Moines couples.

Leader: George, would you and Helen sit in the center of the circle and tell each other one of the secrets that I asked you to think of—a secret that you've never told your mate and that would be most likely to jeopardize your relationship.

Helen: You know, it's funny, but I've been trying to think of some secrets ever since you asked us, but I just can't think of one. Maybe it's because George and I already talk very freely to each other. We tell each other practically everything.

George: I agree. Actually, we just came to this group out of curiosity. Our marriage is wonderful.

Helen: I don't want to make it sound like we don't have any problems at all. We have our ups and downs like any couple, but I have no complaints. (Smiles.)

48

George: Yeh, except I'm very tired. (Laughs.) I don't know why you people hold these meetings at night. I had to drive six hours to get here. I'm bushed. (Lies down on rug.)

Ldr: Helen, you said you tell each other *practically* everything.

Helen: Yes . . . did I? Oh, well, there may be one or two things we haven't mentioned, but . . .

Ldr: Could you think of one of these?

Helen: (Pause) Oh, well . . . let's see . . .

George: (from floor) Go ahead, dear, think of something to make him happy. (Both laugh.)

Helen: (Speaking rapidly) Well, there are some specific experiences that are simply examples of some general agreement that we have made in the past that don't require full disclosure every instant. That would simply overload the lines of communication and possibly lead to completely unnecessary difficulty that could be avoided through mature, judicious judgment. After all, we are adults, and we do exercise some appropriate restraint.

George: (Rises to sitting position) My god, Helen, what does all that mean!?

(Long pause)

Helen: Well, there is one thing I thought of, but I'm almost sure I told you, George. Besides, it's very trivial.

George: It may have slipped your mind if it was trivial, dear. Perhaps it just wasn't important. (Reaches arm toward her.)

Helen: I'm sure I told you anyway.

(Long pause)

Sally: For Christ's sake, what is it?

Helen: I feel so silly saying it.

George: You might as well go ahead, dear. These people will never be satisfied until you do.

Helen: Well, I did tell you about Milton, didn't I?

George: Probably. What about Milton?

Helen: Well, you remember when you slept with that girl a year ago and I was so upset? You told me it was all right if I slept with other men. Do you remember?

George: Milton?!

Helen: I slept with Milton twice while you were out of town.

(Long pause. George looks intently at Helen, shows a flash of anger, then catches control of himself.)

George: (Calmly) I'm glad you told me Helen. I don't like it, of course, but we agreed that we shouldn't restrict each other, so it doesn't surprise me that you did it. (Pause) Uh . . . did you enjoy it?

Helen: Yes, very much.

George: Oh . . . (Begins to pick at fingernails; Sally begins to hiccup in background.)

Ldr: I find it hard to believe your calm, George. It kills me when this happens to me.

George: (Reasonably) You must understand that we made an agreement about this very thing and that several years ago I had an affair that I told Helen about.

Ldr: How does your body feel, George?

George: Not too good, naturally. My breathing is a little labored, and my stomach's tight. I don't know why, but I'm sweating quite a bit, and . . .

Ldr: George, would you put your attention on your fingers? One is cleaning the other vigorously. See if you can be one fingernail and talk to the other finger. Carry on a dialogue.

George: I'm my forefinger. I want to clean you out. I want to press back your cuticle and make you look better. Damn, I get mad at you when you won't give up that last piece of dirt and let me clean you out. Now I'm my other finger. For

Christ's sake, leave me alone. You're not so clean yourself. Let me live my life and you live yours. I don't try to clean you out all the time. I'm just trying to be helpful. Don't push me away. Don't be mad. I don't . . . (George begins crying; continues.) I feel so alone so desperate. I don't know where to turn. (Sally continues hiccuping, louder.)

Ldr: Would you say those last lines to Helen?

George: Yes. Helen, I feel desperate. I don't know why you did it (still crying). I don't want to lose you. (Cries fully, sobs. Helen holds him for several minutes.)

Helen: I don't want to leave you, George. (To leader) Now look what you've done. This was all unnecessary.

George: Why did you do it? And with Milton of all people! (Sally hiccups.)

Helen: I don't know. George, it just happened. I don't know why. (Sally hiccups.)

Ldr: Helen, you're moving away from George.

Helen: Oh, am I, I didn't mean to. I'm sorry. It's just more comfortable here. (Sally hiccups, very loudly. Helen turns quickly toward Sally, says angrily—) Sally, stop that goddamn noise!

Sally: I'm sorry Helen. I've been trying everything I know but it's been going on for 15 minutes and won't stop.

Ldr: Would everyone give Sally his attention. Just stop what you're doing and look at her, acknowledge her presence. We know you're here, Sally.

(Group acknowledges Sally, focuses on her for several minutes. Miraculously, her hiccups stop, she smiles. Helen starts sobbing.)

Helen: (Shouting) That's what I want, George, your attention. Stop taking me for granted. Stop acting like I was a piece of furniture. Sure, Milton isn't much, but he treated me like I was important. He didn't put his nose behind a newspaper every night. He cared about me. And you don't.

George: Oh, god, Helen. I know. It takes a sledge hammer to fall on me.

Ldr: Often people have affairs because there's something unsatisfactory in their marriage. It can be very useful to you two if you could use these affairs to help you know what it is about each other that isn't satisfactory. It helps if you just shout out all these things you've been holding in.

George: Okay. Helen, I know one thing. I don't feel taken care of well enough by you. Why don't you keep the house cleaner? Why don't you have my drink ready when I get home? Why don't you speak up when my friends come over and treat them nicely? Why don't you control the children better so I can relax? And your hair is never combed.

Helen: (Shouting) Well, you're no prize yourself, Big Shot. You're often a big drag when you're home. We never talk about anything. You just give me money to do things but you never talk to me.

George: (Shouts, but restrained) Why can't you leave me alone sometime? You always want me home, or want me to talk to you, or take you someplace . . .

Helen: I don't want you home more . . . I just . . .

Ldr: Would you two be willing to do something to try to help clarify your feelings?

George: I suppose so.

Helen: Yes.

Ldr: Helen, stand behind George and encircle him with your arms so that he can't break out. Hold your hands tight. And George, you try to break her grip and get free of her. If he does get free, Helen, go after him again, and grab him. You try to get her away from you, George. (Helen grips George and they start to struggle. George laughs.)

George: Say, you sure are strong. (Both laugh.) Maybe I don't want to get away.

(He starts to struggle but can't move. His smile turns serious. He starts to pry her hands apart. No luck. Then tries to burst free, moves, swings her around. Helen is tenacious. George gives burst of laughter, then struggles harder. Both get very serious, breathe heavily. George finally gets away, Helen pursues, grabs. George peels off her hands and pushes her away. She chases him around room, he pushes her away. Finally she falls to the floor sobbing. George comforts her.)

George: My god. I never realized.
Helen: That's the way I feel much of the time, George, that you just want to be rid of me. (Several women in group cry and bury their heads.)

(The group broke up a short time later. When they returned the next morning, Helen looked glowing. She had an announcement.)

Helen: I just want to tell the group that when I left here last night I'd never felt worse in the eight years of our marriage. George and I continued this until 4:30 this morning. We told each other everything we had withheld all these years—and some of it was pretty awful. Then we said all the things we like and love about each other, and it was amazing how many of these things we'd never said. Almost more than the negative things. After that we thought we were exhausted, but we started to make love, and it was the most glorious love-making we'd ever had. Fantastic! I never knew it could be like that.
George: (Grinning) Me, too.

Helen: I felt so free, like I wasn't holding back anything from
George. My body just vibrated and pulsated. It was incred-
ible.

George: Yeh. Fuck Milton!

Helen: Then this morning, we got up early—we seemed to have
enormous energy—and went out to a rock overlooking the
river and got married again. We vowed never to hold back
so much from each other.

Mysticism and Spirituality

The spiritual dimension of man is real, and it must be considered along with the body, the self, and the interpersonal. But my unfamiliarity with the spiritual dimension makes this a very difficult matter to write about.

I never thought of myself as even remotely religious. My Jewish upbringing consisted of learning some words—schlemiel, megilla, bupkis—and learning to like delicatessen food. No Bar Mitzvah, no Hebrew lessons, nothing. My scientific upbringing hardened my view that all was rational: the existence of God couldn't be demonstrated, logical positivism had no room for magical thinking, and even agnosticism was a cop-out. I just didn't believe in the hocus-pocus. I was an atheist.

But here's my dilemma. In the earliest draft of this book I wrote a few things that reflected a broadening of my scope and an openness to mystical thought. Good ideas, I thought. The four paragraphs read as follows:

One of the striking differences between Eastern religion and the Western tradition has to do with the connectedness of man and the cosmos. Eastern philosophies seem to emphasize much more the relatedness of all things in nature. Drug takers often report feeling in tune with the universe and being more in touch with the similarities of all things, not only of men but of natural phenomena. This experience leads to a greater interest in such things as the effect of the cosmos on human life (e.g., astrology), the power of prayer on plants, the effect of climate and environment on the human condition, and most pertinently now the almost total interrelation of mind, spirit, and body. This latter insight, understood by many of the Indian yogas, has already made important contributions to the open encounter as will be seen in the discussions of the Kundalini and of some of the specific techniques, such as yoga and meditation, the increased use of silence, and personal centering.

One of the Hindu approaches to feeling brings up another issue that we are just beginning to deal with and that gives promise of leading to greater synthesis. The Hindu mode of dealing with feelings is for a man to train his mind to be the witness to all of his behavior and to observe himself with some detachment. This appears to be in opposition to the encounter entreaty to go into feelings and work them through. Perhaps these methods are not contradictory but represent two stages of human evolution; feelings must be faced directly with awareness and worked through before a detachment can be acquired.

One point at which the open encounter and a mystical viewpoint are mutually helpful occurs when an encounter is going very deep. After hostility is worked through and differences acknowledged as people reach the deeper layers of personality, the similarity of all men becomes clearer. We are all in the same struggle but using different paths with different defenses. The notion that we are all one is given great meaning at these almost mystical moments in the group's life.

It is an exciting development to find a way to connect with the thousands of years of the religious and mystical traditions, and perhaps through an integration of Eastern and Western approaches, both theoretically and in terms of methods, to attain a fuller and more effective synthesis.

Then I gave the draft to members of the Flying Circus, a leadership team formed at Esalen, for comment. Steve Stroud made a remark about this section that puts me in my current dilemma. He said, "Mysticism and Spirituality: In the beginning you promise big things but it is included almost as an afterthought. This could be a moving, beautiful personal note, i.e., (a) encounter movement as a new religion (b) personal quest as search for God, (c) how this quest is turned on, shut off, (d) inner perception vs. outward projection. Personal Note: You know that you are *God*. Tell your own genesis in discovering this. You have a strong spiritual side (which you hide) that others could profit from. In my opinion, if this isn't the hardest, most time-consuming chapter for you to write, it isn't finished yet. Personal Suggestion: Forget your readers and write this book to satisfy yourself. Personal Gift: I'll feed you if it takes so much time to write you get hungry."

This beautiful, intimidating note forced me to try to live up to Steve's perception. I must hide my spiritual side even from myself, but I do want to find and express it. The first memory I had of the change in my orientation as an atheistic scientist came on my first LSD experience. At one point I was lying on the floor, arms and legs out, and my whole body was vibrating. My hands and feet were connected with the universe. I was vibrating with the cosmos. The feeling was one of ecstasy and orgasmic harmony. I was fully in tune with everything. Then I looked in the mirror and my face changed into Buddha, then Mephistopheles, then a Mongol—it was all within me.

When I came down from the trip I began to analyze these

experiences from the standpoint of a sound scientific base, considering probability, theory, and . . . but that lasted only a few
seconds. I didn't want to try it. The scientific analysis was drag-
ging me down from the euphoria and ecstasy of the experience
to a kind of snivelling, persnickety way of being. I didn't care
if there was a scientific explanation. Science was something that
helped keep my muscles tight. It made sure I didn't soar anywhere or let everything go. It made sure that I didn't let all my
muscles relax and experience whatever happened. It forced me
to weigh, evaluate, criticize, be cautious, respectable, replica-
ble, responsible, uncriticizable.

I began to get mad at science and the education I had received. Why hadn't they told me, why hadn't I realized, that
scientific explanations were only one way of seeking truth?
Other influences cannonaded me. Mike Murphy, Esalen's president, meditated several hours every day. Meditated! Sat there
thinking of nothing for hours! I tried it and it wasn't bad. On
occasion I began to get that ecstatic feeling again.

The whole Esalen community was much more spiritual than
I was, I thought, although Steve's remarks now make me doubt
it. But several people who participated in spiritual activities—
meditation, yoga, prayer meetings—looked awfully good. They
seemed clear-eyed, lean, and serene. I sometimes seemed fur-
row-browed, paunchy, and agitated. What was going on? I had
that vague feeling again that there was a vast secret that everyone knew but me, that I was way behind, that perhaps the
whole encounter thing wasn't "where it was at," as some people
put it.

Then one day Baba Ram Dass came to Esalen to stay for four
months. I knew him; he was Dick Alpert, a kind of bright,
smart-alecky kid who taught at Harvard just after I left. I'd met
him a few times, known him a little, followed his exploits when
he and Tim Leary got involved in LSD. Now here he was back
from a trip to India, spending about a year's training to be a holy

man. Dick Alpert, complete with beard and sheet. Phah, said I, but I noticed his eyes were very clear. I went home that night and looked in the mirror. Several little veins kept my eyes from being that clear.

Ram Dass elected to be at home every afternoon in a house about twenty miles from Esalen. After fighting with the idea that I was too important to go twenty miles to see him, I went, twice. During my visits I went through myriad emotions. Jealousy was large; he seemed to know a lot, turn people on, maybe more than I did; he was serene, attracted large crowds, and made some extraordinarily profound statements, statements that again reinforced my idea that there were all kinds of secrets that I didn't know.

I seized on his weaknesses. When he was Dick Alpert he used to brag about how people came to him, endless anecdotes about girls calling him up late at night. And now look, he'd set himself up so that people had to come to him. And maybe he's just found a new shtick. Last year he's turning people on to LSD, this year it's the mystical trip. I'll trust him more if he returns to India (he's already extended his stay here a year). And he's still self-aggrandizing. Listen to him read his press notices from New Hampshire. Call that enlightened?

That was the skeptical, threatened scientist talking. I also saw great changes in Dick and heard great profundity that made me think a great deal. He had something. He was something. He seemed like a whitewashed wall. I could still see some of the brown—the old Dick showing through—but I could also see that the white covered large areas and made a great deal of difference. So here was a contemporary taking the mystical trip, and being very impressive.

At the Esalen residential program several people were invited to present their approaches. Dorothy Nolte presented Rolfing, John Pierrakos gave us bioenergetic analysis, and Charlotte Selver presented her sensory awareness method. The striking thing about their presentations occurred after the formal part was over and we could chat about how they themselves regarded their work. In every case they referred to a belief that they were working with energies in the body that were not the known ones of electrical current, blood circulation, or breathing. It was some other energy, cosmic energy.

At about this time I found that I was enjoying sharing in the magical, mystical beliefs. It had nothing to do with whether or not they were scientifically valid, but simply how it made me feel to believe them. The whole Esalen environment is shot through with mysticism. The land is the former burial grounds of the Esalen Indians and the natural hot springs have long been felt to have magical healing powers. The confluence of ocean, hot springs, and mountain stream makes the location unique and invested with a magic. I found when walking the grounds at night—hearing the ocean, seeing the stars, the canyon, the trees, sitting in the hot baths—that there was a special feeling here. Mystical, spiritual—I couldn't tell—but special, uplifting.

Many residents believed in astrology, the *I Ching,* Tarot cards, Karma—one meaning of which is that whatever one is destined for will happen.

I started opening myself up to the possibility that these ideas were not totally false. But I had to do that by finding some scientific basis for their truth. Someone mentioned that the moon has a large influence on the tides, so why not on a person who is about two-thirds water. Hmm. A reading from the Tarot or from the astrological charts didn't seem markedly worse than a reading from psychological tests. And the idea that whatever is supposed to happen will happen greatly reduced my anxiety about the future on several occasions and even made some unpleasant events, like deaths, much easier to deal with.

In fact, it was around the issue of death that I came to realize that I was beginning to really believe some of these views. In the summer of 1969 my father was overcome by a stroke that left him totally unconscious. I flew back to Connecticut and spent several hours with him alone in the hospital. Both on the trip back and while talking to him I found myself believing in spiritual things, like reincarnation and the body-mind identity. This is what I wrote on the plane going to see him in the hospital:

Dad's stroke—going.

My God—men have landed on the moon and my father's dying—on the same day!

Dad, I feel good about going to you. It's right. I want to tell you all. My feelings are awfully far from my consciousness. Intuition says that this trip is of great importance. It's hard to feel it. But I do cry periodically. For what might have been, and for what might be—with my children. I love them (tears).

Maybe the resolution of you will free me. That's in the back of my mind. Also embracing the spiritual seems closer as I approach Danbury. All of a sudden the reality of mysticism is clearer. I really feel reincarnation will happen with me and you. We have learned a lot this time around. Next time we could do it better.

Levels and levels. There are so many. And they recur. And they are all true. The mystical ones too. But you kind of intimated that, Dad. You always appreciated the mystical. More than I did.

It never fully happened. That's why we need another incarnation. My father was better than yours. You used to say that, and it's true. I have the self-insight you never had. You had to stay on top of everything on the outside. The only place you showed insecurity or weakness was in your body. Gout, arthritis, diverticulitis, high blood pressure, glaucoma, and a stroke. You ravaged your body. Next time you'll know better. Somehow you taught me something that allowed me to seek out an understanding of how people express themselves through their bodies.

This is one of the things I want to tell you. You are O.K. You gave me a lot and you didn't give me a lot, and you fucked me up—but what you gave me allows me to overcome the deficits and come out with a powerful being. I'm capable of almost anything and I'm almost certain to make a big impact on the world. And you contributed mightily to it.

I keep thinking of old times, the ball games, the travel through the midwest, the FDR period, capitals of the states, the order of the presidents, Lou Gehrig, the White Sox, irony. You made it, Dad. You lied sometimes, but you were mainly very honest and very moral. I'm honest and moral. And I'll talk a lot of people into being the same. You *were.* Your customers trusted you. I admired that. You wouldn't load them up with merchandise they didn't need. And I admired *that.*

Wait for me, Dad. Don't die yet. I must tell you these things. I must tell you—it's all right. *You are all right.* You did what you could. And it was good.

You needed someone to tell you how great you were. I just lately came to realize that your hero stories were a cry for help. But your parents wouldn't let you be weak and moody.

I tried once to talk at a deeper level about your divorce from Mom but you didn't seem to want to. So I gave up. We didn't reach each other at that level. I think we can reach each other at a deeper level and that's the main reason I'm here.

Toonerville Trolley. My seat partner mentioned this and it brought back a series of memories of childhood. I often felt that I had been deposited into the world by the T.T.

Funny, it's only when I hear music or drink a little that these sentimental feelings come through.

We are much alike. And you have given me the tools to overcome some of the weaknesses we both share. This is one of your great gifts. And you are an honest man. I trust you. And you help me to be honest, too. I'm proud of your flight back to California during the loyalty oath. You were just right. You said I was morally right but practically, I would jeopardize my career. It just happened that my career flourished anyway.

I think I've said all I have to say. Almost. I believe firmly that we will meet again in another incarnation. And the almost? The almost is because the last thing I want to say to you is—I love you, Dad. You were a good father. I love you.

Goodbye.

He died about a week later and it was easier for me to deal with because I felt, and still do, that we will meet in another incarnation.

Steve's words come back to me now. Maybe it is true that my lifelong quest for realizing my potential, even making a career of it, is the same as looking for the God within me, and urging everyone else to find the God within himself. Yes, it feels right; that's where God is, at least. I can accept that. I've always had a propensity to go inward. Even as an adolescent I never could get excited about speedy transportation by means of flying, of going out and around. I felt it would be much more efficient to expend our financial and technical energies going through the earth. Imagine, if we could drill holes through the earth, travel to the other side of the world would be a matter of hours, not days. This elegant solution resulted from going inward.

I feel that about people. The ultimate answers are in each of us, inside our skin. And for me now, as open encounter proceeds and gets more profound, as intrapsychic methods get deeper, as the place of the body becomes clearer and as the mystical and spiritual dimension becomes more of a reality to me, I see man's unity and oneness more clearly, and his realization of himself comes closer. Open encounter seems to be a key to unlock the door going down the right hallway. The corruption and hypocrisy seem ugly and perhaps soon unnecessary.

Kundalini Yoga

The concepts used for the spiritual level of man are not entirely clear to me, since this is an area in which I am a neophyte. The formulation that appeals to me most so far is from one of the Indian yogas called Kundalini. It is remarkably consistent with the conception I'm presenting here.

The Kundalini is the Grand Potential or the Supreme Power (received from the earth) in the human body. The aim of the yoga (life path) is to arouse this power and purify the elements of the body. The Kundalini takes the form of a sleeping serpent, coiled at the base of the spine. To gain full realization, the Kundalini power penetrates seven chakras, or centers of the body, located along the spine. Only then can a man realize his full (cosmic) potential. The serpent must be awakened and then rise through these chakras (roughly characterized):

Chakra:	Location:	Meaning:
1.	Base of spine	Grand potential, Primitive energy
2.	Level of genitals	Sexual energy
3.	Level of navel	Assertiveness, Anger
4.	Level of heart	Affection, Love
5.	Level of throat	Communication, Expression
6.	Level of pineal body	Intuition
7.	Top of head	Cosmic consciousness

In the yoga, the usual methods for attaining a breakthrough of the chakras is meditation. Each chakra is meditated on until a surge of energy is felt up the spine, often accompanied by great heat. Perhaps some of the body methods developed in the West, especially Rolfing and bioenergetics, would be other methods for aiding the Kundalini energy to rise through the spine.

The Kundalini framework is very comprehensive for understanding the approach of open encounter. It recognizes the importance of the body through centering all the activity there; the intrapsychic through the method of meditation to reach these centers; the interpersonal in the meaning given to each chakra, such as assertion and affection; the intellectual through the expression and intuition chakras; and the spiritual through the crown (seventh) chakra and the whole object of the rise of the Kundalini energy, namely, cosmic consciousness. It thus incorporates in the compact framework of the body the vital elements of man.

Further, the order of the chakras is important. I've seen several people try to attain a higher chakra without going through the lower ones. On lower levels this phenomenon is very typical. A man in an encounter group is having difficulty establishing a love relation (fourth chakra) with a woman in the group. She reports that she feels some phoniness in his approach and feeling. What frequently results is that he has a sexual desire (second chakra) for her and is not acknowledging that this issue must be dealt with first. Or sometimes he has great hostility toward women (third chakra) that he is also not dealing with. The order of chakras supports the idea that in order to reach the highest levels of joy and ecstasy, or even real affection, the sexual and aggressive feelings must be dealt with satisfactorily.

On the higher chakras the same principle seems to apply. One man took LSD with the object of having a cosmic and spiritual trip. He felt ready for this step and had prepared himself for it. However, he spent most of the trip vomiting around an unresolved resentment of his mother (third chakra). He had tried to skip over the third chakra to the seventh. Another man in a psychotic state was apparently able to reach moments of great mystical purity (seventh chakra), but he would be pulled back from these quickly by a need to compete with the men (third chakra) near him, either physically, intellectually, or in terms of penis size.

In the case of Baba Ram Dass, he went to India to attempt to reach the seventh chakra through the discipline of a guru and meditative methods. My impression of him was that he was succeeding but that the impediments were his inability to overcome competitive feelings (third chakra) and resolve affectional relations (fourth chakra). The ways in which people attempt to reach the higher chakras are a spiritual discipline especially involving meditation, sometimes psychoses, and some psychedelic drug trips. I'm not sure how rigidly the sequence operates and I'm sure that, like all sequences, many things happen at once, but the general principle of not skipping chakras has been extraordinarily illuminating.

Several students of the chakras have attempted to reconcile them with Western anatomy. The most extensive attempt is made by Vasang G. Rele in a small book called *The Mysterious Kundalini: Physical Basis of the "Kundalini (Hatha) Yoga" in Terms of Western Anatomy and Physiology.* (One of the charming things about the book is that the foreword is written by a man who completely disagrees with the thesis of the book.) I found the ideas quite fascinating and offering a bridge between East and West. Rele feels that the chakras correspond to the plexes (centers) of the autonomic nervous system, and that the Kundalini energy herself corresponds to the right vagus nerve. Rele's brief description of the general idea will give the flavor of his approach:

Normally, the central nervous system is well developed as regards its response to external stimuli, while the sympathetic nervous system lies dormant. When the latter is made active by Pranayama (breath control) and by certain other processes described in the Hatha Yoga, a person develops the power to do certain things which are beyond the scope of an ordinary individual. Actions done by these persons are regarded as miracles, though to a Yogi, they are not so. They are due to a latent power within, but it requires to be converted into active energy. A Yogi, when he develops his autonomic nervous system, becomes so engrossed that the . . . knowledge of his relations with the external world are held in abeyance, and he sees his Self pervading the whole universe and becoming one with it.

This is a good description of the aim of spiritual enlightenment coming after the chakras are overcome.

The correspondence between chakras and plexes (joining of nerves) of the autonomic nervous system is given more systematically, though almost identically, in *The Chakras* by C. W. Leadbeater, one of the authorities in the field. For those with some knowledge of anatomy, his chart with technical terminology may be useful:

There is some slight controversy over the second chakra. The genital interpretation is given in most Indian texts and is the one I shall use here. The crown chakra (seventh) is not connected with any of the sympathetic plexuses, but is presumed to be associated with the pineal body (an organ for which Western science has not found a function) and the pituitary gland.

Thus the Indian tradition has attempted to give its mystical belief a scientific base. If these nerve plexuses are stimulated they could well provide a diffusion of energy, and perhaps such diffusion is blocked by the emotional problems expressed as physical tensions interfering with the transmission of this nerve energy.

This is by no means an adequate rendition of the Kundalini. It omits, for one thing, the concept of several bodies that coexist simultaneously. I simply want to introduce this conception of Kundalini and chakras in order to relate it to my scheme. Besides, I don't know much more about it. The interested reader

Chakra	Position on surface of body	Approximate position of spinal chakra	Sympathetic nerve plexus	Chief subsidiary plexuses
1 Root	Base of spine	4th sacral	coccygeal (Impar)	(This is convergence of pelvic plexes)
2 Spleen Genital	Over spleen over genitals	1st lumbar 2nd sacral	splenic hypogastric	
3 Navel	Over navel	8th thoracic	celiac or solar	Hepatic, pyloric, gastric, mesenteric, etc.
4 Heart	Over heart	8th cervical	cardiac	pulmonary, coronary, etc.
5 Throat	At throat	3rd cervical	pharyngeal	
6 Brow	On brow	1st cervical	carotid	cavernous, and cephalic, ganglia, generally

is referred to the two books cited above and A. Avalon's *The Serpent Power.* All three of these books can usually be purchased through metaphysical bookstores.

The Integration of the Individual

Work to unblock or strengthen man's life flow is best done by treating the physical, emotional, and interpersonal levels as a unity and letting work done on one level be supplemented by work done on the others. Using a combination of methods appears to me to be the most effective approach to realizing the human potential. Ignoring any of the levels greatly decreases effectiveness. I have noticed that many practitioners in the area of the human potential who concentrate on one level to the exclusion of the others reflect this imbalance in their personalities. Several body people and those who work with intrapsychic techniques have difficulty with interpersonal relations. They often have trouble encountering openly and meeting other people on their own level. Similarly, some who are interpersonal only have uncared-for bodies and not a great deal of sensitivity to individual defenses and dynamics. In my case I think that at least the spiritual dimension of which I am just becoming aware is deficient both in my method and in my personality, and as it becomes more of a reality to me it will be incorporated more organically and gracefully into my approach.

In order to integrate the various levels of functioning the Rolf technique of body integration will be used as the focus. The basic philosophy of Rolfing is that all bodies are aberrated in some way due to the physical and emotional trauma of life. The body needs to compensate for these trauma in order to stay upright against the gravitational force. If the body is in correct alignment it operates in accord with gravity and remains upright simply by being balanced with a minimal expenditure of energy. If the body gets out of that position, say by the head being bent forward, gravity pulls down on the head, requiring other muscles, probably in the back and the back of the neck, to compensate for the gravitational pull and prevent the person from falling on his face. So for each aberration there must be some tight muscles. Here's a hypothetical example:

Suppose an infant, in learning to walk, feels his mother doesn't want him to approach; he therefore anticipates being punished or rejected. Hence his step is tentative, part of his body going toward his mother and part shrinking away as he steps forward, thus pulling his weight to the back of his foot and his calf, which tighten. In order to prevent falling backward, the upper front leg muscles tighten. (You might try this out as you read.) Then, to keep the body in balance, the muscles in the small of the back tighten. Then the head goes forward and the neck muscles tighten in order to keep the body upright. If this pattern persists into adulthood, the person has an unstable feeling because his feet aren't solidly on the ground, his legs are very tight, he might have lower back pains, his head goes forward, and probably he tires easily in his neck and shoulder muscles and loves an upper back rub. Further, the blood supply is diminished in the areas of tightness. His forward head makes his breathing more shallow. Probably the muscle tensions put pressure on the nerve ganglia and endocrines, thus reducing their effectiveness.

The Rolf technique attempts to liberate these tensions. Since the body is a complex system of muscles and other tissue, it is necessary to view the Rolfing procedure in terms of an overall conception of the body. A muscle pain in the back of the neck could yield only temporary relief to a local massage around the neck, since its basic cause may be connected with the back of the legs, and ultimately, as illustrated, in the feet. Repositioning of the feet might be a much more effective treatment for the neck pain than a neck massage. For this reason, the Rolf technique treats the body as a whole, almost regardless of any specific physical complaint.

The Rolf technique involves ten hours for the basic sequence, although many people go beyond that. Each session of about an hour has a specific set of physical movements devised by Ida Rolf. The ten sessions constitute a unit, and the entire body is covered systematically in that span. Each session is devoted to a loosening and lengthening of specific muscles and fascia, the thin envelope of connective tissue that surrounds each muscle, muscle fiber, and muscle group. This loosening leads to a repositioning of these tissues and a migration back toward their natural position. The procedure is to give the Rolfee a deep fascial reorganization, using the fingers, knuckles, and elbows in an attempt to free the muscle attachments and release the chronic tensions. The procedure is painful to the degree that there is muscular tension, although the handling of the pain is an interesting problem in itself. Many Rolfees learn how to adapt to the pain so that it is not unpleasant; on occasion it may be pleasurable or even ecstatic. My instruction to each Rolfee is to put all of his attention on the spot where my hand is and try to relax that spot. If I feel him tighten up I will withdraw my hand, give him time to relax and begin again slowly enough to get in tempo with him.

This procedure is very important in terms of the theory above. The more the Rolfee can relax and let me apply pressure, the more that part of the body is free of tension. When the tension is voluntarily released by the Rolfee, this is equivalent to working through a psychological problem (as in a guided daydream fantasy), usually without the need for intellectual interpretation.

One way of viewing the first six Rolfing sessions is to focus on the pelvis. The pelvis has many muscle attachments and is pivotal in the body, due in part to its central position. Because the pelvis is central, if it is out of position, it throws off structures

both above and below it. Rolf feels that the pelvis should be
relatively horizontal so that it provides a floor for the abdominal
organs to rest on. This is in contrast to the Lowen conception,
which has the bottom of the pelvis (symphysis pubis) tilted
backward so that the abdominal organs hang free in front. (I
prefer the Rolf conception.) The ideal Rolf structure has a
straight line going through the middle of the ear, shoulder, hip,
knee, and ankle. Each of the first six sessions deal with different
muscles that attach to the pelvis.

Another perspective on these six sessions is that they deal
with layers going from the outside in. Right beneath the skin is
a layer of fascia, a substance like the fine, white network that
is under the skin of an orange. There is also a fascial layer
around each group of organs, each organ, and each tissue within
the organ, down to the muscle fibers. Everything has its own
wrapping. Because of the physical trauma described, these fascial envelopes get dried up and stuck. In order to get to the
muscles, these fascial layers must be stimulated, blood supply
restored to them through pressure, and they must be unstuck,
released, so that the muscles and other tissues can expand
freely. After fascial freeing is accomplished, the Rolfer can go
deeper into the body and work directly on the muscle wrap-
pings. The first three sessions are concentrated primarily on
freeing fascia and the later ones on freeing specific muscles,
each session allowing the practitioner to go deeper into the
body as it is prepared for a deeper letting go. This sequence of
sessions is largely dictated by the body. When one part gets
worked on and released, an imbalance is caused due to the lack
of release of the complementary muscles. These latter will often
look and feel like they need lengthening.

Session One. The first session is aimed at lengthening the
distance between the bottom of the rib cage and the top of the
pelvis on the assumption that everybody has been jammed

down into the pelvis and needs more length to allow the abdominal organs more freedom. The first session loosens the outer fascial layers of the body and frees the muscles around the rib cage so that breathing is fuller and deeper. The deeper breathing puts more oxygen in the blood and helps the blood carry off toxins more efficiently. Also, the tension around the heart muscle is released so that blood flows more freely. This leads to a general feeling of well-being. Also, the top front of the body from the sternal notch (the point between the collar bones) to the navel is lengthened. These effects are caused by deep manipulation around the thorax (rib cage), then around the hip and upper leg, giving more mobility around the hip, and then straightening the spine.

The emotional reactions to this session (as to all the sessions) are varied, depending on the person, but I shall cite some of the common responses. Work on breathing, especially releasing the diaphragm (the muscle under the rib cage) often brings associations of suffocation fears or hospital situations. Frequently people will feel terror, and remember a hospital situation when they were given ether. One surprising result is that an operation in which the person felt no fear sometimes comes back at this point with great terror. What apparently happens is that the feeling associated with a traumatic event is cut off immediately at the time it occurs by locking it in some muscles that then become chronically tense and probably painful to pressure. These sensitive areas can often be discovered simply by imagining someone pushing hard at all of your muscles—stomach, behind the inside ankle bone, in the groin, everywhere. Some of these places will feel painful even in the imagination. When these muscles are released, the fear comes out and can be worked through, thus allowing that muscle to resume its natural state, as well as all the muscles that it has affected. Often there is a hollow at the breast bone (sternum) in the middle of the chest that is related to important emotional events, perhaps to fighting and being hit in that area. One man yelled "Brother!" to express his pain whenever I would press on that spot. This opened up a lot of feelings about his brother that he had never realized. He had followed a pattern of withdrawing from his brother (pulling back his chest) rather than asserting himself (sticking out his chest). The expression used to respond to pain is often significant, as in this case of "Brother." In another case, the phrase "Oh, God!" was used by a former Episcopal minister, apparently not yet totally free of his earlier role.

This session often reveals a fascinating difference between the front and back of the body, especially in the upper part. Some people are very tense in the front of the chest (pectoralis major, intercostals) and feel great pain there, while their back muscles (erector spinae) are relaxed and easy. Psychologically, these people tend to be very "up front." They react spontaneously and tend to be quite open. Other people have no tension or pain in front but show great holding and pain in the back muscles. They tend to be delayed reactors, those that play it cool and react later. One psychiatrist was a good example. Whatever was said to him he would accept, but a day or two later he'd respond strongly. It was as if he let what was said go through him where people could see, his chest, and he would catch it behind his back and deal with it there. He had the same syndrome in the other direction. While I worked on his chest he was apparently calm, but his feet were sweating profusely.

Another fascinating hypothesis concerns breathing. On several Rolfees I have noticed that chest breathing takes place when feeling is being avoided. When breathing is abdominal there is much more emotion. While I was Rolfing one man in the first hour he was quite calm and clinical as I worked on his chest, and he was breathing almost entirely with his chest. Following the first session I put him into a fantasy, and he started talking about his feelings for his wife, who left him for another man, and his children about whom he felt guilty. As soon as he started feeling grief and anger his entire breathing pattern changed. His stomach started moving fully and rapidly and his emotional state changed from objective coolness to sadness, crying, and hatred. Apparently the deeper feelings involve lower breathing to express. If a person wants to block off these deeper feelings he breathes only with the chest.

The first session covers the area of the fourth chakra (heart), the chakra of love and affection. The effect of freeing this area is seen in most cases when the Rolfee ends the session with a feeling of well-being and a glow, often "high." Part of the session involves releasing the tension of the rib cage, which in turn increases the blood flow to and from the heart. This flow of the life fluid results in a generalized warm feeling.

Interpersonally, the first Rolf session covers both affection and inclusion. Affection is stimulated by opening up the feeling around the heart and helping the blood flow more freely, for lack of personal warmth is often accompanied by a constricted heart, not letting the life fluid out. (Perhaps this is related to heart trouble.) A full feeling of love requires a strong and full pumping of life blood throughout the whole body. A "broken heart" is often accompanied by tight feelings in the heart area. To a loved one, "I open my heart to you" is probably literally true. The nearness of a loved one can cause a heart's fluttering and fast beating. It is characteristic that a happy love relation brightens all of life; it gives a general glow to everything as the strongly beating heart sends nourishment to the entire organism. Similarly, an unhappy love situation darkens the whole world. Since it would be difficult to tense the heart in such a way that blood would flow in but not out, it would seem that giving love and taking love would be closely related.

Indeed, in some early research I did measuring inclusion, control, and affection (*FIRO*, p. 57), one annoying result was that I could not make up a scale measuring the amount of affection a person expressed to others that would be significantly different, in the sense of a low statistical correlation, from a scale measuring how much affection a person wanted from other people. This was such a difficult task that on a later questionnaire (LIPHE) I simply combined the two scales into one. Perhaps the centrality of the heart as the center of an inflow-outflow would suggest a reason for my test-making difficulties.

Inclusion is related to the first session through breathing. Breathing is like the starter on a car; it is the in-out decision-maker for biological life. If a person chooses not to enter into any activity, not to commit himself, not to feel anything, he can accomplish this by not breathing, or to a degree, by breathing very shallowly. Lowen feels that the depth and quality of breathing derives from early contact with the father, shallow breathing indicating a holding back, a reluctance to express oneself fully and as an equal, a reluctance to enter into a deep exchange.

This is very similar to the inclusion phenomenon in a group, where the degree to which a person chooses to give himself to the group, to commit himself, is determined in part by his assessment of the place he will be allowed to take in the group. He sizes up the situation and decides on the amount of energy he will devote to the group. He can play it cool, breathing so as not to be detected, or he can throw himself into it with great energy, necessitating breathing deeply. One of the best methods of getting someone involved in the group is to get him to breathe heavily through wrestling, pounding, screaming, or anything that requires heavy breathing. After that he almost inevitably feels more present. This also helps to specify more of the body truth that keeps bullshit to a minimum. If a group member is working on any feelings in the area of inclusion, the focus can be on his breathing. If he begins to shorten it he is probably withdrawing; if he starts to relax and breathe deeper, he is committing himself more. Respiratory ailments are probably related to inclusion problems.

Session Two. The second Rolf session focuses on the feet and ankles, which then have an effect on the pelvis and back. The back is worked on at the end of the hour and lengthened to match the lengthening of the front in the first hour. The feet are of vital importance psychologically because they are the contact with reality, the ground, and gravity. Physically, an imbalance at the feet throws off the balance of the total structure. The Reich and Lowen people feel that the feet represent primarily a person's relation to his mother—whether the infant tried to walk too soon, running after the mother, thus getting bowed legs; or anticipating rejection, walked very tentatively; or feeling overwhelmed, thus "digging in his heels," or being very careful to avoid criticism by tiptoeing, and so forth. There is a whole method, zone therapy, based primarily on the feet, using different parts of the feet to relate to specific body parts. I suspect this is a method worth looking into and redeveloping, for work on the feet often leads to profound changes.

In one instance a man's right foot and left calf were very tense and cramped, and working on them caused him great pain and anger. I asked him to do some gestalt therapy on them by carrying on a dialogue between the two. Soon his calf was excoriating his right foot for not stepping out enough, for not stretching out and initiating movement for the whole body. He wasn't carrying his weight, said the calf. This dialogue helped the man to recognize his own passivity and his annoyance with it.

Another man found great pain in his feet as I worked on them and had to keep them moving. I asked him to keep them moving until he found out what they wanted to do. "Run away," he said, "I want to run away." He immediately thought of both his immediate situation, in which he was unhappy with his marriage, and his early childhood situation, when his father pressured him to become a doctor. The feet had evidently prepared themselves for running many times but had never been able to complete the act. The result was great tension in the muscles and fascia of the feet.

Along with the foot, there is a great deal of change all the way through the body. Aligning the ankle joints so that they are moving horizontally and freeing the feet so that they walk parallel, and so that the weight is balanced over the sole of the foot, helps to realign and straighten the body by decompensating the compensations that the body has been making for its imbalances. Frequently, what appears to be a neck pain or a back pain can be alleviated by work on the feet because the back pain is a compensation. Psychologically, successful foot work can make a great deal of difference in how the person stands in the world. Often much more grounding, more firmness, more of a sense of the self as a stable person follows from this work. Having both feet on the ground and not being afraid to step out can be exhilarating feelings.

Session Three. The third session centers around the sides and the trunk of the body. It is also concerned with freeing the superficial fascia, and concentrates on widening the sides to allow deeper breathing and balancing the lengthening in front and back. It aims at releasing a key muscle of the trunk (quadratus lumborum) that connects the bottom (12th) rib to the top of the pelvic bone (crest of the ilium). This muscle when normal anchors the rib cage and maintains the distance between the ribs and the pelvis. When it gets thickened breathing is affected and the ribs and pelvis are jammed together. Revitalizing this muscle thins out the middle of the body, often making it appear that the person has lost weight when, actually, the "spare tire" around the middle has disappeared because the distance between the ribs and pelvis has increased.

The psychological feeling is of greater awareness in the center of the body. In my experience the back and sides of the waist tend to be remote from the awareness of most people. The area from the rib bottom to the pelvic top is often untoned, the temperature of the skin cooler, the accumulation of fat greater, and sensation diminished. I suspect that the main result of successful work in this region is very subtle and has to do with helping a person get "centered." The work down the sides is primarily aimed at separating the side muscles that get stuck together (latissimus, serratus anterior, teres). This, too, is related to awareness.

The right-left split has been classically related to the male and female side. One girl represented this beautifully. As I worked on her right side, I found the tissue tough; her right shoulder went forward and whenever she felt pain, her fist and jaw clenched, she said "Shit!" and a flash of anger would come over her. On the left side her skin was soft and spongy, her shoulder was back and pain would result in her melting, often followed by tears. The pain was much greater on the left. The overall appearance was of the tough, male, right side protecting the soft, feminine, fragile, left side. This matched her position in the world, where she was a professionally successful woman of great femininity. She turned on one side or the other. A freeing of her body can help her build toward an integration of the two parts.

The third session also goes into the muscles of the buttocks and begins to deal with pelvic structure at a lower level. In some people this releases muscle tensions that are involved with feelings about homosexuality. Here is a report of a Rolfee who had such an experience:

"My third Rolfing was my most liberating experience. Sexually, it put me in contact with previous experiences, dating back some twenty-odd years. Specifically, I remembered a male individual with whom I consented to have sex, but which turned out to be physically and emotionally disturbing. I was 13, a virgin, and I was very curious. When the sex act became painful (my partner was trying anal penetration), I resisted, complained, and asked for the act to cease. My partner was too far into his own trip to care, and so I had to endure until he climaxed. Although the experience was never completely forgotten, I tried not to remember it. It was during and after my third Rolfing that the vivid memory came back to me, and with the memory fully exposed, I've felt a great sense of relief."

Session Four. Session four returns to the bottom half of the body. Consecutive sessions never work on the same area of the body, thus easing the physical strain on the Rolfee. This session is aimed at freeing the pelvis from below by releasing the big muscles at the side and back of the upper leg (adductors and hamstrings), the muscles that attach to the lower end of the pelvis (the ramus of the ischial tuberosity). Work on the legs continues, extending upward from the ankle for the first time and also getting into the genital areas for the first time. The legs are frequently full of emotion, often very specific, sometimes going back to unique incidents like being tied and bound around the legs and put in a dark closet when young. One girl actually had a fear reaction where her Rolfer reached the back of her leg slightly above the knee. Her immediate association was with a feeling of great embarrassment when she had to wear a skirt to school for the first time. She had always been a tomboy and felt very comfortable in that role, including the long pants. The quick switch in roles symbolized by the skirt made her very uncertain. Apparently this was dealt with in part by tensing the muscles at the point where the skirt contacted the skin. Release of this muscle brought out the old feelings surrounding the incident.

Another man felt great emotional pain when I released the muscles around his knees, and he immediately remembered embarrassing situations involving wearing knickers when he was a boy. He was the only boy in his elementary school graduating class who wore knickers, and he remembered one little girl snickering when he crossed the stage. This brought back strong feelings of embarrassment, anger at the girl, anger at his mother, and a still-felt longing to be like everyone else. Dealing with these feelings in a follow-up fantasy helped him to work them through.

The muscles around the genitals are often very tense and bring out feelings of being permanently injured by the Rolfer, or of being sexually violated. Early castration fear takes the form of tightening the muscles around the genitals, including the adductors (inside top of leg). These muscles are also held tight to stop urination when toilet training has been a traumatic event. So the possibility of emotionally laden material is very great during this session. The area corresponds to the second chakra, the seat of sexuality.

Session Five. The fifth Rolfing session deals primarily with two muscles. One is the large stomach muscle (rectus abdominus) that attaches at the ribs at their point of separation from the breast bone (5th, 6th, and 7th ribs), goes over the stomach, and attaches right in the center of the pubic bone (symphysis pubis) just over the genitals. It's the muscle men beat on when they want to show how hard their stomach is. The other muscle is the psoas or iliopsoas, a fascinating muscle. It is deep inside the body and attaches to the lower portion of the spine, crosses over the pelvis, and ends at the inside upper part of the large bone in the upper leg (lesser trochanter of the femur). It therefore connects the top part of the body to the bottom, the spine to the leg, and is very crucial for all pelvic movement, general body balance, and sexual movement.

This area covers the third (navel) chakra, supposedly the seat of power. The psychological responses during this hour support this notion. Feelings of terror, fear, and anger are very commonly released when these muscles are relaxed. If a child is motivated to strike out either with his arms or legs (try it), the stomach area is tensed to stabilize the body for the blow. If this pattern is repeated often, and external circumstances like parental prohibitions prevent the full expression of the anger, it can result in chronic tension of the muscles in the stomach area. Further, the stomach muscle attaches at the lower end near the sexual area and sexual tension affects it, so that feelings of fear of sexual attack, injury, or violation can be stimulated during this hour. With one man the work on his stomach uncovered his passivity and lack of aggression. He was very disturbed for days afterward, and reports that he has since become much firmer in his relations with girl friends and business colleagues. Another man was filled with terror as I started working in the stomach area, and he had great difficulty sleeping. He reported:

"I felt, during the session, that the entire front of my trunk had been unstuck and softened up—unhinged in a way that caused me to tremble (and flap) from sternum to pelvis like a reed in the wind. I trembled some during the session, but the trembling increased during the day and night following the session. My stomach was sore and burning. The fantasy I had during the session was of being small and helpless and held down and tortured—the feeling was fear and humiliation and some sobbing began. I felt very sorry for myself, and then tears of self-pity gradually changed to anger.

"The most marked emotional result was the two days of panic and sense of angry depression. There were moments of terror that I was about to 'go down the drain,' dissolve, vaporize, lose my control, my identity, and, to put it bluntly, go mad. This overwhelmed, or nearly overwhelmed, me off and on for several days—a sense of unreality, of a plastic, flat, nightmare world, and the feeling that either I or they were zombies.

"It was a deeply unsettling experience which seemed to cut a charge of anger loose to drift freely through my bloodstream until it dissolved (or was eliminated and/or passed out).

"When the terror of the experience had been endured and

the panic had subsided, I knew that I had gotten a life-giving message from my body."

Frequently behind the fear and anger is a feeling of despair and depression, a hopeless feeling of "what's the use." In contrast to the first session, when the heart chakra release leads to a feeling of warmth and well-being, the Rolfee is frequently left depressed after the fifth session. After he vents his spleen he is sad. Of course, being in touch with this anger and sadness can be very valuable in working through the related feelings. Interpersonally, the area covered is closely related to aggression, assertion, anger, fear, and feelings generally dealt with in the control area. In a group when someone is working on a control problem, it is valuable to watch his abdominal area and keep him focused on it. If he begins to intellectualize, his awareness of the tension usually leaves, an indicator that he has begun to defend against his feelings. He must get back to those feelings if he really wants the issue worked through.

Session Six. The sixth session deals with the backs of the legs, the small internal muscles connecting the pelvis and the leg (rotatories), and the muscles and ligaments around the sacrum and tailbone (coccyx). This area covers the first chakra, the point at which the Kundalini energy is stored. The backs of the legs for many people are very alien, difficult places to have much feeling, since they are far away and out of sight. Awakening the energy in those parts often gives rise to a startled reaction, new sensations the person rarely felt; a whole new area of the body comes alive. There is frequently a great deal of holding behind there, for it bears the brunt of presenting a relaxed, stable image. Like the Wizard of Oz, in order to present a good "front" to the world the back must work very hard; in this case it comes out as much holding and tension in the back of the legs, the buttocks, and the lower back.

One of the rotatory muscles, the piriformis, I find fascinating.

Like the psoas, it is a muscle that attaches the top and bottom parts of the body, attaching at the inside of the sacrum, the triangular bone at the base of the spine, and the top of the leg bone (greater trochanter of femur). Freedom in this middle part of the body allows a free flow of energy through the pelvis and genitals into the legs. It's therefore central to the integration of body flow.

This area is also the repository of many leftover feelings from anal training. If toilet training occurred before the anal sphincters were developed, the anus had to be held closed by the muscles of the buttocks, thus a release of tension often releases early feelings about anality. As in the third hour, homosexual feelings are also elicited in men, often around the anus, the receptive organ.

Interpersonally, control issues are often related to the backs of the legs, primarily as resistance to control. The extensor muscles, the ones that extend muscles to their full length, hold the body rigid and resistant to pressure. This could apply to the back of the legs up the whole back. Wanting to control others is expressed through the flexors, the muscles that bend the joints, as in pounding the table or striking. Tension in the back of the body is related to "digging in your heels," "stiffening the backbone," and "bowing your neck," generally the postures of resistance. The person who resists control need not also wish to control others; he may have tense muscles in back, but not in front.

In a group, whenever the issue of resisting control is broached, attention should be focused on the muscles in the back of the body. They could be massaged while the person is working since any loosening would help the person break through his block and have the blocked material more available. Also, the relaxing of felt tension is another instance of the specification of truth in the body. If the tension on these parts disappears during the encounter process, it is a good sign that some defensiveness has occurred and the work being done is not effective. The other possibility is that the problem has been worked through and relaxation has been attained. Which explanation is pertinent is usually evident from observing the person.

Session Seven. The seventh Rolfing session deals with the face and neck, covering both the fifth (neck) and sixth (between eyebrows) chakras. In many ways, this session is quite interesting, partly because of the many nerve plexes in the face. Release of these plexes often gives a rush of feeling leading to a euphoria. The muscles of the neck are released first (trapezius, levator scapulae, sternocleidomastoid, splenius, longissimus), then the jawline is worked on and the mouth is entered to release the muscles that go down the neck (suprahyoids) and to the spine in back of the neck. Then the openings in the nose (nasal meatuses) are opened and the external facial muscles drawn back. Each of these actions can give rise to profound experiences. Work on the neck was very crucial for me and is often closely connected with control, specifically masculinity problems. In many men in particular, masculinity is closely tied to the neck muscles, particularly those in back (trapezius). Building up those muscles makes a man look like a wrestler or middle guard in football. They usually also develop wraparound shoulders. The head is then jammed down into the neck and actually feels protected by the neck and shoulder muscles. As I mentioned earlier, when my trapezius was freed and my neck rose out of this muscular cage, I felt very strange and vulnerable and exposed up there where people could see me.

The throat muscles generally hold onto fears of expression. They represent inclusion problems and often go together with breathing. Breathing is held back by a tight throat. The child who wanted to yell at his parents but wasn't allowed to held it in his throat so that his voice is strained or too soft. Throat illnesses come easily, coughing is common, and sometimes laughter is stopped prematurely because the tight throat and shallow breathing prevent a true belly laugh; all the laugh must be from the throat upward and attempts to laugh more heartily result in coughing. Attention to the voice is very important when working on inclusion problems, especially because it represents expressiveness and contact with others. Fear of inclusion is often accompanied by a tight throat and a soft, unintelligible voice. Noting the variations in the voice tells where the person is in terms of his inclusion behavior. This is consistent with the throat chakra being the center of communication.

The bottom of the jaw is often the place where tears are held from prematurely stopped crying, as described earlier. The jaw muscle itself (masseter) often holds much anger due to biting inhibitions when young. This is a good body part to watch when control problems and anger arise. Dental problems caused by excessive grinding (bruxion) are often traceable to repressed anger. The position of the lower jaw is determined largely by the tightness of the masseter. This means that if a small child was unable to speak up to his parents, he would tend to hold back on his jaw muscle, thus pulling his lower jaw back. This results in an overbite (buck teeth) and sometimes a lisp, since the upper and lower teeth must be almost together to make a proper *s* sound.

Work in the nose often opens up the passageways and helps sinus conditions. These are sometimes related to repressed tears, and these tears can sometimes be reached this way. I had some very important experiences when the external facial muscles were worked on. I have a prominent vertical line between my eyebrows. As it was being smoothed out by being drawn toward my ears, I had a feeling of openness in my face and my eyes seemed to open wider and see more. My feelings around my intent squint led me to remember being expected to understand everything I was told. When any information was presented it was essential to put all of my attention on it, which meant squinting both to concentrate and to appear to be concentrating.

Another memory that came back was a picture of myself being somewhere with many people and looking intently for something. The main motive for my intent look, I suddenly realized, was to stop those people from looking at me. If I were so focused on something external, maybe they would be, too. So I was trying to divert their attention. This happened particularly when I'd enter the college library in order to pick up a girl. I didn't want people to look at me while I was engaged in this nefarious activity, so I would look very intent and stride purposefully, hoping that they would think I was simply involved with something legitimate and then not notice me. Working on these feelings allowed me to open my face more and really look at things and people.

The work on the neck and mouth often helps to bring the head back over the spine. Many people's heads are too far forward, since normally, the ear is over the shoulder. As current slang puts it, "Get your head on straight." A straight head represents much greater presence and firmness in the world. It is not cowering or protected, it is simply there for all to see. Along with the stabilized legs and their relation to the ground, the solid center, the increased breathing and circulation, and the longer energy flow throughout the body, the whole organism begins to feel more energetic, more centered, more self-accepting, and more together.

Sessions Eight, Nine, and Ten. The process to come together, as the Beatles say, continues through the final three sessions. The eighth and ninth work more intensely on the top half of the body around the shoulder girdle, and on the bottom half around the pelvic girdle. The tenth session simply begins at the bottom and works all the way up, working on the major joints: ankle, knee, pelvis, and shoulder. All three sessions are tailored to the

Rolfee picking up areas that need more work and concentrating on the special problems of each person. They are different in method since the outer fascial layers have now been loosened and the muscular structure is much more plastic and flexible. A Rolfer can often almost sculpt some muscles into place at this time. Furthermore, these sessions afford an opportunity to get it all together, to look at the total structure and work at distant but related parts.

The reactions after these hours are often very intense, perhaps due to the fact that they cover larger areas of the body picking up more feelings, and partly due to the fact that they are focused on the integration of the whole body. Improved flow of body energy is a common feeling. Following is the report of one girl after her tenth Rolfing. It is a good example of the mixture of specific memories, total integrative experiences, and a new organization of the body and emotions.

"Before the hour began, in some sort of anticipation I felt a tingling all through my body, somewhat as though I were to meet a lover.

"My feet and legs were worked on first. There was some physical pain, though not overwhelming. I began to notice that I could feel the muscle manipulation in my arms, and only pain in my legs. Then, energy was shooting through my arms and out of my hands, as if I had been continuously, electrically shocked. I was aware that I could still feel nothing in my legs other than occasional pain. I finally asked the Rolfer to stop for a moment and gave him my hands. I felt some of the energy pass through me to him. When he began to work on my calves again, I placed my hands over my thighs and, slowly, the energy build-up in my arms began to subside, and I felt energy passing through my legs. I felt more even, and then began to experience a feeling of warmth and love. If an entire body could smile, that's what mine would have been doing.

"While the muscles next to my spine, my rib cage, and my

sides were worked on, there were moments of intense nerve pain—a dull ache, like a toothache all over. Following different manipulations, I took deep breaths and noticed that each successive breath was much deeper and fuller than the preceding one. In about the center of my back, to the left of the spine, I felt a sharp, quick pain, after which I burst into tears, crying, not from pain, but through a mixture of emotions. I found myself in an operating room, about to have my appendix removed (age 7½). I smelled the hospital, the ether, and almost cried out 'No, don't!' in response to the ether mask being put over my face. I felt helpless and alone. Still crying, I experienced myself completely nonverbally, as if I were a baby being thrust out into the world. Almost simultaneously, I found I was able to comfort and love myself from inside—as though I had cried out for something and received it.

"My upper back, arms, and neck were worked on, as well as my abdomen and pelvic area. At the end of the hour, when I stood up, I felt shaky, unfamiliar with my body, and moved very tentatively. I was instructed to keep my waist back and lead with the top of my head when moving forward. This helped to build a new structure within which I could move more comfortably.

"In the first few hours following the processing I felt very relaxed, light, and whole. I enjoyed, quietly, everything I saw, heard, and did. My experiences had a pinpoint type clarity.

"The two days following the session were a potpourri of everything. I felt wonderful the next morning, tired the next afternoon, and after a nap, entered a world of slowed-down perceptions. My body ached all over, I cried for no apparent reason, and I found myself daydreaming a lot.

"I feel as though little bits and pieces from all parts of my life are flashing by, becoming integrated within my being. The emotional experiences are real, but I'm aware that they are passing as they are occurring, and I have little difficulty going

through them. My pace seems slowed down and more meaningful."

From the considerations presented so far, I would like to
extract two general principles:

1. Any conflict not resolved at one level of organization must
be dealt with at the next lower level. This means that unresolved intellectual problems must be dealt with by bodies,
unresolved administrative problems by employees, unresolved
parental problems by children, and so forth.

2. Problems can arise at either the conscious or bodily level
and are best resolved by a combination of physical and psychological techniques.

To illustrate the first principle, I'd like to present a personal
example that also illustrates the importance of combining both
approaches.

I've had a sore left hip, off and on, for about ten years. Seven
years ago or so, I had a medical doctor look at it. He X-rayed
it, found a slight calcium deposit, diagnosed it as bursitis, and
gave me a cortisone derivative shot. It felt better for a while,
but soon was painful again.

I was Rolfed, and was told that Rolfing the hip would take
care of the pain. It would release the tension in the muscles,
which would allow the bones to return to their normal position,
and the irritation would disappear. It did for a while, but soon
the hip was hurting as before.

A girl friend didn't like the way I walked, especially when she
was mad at me. "It looks like you're holding everything in. Your
feet hardly touch the ground." I'd been proud of that. I could
always run fast partly because my feet didn't stay on the ground
long. But I could see what she meant. I didn't thrust my pelvis
forward like some other men did.

All of a sudden my hip started to hurt severely, so I took a
fantasy trip about my hip. I had an image of starting to lunge

forward to the right with my left leg stationary, thereby inhibiting the lunge. As I wobbled back and forth a few times, I could start to feel the irritation in my left hip. An association came to me. I've always had trouble initiating. I can respond well, but I'm a poor self-starter. For example, I never know what to do when I take my children for a weekend. And I recently discovered one reason I've wanted to become famous. I don't have to initiate. When I go to a gathering and someone has heard of me he usually will start the conversation. Then I can react, which I do better than initiate. I was always very bad at picking up girls in bars for the same reason. It was all right if they began. It's even true for my cars, probably not accidentally. The most frequent problem I have with cars? The starters don't work well.

The mystery of my hip was beginning to clear up. The left hip is where my body was dealing with my unresolved problem of initiating action. I would start to initiate action, then get frightened and stop. I couldn't resolve this problem on the conscious level, so my hip joint kept getting irritated by the continued back and forth motion.

I started stepping out with my left leg, taking a full stride, and amazing things happened. The soreness in my hip, which had become severe, was greatly diminished. I assume that there is a calcium deposit there, so it will take a little while for it to be absorbed and the pain to disappear entirely. The muscles around my pelvis started to get unstuck and I felt much more sensation in that area down to my genitals. It felt wonderful to walk. I spent half a day just walking up and down the hills of Monterey.

Other things started to come together. I have a rotation in my pelvis with the left side back. Of course, I inhibit walking motion of my left leg. And I have a spare tire around my middle. As I walked with the full left stride, I noticed the roll of fat start to move. With my old way of walking, which held the whole pelvis still while just the legs moved, the spare tire didn't move at all. That's why it accumulated there—no action.

Further, my front, upper legs are very heavily muscled, too much. This, too, made sense, since these muscles had to power the legs unnaturally. With my new way of walking, the propulsion power was distributed through the upper leg, the buttocks, and the small of the back. I experimented. It's like the difference between throwing a ball with the shoulder stationary (try it) and throwing it while letting the shoulder follow through. In the first case the shoulder muscle (deltoid) is under greater strain.

Suddenly, everything made sense: my conflict over initiating, the comment about my restricted walk, my painful hip, the spare tire, the pelvic rotation, the overdeveloped upper leg. The left side as initiator started to make sense, too. The military march always begins with the left foot: left, right, left. In boxing, you lead—that is, initiate—with your left glove. Runners almost always line up at the starting line with the left foot forward. My right side seemed much less problematic. No soreness there.

But then I was telling all this to a friend. "But my problem is on the right, I can't follow through," he said. As we watched him move, his right arm was held back. And this is indeed the way he is in the world. He has no trouble initiating interpersonally, but he does have trouble following through and completing things. He was in his forties and hadn't really finished anything. The right side held back. The opposite of my problem. Once I get started, I usually follow through and complete things, like this book. I'm effective. If I can get started.

Hypothesis: A hip rotated with the left side back reflects conflict over initiating; right side back reflects conflict over carrying through and completing. Again, boxing gives the paradigm "the old one-two." One, the left hand initiates the action and sets up the opponent, and two, the right hand finishes the job with a knockout punch.

Lots of problems are raised. What about left-handed people? What's the difference between a hip rotation and a shoulder rotation? (Maybe the hips reflect a more hidden feeling?) What does emerge is a clear instance of the close relation between the body and feelings. When I realized and worked on the conflict over initiating, both by realizing it and starting to deal with it —psychologically by trying more initiating, physically by striding differently—then the hip no longer had to bear the brunt of my failure to take responsibility for my conflict at the conscious level. The hip started to hurt again whenever I stopped initiating appropriately. I had now learned to read my hip's signal.

The second principle arises from a difference between the Rolf and Lowen approaches. Rolf stresses physical causes of tension, while the bioenergetic theory is psychologically oriented, emphasizing emotional bases of trauma. I think chronic muscle tension can have both origins, and regardless of whether the tension has a physical or emotional origin the other level gets involved. An analogy to an automobile may clarify this concept.

There are two types of car troubles. One is due primarily to driver error, like riding the clutch and gradually wearing it down. The other is due to a defective part, like a poor electrical connection that prevents the turn signal from working. In order to fix the clutch it may be necessary to replace the mechanical part. But whether or not it needs replacing, the driver must be taught not to put his foot on the clutch excessively or else the same trouble will recur. In the case of the poor electrical connection the trouble is cured primarily by replacing the defective wire. In both cases the complete treatment of the cure involves working with both car and driver. But in the first instance the emphasis is on the driver, while in the second it is on the car.

The bad habit corresponds to a psychological difficulty that begins to cause physical damage, like worry leading to an ulcer. The faulty wire corresponds to a physical trauma that begins to cause psychological difficulties, like a poorly set broken foot that leads to feelings of psychological instability.

Both muscle tensions, regardless of cause, produce a tightening of the fascial envelope around that muscle that makes it more difficult for the muscle to return to its normal position. Perhaps if the muscle tension is simply the result of a physical trauma, pressure by the Rolfer with the cooperation of the Rolfee can bring about a release of the muscle, since it is primarily a physical holding and can therefore be released by physical means. This may correspond to the type 2 and 3 kinds of tissue. "I will relax if you support me" and "I will relax if you support me and put pressure on me." If the tension is of psychological origin, then, in addition to the fascial contraction, there is an unconscious holding onto the muscle because of the fear and conflict it represents.

During the Rolfing process there is usually a clear distinction between physical and emotional pain. The first results simply from the pressure on the tissue, the second includes feelings of fear, anger, grief, and other strong emotions. With the emotional pain, probably due to the first (clutch) type of tension origin, psychological work must be done with the Rolfee to help him get through the fear so that he can relax the muscle. This type of work is not as necessary for pain that is purely physical in origin (faulty wiring type).

In terms of energy cycles, the muscle tensions are usually feelings held between the preparation and performance stages. To allow for the completion of the energy cycle is to free the muscle from being chronically contracted and allow it once again to function normally. In order to complete the energy cycle the performance and consummation stages must be discharged. Completing the performance stage means dealing with the feeling generated during and after the energy cycle.

Performance is primarily a physical act, while consummation is more of a psychological act. Both are required to complete the cycle.

Suppose the tension is in the arm and relates to an early, inhibited desire to hit one's parents. In order to complete the performance aspect of the energy cycle the arm must complete the hitting motion—probably a pillow representing the parents would do. The consummation phase of the cycle involves dealing with the guilt, anger, or whatever feelings are generated by the act of hitting. If only the hitting is accomplished, the feelings are still unresolved and the cycle is simply blocked one stage further along, after performance and before consummation. If the working through of feelings is accomplished without the physical work the muscle is left contracted in its stiffened fascial sheath. This underscores the importance of dealing with both the physical and psychological aspects of a problem in order to achieve complete discharge of the blocked energy.

Following is a summary of how the individual levels of the personality are hypothesized to be related.

TABLE I: INTERRELATIONS OF INDIVIDUAL LEVELS

	Inclusion	Control	Affection
Problem	In or out	Top or bottom	Near and far
Interaction	Encounter	Confront	Embrace
Self-concept	Importance	Competence	Lovability
Body	Energy	Centering	Acceptance
Sexual response	Potency	Orgasm	Feeling
Physiology	Senses, skin Respiratory Digestive Excretory	Nervous Muscular Skeletal Endocrine	Reproduction Circulation Lymphatic
Lower chakra Meaning Rolf session	Sacral (1) Grand Potential Six, nine	Navel (3) Assertion Three, five, nine	Genital (2) Sexuality Four, five, nine
Higher chakra Meaning Rolf session	Throat (5) Expression Seven, eight	Brow (6) Intuition Seven, eight	Heart (4) Affection One, three, eight

The Group

Every group—an encounter group, a social group, a board of directors—has the same characteristics as an individual. It has what for a corresponding person we refer to as a body, a self, interpersonal relations, and a spiritual dimension. Every group goes through the developmental stages of inclusion, control, and affection that we traced in personal growth. During these stages the same phenomena that occur in the individual also occur in the group.

To develop the parallel, it is useful to think of an individual as a group. He is made up of many parts just as a group is made up of many people. In the course of an infant's development many ambiguous figures in his environment are gradually brought into focus. These figures are then incorporated into his being to various degrees and exert a differential influence on his behavior as he develops and on his later behavior as an adult. The problem of integrating his parts into a coherent personality parallels the problem of weaving group members into a coherent whole.

An individual may be conceptualized as a group in which he is struggling to become the leader. This group is composed of all parts of people whom he has incorporated into his own ego. Just as some groups seem to be dominated by one group member, so may an individual be influenced by a particular person; just as external forces influence group behavior, so do an individual's external personal relations affect the interaction of his influences; just as a group at times acts as if it were torn by dissension, so does an individual's behavior at times reflect internal conflict; just as groups vary in cohesiveness, so do individuals vary in their integration; just as groups become immobilized and unproductive, so do individuals.

The analysis of an individual arriving at a decision is the internal working out of interacting parts within him to reach a decision. The group equivalent to individual behavior is a group decision as opposed to idiosyncratic actions.

Each social entity—person, group, country—must deal with its environment or outer reality, with its own internal emotional forces or interpersonal needs, and with those factors involved in task accomplishment, such as intelligence and other abilities.

In its relation to outer reality, each entity has inclusion, control, and affection problems. Each entity must establish and maintain sufficient contact and interaction with outside groups and individuals in order to avoid its own isolation, but it must not engage in so much contact that it loses its identity. The entity must also establish and maintain sufficient control over outer reality so that it can function satisfactorily without outside interference, and yet it must not assume so much control that it is forced to undertake more responsibility than it can handle. And, furthermore, each entity needs to establish and maintain sufficient closeness and intimacy with outside reality so that it can feel the pleasures of friendship and affection, and yet there is no need to experience so much intimacy that its actions become distorted and detrimental to group objectives (affection).

As for interpersonal needs, the entity's existence is greatly dependent upon each of its internal units, like a group member feeling that he is part of the total entity. The desire for inclusion becomes a motive for efficiency in activities, such as notifying members of meetings. However, group members must also be allowed to maintain some degree of distance from other group members and some degree of individuality (inclusion). It is necessary for group members to influence each other to some extent so as to make decisions and to establish behavior patterns in order to restrict the amount of control some members have over others. The institutional procedures of majority rule and consensus are often used to balance control relations (control). People must relate to one another with sufficient warmth and closeness for group processes to occur. If there isn't enough freedom to express feelings among members, then productivity suffers because energy is tied up in suppressing hostile impulses. However, excessive intimacy and closeness may detract from the main purposes of the group and may personalize task issues to an undesirable extent. Hence it is necessary to balance the degree of closeness in groups (affection).

At the level of intellectual, or task, behavior, the precise functions of the entity include at least the following: the establishment and clarification of the hierarchy of entity goals and values; the recognition and integration of the various modes of problem-solving existing within the entity, and the development and utilization of the full potential of each group member.

One theory of group leadership distinguishes ten types of leaders, that is, a person around whom a group forms as a result of eliciting common feelings from group members. These types suggest ten ways in which individual personalities are integrated, ten kinds of ego integration. One way groups are formed is through the central person as an object of love. Another mode makes the central person the object of aggression. Perhaps these two processes occurring within an individual may be distinguishable by strong feelings of self-love on the one hand and of self-hate on the other.

Another type of group formation centers around a common-conflict solver, a person who resolves enervating conflicts in other group members. When there is a great deal of conflict within an individual, he may select an influence that is not a source of conflict in order to orient his own ego, thereby allowing him to solve his problem. One might wonder, however, about the stability of such an individual; in groups this formation is a very volatile one, since the leadership pattern is dependent only on the immediate conflict.

One application of looking at the individual as a group has been made by certain psychotherapists (although their theoretical basis may be somewhat different). The gestalt therapists and those in sociodrama use the multifaceted personality. For example, the therapist may say (in an appropriate situation), "Imagine someone inside your head saying to you, 'You are a mature adult,' and someone else inside your head saying, 'You are an immature child.' Make them have a discussion or argument with each other until one wins. Act out each part." The therapist is helping the patient understand the nature of a conflict by assuming that his personality is made up of introjected people. Often the patient will visualize his father, or himself at an earlier time, or as his mother, or boss, or some other significant figure in his past as one of the people in his head. The internal conflict he is presently experiencing can then be understood as a struggle between parts of "others" that he has internalized.

The three phases of group life follow the three interpersonal need areas and go in the same order, inclusion, control, and affection (the stage of group integration). When the group begins to separate, the phases are run through backward until the group ends (the stage of group resolution). Usually within each phase the group leader relation is dealt with first, then the member-to-member relation. In the individual these stages also occur in the same order, first in childhood, then in adolescence, then in adulthood (see *FIRO*, pp. 175 ff.).

Recently a member of a group was asked, "How would you describe what happened in this group?" She replied, "Well, first you're concerned about the problem of where you fit in the group; then you're wondering about what you'll accomplish. Finally, after a while you learn that people mean something. Your primary concern becomes how people feel about you and about each other." This spontaneous response constitutes a splendid statement of the principle of group integration, and the inclusion ("here you fit"), control ("accomplish"), and affection ("feel") phases.

Inclusion Phase. The inclusion phase begins with the formation of the group. When people are confronted with one another they find the place where they initially fit. This includes being in or out of the group, establishing one's self as a specific individual, and seeing if one is going to be paid attention to or ignored. Anxiety about inclusion gives rise to overtalking, withdrawal, exhibitionism, and reciting hero stories. But the basic problem of commitment to the group is present. Each member is implicitly deciding to what degree he shall become a member of this group, how much investment he will withdraw from his other commitments and invest in this new relation. He is asking, "How important will I be in this setting? Will they know who I am and what I can do, or will I be indistinguishable from many others?" This is the problem of identity.

The main concerns of the group in the inclusion phase are energy and boundaries. The group is energized when its members commit themselves to the group. Lack of group energy leads to the group's ending, just as lack of individualizing leads to an individual's death. The boundary problems for the group are expressed in terms of requirements for membership and staying or leaving. The relation of the group to the outside world parallels the relation of an individual to other people.

The physical aspects for the individuals in the group generally have to do with the skin, the senses, and breathing—essentially the boundaries of the person and how they will be penetrated. One of the quickest ways to engage feelings about boundaries is to have people sit near each other in a circle, shut their eyes, imagine that all the space around belongs to them, and then move their arms around. (Try it.) The reaction to touching another person is a very fast way of recognizing inclusion feelings. For some it is reprehensible to have their boundaries penetrated by a stranger; for others, it is like being rescued from loneliness; others curl up, willing to cut down their own space if they can just remain undisturbed.

A more direct way of involving the body boundaries in this phase is to ask everyone to be silent with eyes open and to touch faces, mutually, two at a time. This makes very clear, with physical reactions, what feelings of inclusion are.

Breathing also involves commitment. I frequently ask everyone to breathe deeply for several minutes, or engage in some activity that increases breathing, like jumping up and down or screaming. This brings a person more into the present so that he is more engaged with the current happening.

An advanced stage of group inclusion occurs when all members touch or breathe together. This is analogous to an integration of body parts as parts of the same organisms. If a group member is missing or has not been integrated into the group, the sense of loss is felt, just as an individual's alienation from his pelvis or the back of his legs is felt as some level. Successful group work to incorporate all members often results in a euphoric feeling, similar to being made a whole individual. Usually the group can function better thereafter because the hidden energy tied up in concern over that member can be used more productively.

One characteristic of groups in this phase is the occurrence of what Semrad has called goblet issues. The term is taken from the metaphor of a cocktail party where people pick up their goblet and figuratively use it as an eyeglass to size up the other people at the party. Goblet issues are those that in themselves are of minor importance to the group members, but that function as vehicles for getting to know people, especially in relation to one's self. Often the first decision confronting a group becomes a goblet issue. These discussions are long and inconclusive; however, during the talk there has usually been a great deal of learning and at the end group members all have a much clearer picture of one another. Each person knows better who responds favorably to him, who sees things the way he does, how much he knows compared to the others—his identity in the group. Contrary to outward appearances, goblet issues do serve an important function, and groups not permitted this type of testing out will search for some other method of obtaining the same information, perhaps using as a vehicle a decision of more importance to the group.

One implication of this theoretical point suggests techniques for beginning groups, including involving the body. Rather than allowing the group to get seduced into the content of goblet issues, it is more valuable to get to the underlying issue of inclusion. In a recent group, everyone first sat in a circle and started to chat, while one person sat out of the circle. The group leader ignored the verbal content and asked the group to stand up and form a tight circle; he invited the outside member to physically break into the circle. This immediately mobilized inclusion feelings for all members through their own participation and through identification with the breaker-in. The group was thus forced to experience the basic feelings they had at this point and to see that their efforts at making talk were just ways of dealing with breaking into the group.

The technique of breaking in is another example of a group inclusion problem dealt with at the physical level. Feelings about being in and keeping others out are quickly reached through experiencing the physical struggle. On the individual level, this activity is equivalent to one body part that has been chronically tense and lifeless beginning to stir, relax, and threaten to join the rest of the body, as for example, the muscles in the back of the neck.

Control Phase. Once members are fairly well established as being together in a group the issue of decision-making procedures arises. These involve problems of sharing responsibility and its necessary concomitant, distribution of power and control. Characteristic behavior at this stage includes a leadership struggle, competition, discussion of orientation to the task, structuring, rules of procedure, methods of decision-making, and sharing responsibility for the group's work. The primary anxieties revolve around having too much or too little responsibility and too much or too little influence. Each member is trying to establish himself in the group so that he will have the most comfortable relation to the other members with regard to control, influence, and responsibility.

At this phase physical confrontation methods such as wrestling and arm wrestling are effective in allowing underlying feelings to emerge. Also, tests of intellectual ability help to bring out feelings of competence and competition.

Whereas the body problem in inclusion was getting everyone involved, the control problem involves organizing these parts into a functioning whole. As with the body, the object is to find out the unique characteristics of each group member, to help each member function to his full capacity, and to have all the participants working together to function most effectively.

One example will clarify the group-individual analogy. In a family group, the phenomenon has been widely noted that once a family member has been placed in a certain role it is very difficult for him to get out of it, because the family as a system has adapted to his role placement. For example, placing a child in the role of a schizophrenic allows the hostility between other family members to be focused on him as a scapegoat. If he were to get well, the other family members would have to face their hositility toward each other and themselves, thus they exert a strong force, often unconscious, toward keeping the child schizophrenic. Similarly, if a body part, say the legs, is chronically tense and misaligned, perhaps the back, the neck, and the head have all compensated to keep the system, the body, upright. If the legs are released from their tense state, then these other parts have to get out of their familiar patterns and adapt to new, unfamiliar patterns. Therefore, they act against the legs changing.

In the case of both the family and the body the solution is that all of the parts have to be worked on simultaneously. The recent recognition of the importance of family therapy is a realization that working only with a schizophrenic without relating to his family is not an adequate or efficient approach. Similarly, the Rolfing philosophy recognizes the body as an interconnected system requiring many body parts to be worked on simultaneously in order to correct imbalances.

The implications for group leadership are that encounter groups are interconnected systems, not just individuals in a group setting, and it is essential to be aware of all the interconnections in the group. Just as with an individual at the control stage, a group is concerned with internal regulation, centering, and efficiency. While the individual uses his nervous and muscular systems for these functions, the group uses administrative procedures after working out their own various abilities and relative positions. Coordination of its parts into an efficient working system is the group correlate of centering.

Affection Phase. Following a satisfactory resolution of the problems of control, problems of affection become focal. It is typical to see positive feelings, direct personal hostility, jealousy, pairing behavior, and, in general, heightened emotional feeling between pairs of people expressed at this stage. The primary anxieties have to do with not being liked, not being close enough to people, and excessive intimacy, each member striving for his most comfortable position in giving and receiving affection.

Methods involving touch and physical closeness help clarify affectional feelings. As I begin to write about the physical components of the affection phase I find I'm having trouble, which makes me suspect that it's an area I haven't worked out very well for myself. The heart is the primary affectional organ along with circulation (as in blood brothers) and the sexual organs. The external touch of inclusion advances to interpenetration in the sexual act, an expression of affection. At this time, closer physical contact, like hugging, between two people becomes common, a warm feeling. These hugs seem very natural now, while they were uncomfortable at the beginning of the group. Leo Litwak, a reporter for the *New York Times,* recognized this phenomenon in his excellent story about an open encounter workshop. He noted how uncomfortable he felt when he arrived at Esalen. "I was somewhat put off by what I considered to be an excessive show of affection. Men hugged men. Men hugged women. Women hugged women. These were not hippies but older folks like myself who had come for the workshop. People flew into one another's arms, and it wasn't my style at all." At the end of his five-day workshop he wrote: "Our group gathered in a tight circle, hugging and kissing, and I found myself hugging everyone, behaving like the idiots I had noticed on first arriving at Esalen." This is a typical response. In the affection phase, the desire for total body contact flows easily, while in the earlier phases it is stiff and forced. Not being aware of this evolution, passing observers often get a distorted view of workshop behavior.

Affection problems for a group as an entity parallel individual affection problems, especially in acceptance, distribution of warmth, and sexuality. The problem of group loyalty or liking for the group by its members is the correlate of an individual's self-love.

The fact that these group phases exist, combined with the availability of various group techniques, leads to a very effective method for rapid group diagnosis. An assessment of where the group is in relation to its inclusion, control, and affection issues gives a good picture of its present state. The best three methods I've found for doing this are the blind milling (inclusion), the dominance line (control), and the high school dance (affection). Briefly, the blind milling gets people in physical touch with each other. Discussing their reactions to that experience usually brings out feelings of belonging and other inclusion issues. The dominance line activity asks people to form one line, with dominant people at the head and submissive people at the rear. This exercise brings out feelings about competition and power issues. The high school dance requires each member to select people attractive to him and arouses feelings of intimacy, sexuality, jealousy, rejection, and other strong emotions.

I recently ran a two-hour microlab that was outstandingly good. The response from the group of about 800 students (divided into groups of 6) was exceptional, so that as a parting, it seemed to me appropriate to have us all sit, shut our eyes, hold hands, breathe together, quietly say the syllable OM, then bring it up to a very loud volume, hold it, bring it down slowly, then silent, and feel the energy in the room going through each person. The effect of this was electrifying. Standing at the front of the room I could feel the energy crackle up the front of me, leaving me almost breathless. The whole group remained silent for about ten minutes. It was a remarkable experience and seemed to me to be somewhere between the affectional and spiritual states.

This state is also reached by the organism on occasion when Rolfing reaches an advanced stage. Something happens, often after the tenth session, when everything seems together and the body feels warm and whole and integrated. The affectional part has to do with the energy flow between the heart and the genitals, when affection and sexual feelings go together without blockage between them. Aha! I know now why I'm having some trouble with this section. I haven't yet had the experience of feeling that unblocked connection. I know what I've written is true, but only intellectually, because I still have too many blocks between the heart and the genitals to be able to experience the flow. Some day, perhaps.

Inclusion, control, and affection are not three distinct phases. Each area is emphasized at certain points in a group's growth, but all three issues are always present, though not always of equal importance. Some people are fixated on control and authority problems, some on affection problems. If their concern is strong enough, they focus on these the whole time, to the exclusion of the other areas dealt with by the group. For any person, his area of concern will be the sum of his individual problem areas and those of the group's current phase.

A good analogy for the developmental phenomena is given by tire-changing. When a person changes a tire and replaces the wheel, he first sets the wheel in place and secures it by sequentially tightening each bolt just enough to keep the wheel in place and make the next tightening possible. Then the bolts are tightened further, usually in the same sequence, until the wheel is firmly in place. Finally, each bolt is gone over separately to secure it fast. Like the bolts, the need areas are worked on until they are handled satisfactorily enough to continue with the work at hand. Later they are returned to and worked over to a more satisfactory degree. If one need was not handled sufficiently on the first sequence, on the next it receives more attention.

In the inclusion phase extreme behavior revolves around excessive withdrawal or exhibitionism. Preoccupation with leaving the group or not getting involved is frequent. Often dissociation from the here and now is observed. Shallow breathing, faulty seeing and hearing, and even skin rashes and the like can be expected more frequently at this stage.

During the control phase there is often a great deal of preoccupation with the group's delinquency and prolonged discussion revolves around the topic of the members doing what they were not supposed to do. This type of problem occurs frequently as the struggle between work and gratification. Such delinquency is often accompanied by a great deal of wrestling, resistance, and complaints, and palace revolts are not uncommon at this time.

Frequently, when groups are dealing with the affection area, the problem of separation arises. Each person has his own method for easing the pain of separation, a pain that all of us must endure beginning with the separation from the mother at birth to separation from all living mortals at death, and including moving to new schools, new neighborhoods, losing friends and lovers, and having friends and relatives die. For some people, preparing for separation becomes so important—perhaps because the associated pain is so great—that it becomes a character trait. A person may never allow himself to become very involved with anyone because the anticipated leaving is too unpleasant. Others use gradual withdrawal. Lateness, absence, and daydreaming increase, and more time is devoted to a new activity so that the transition is easier. At this point in the group's life, one can expect that death and illness will become more frequent topics, an unconscious displacement of the separation concern.

Some people demean the group. They are trying to convince themselves, "You see, I won't miss such an unimportant group." Sometimes the blame is shifted by attacking the group and forcing other people to do the rejecting. They then don't have to take responsibility for leaving; they had no choice. This is common in marriage where the person who wants to leave will so antagonize his (or her) partner that she (or he) will finally initiate a divorce. One of the most common methods of handling separation is the reunion phenomenon. Group members make elaborate arrangements for the group to meet in the future. In almost all of these situations the plans never come to fruition; they simply make separation easier by colluding on the fantasy that there will be no real separation.

Usually the most successful way to separate is to work out any unresolved problems so that the group experience becomes a part of the person and none of his emotions are left in the group for him to work them out on future people. An example of this is a child with unresolved fear and anger toward his father who then feels that fear and anger toward all future authority figures. Semrad once said, "Decathexis (withdrawing involvement) proceeds memory by memory." Often, when one member feels that his reaction in an earlier meeting was misunderstood, he will recall the instance and explain what he really had meant to say, so that no one will be angry with him. Or perhaps a member wants to tell another what an important comment that member made in an earlier meeting and how much better it made him feel. After this process, the group members seem more capable of accepting their separation and resolving their relations.

The need for separation techniques can be put in terms of group energy cycles. When some energy cycles in the group life are frustrated, a feeling of uneasiness and incompleteness and some body tensions usually result. This has to do mostly with the resolution of relations between members. Separation from the group is another issue and usually focuses on how the experience can be made a part of the self and carried over into one's other life. A feeling that the group experience will have no effect on subsequent life leads to sadness, while a feeling of a permanent difference leads to elation.

In the process of resolution there seems to be a particular sequence in which these problems are dealt with. The personal positive and negative feelings are dealt with first, as in the examples above (affection). Next, discussion focuses on the leader and on the reasons for compliance or rebellion to his wishes (control). Later come discussions about the possibilities of continuing the group, about how committed each member really was, and how they feel about leaving each other (inclusion). This evolution reverses the formation sequence by first withdrawing the affectional ties, then the control problems, and finally the inclusion phenomena.

Another closing issue is the problem of transferring the experience to outside life. A frequent statement is: "I can encounter here because you are all willing, but what can I do when I return to Sheboygan and nobody understands me? Will what I feel now last?" The person is preparing to negate the entire experience through not retaining it. His fear can be resolved by asking such questions as: "Whom do you know you could touch more? Whom, in normal life, could you express anger or affection to? How could you do it?" Here is another point at which the similarity between a group and an individual is quite clear. The degree to which any change in a person is permanent depends on the degree to which he makes changes in his physical structure. If in the course of an encounter group a person experiences deep feelings, goes through many deep emotions in his body, perhaps cries, feels angry, wrestles, or dances, then the changes probably affected his actual physical structure. If he were Rolfed, that structure was changed directly. If, on the other hand, his experience was entirely intellectual, simply understanding his problem without much involvement of the rest of his body, there is very little likelihood that his changes will last.

In organizational behavior there is an almost identical theory of change. If an outside consultant is to make a permanent change in an organization, his suggestion must be made into a tangible change, such as a new organizational chart, a new committee, or a new appointment. If there is no such change, then the chances of the suggestion having a permanent effect is greatly reduced. In both cases the permanence of a change in the unit, a person or a group, is a direct function of the degree of structural alteration of the person or group.

An understanding of the developmental cycles in groups helps to orient the group leader to what may be happening in moments of great confusion. It suggests areas to look for that may be underlying the open phenomena in the group and helps to focus the group on the basic issues. If there is competitive strife, no matter how gentlemanly it is being expressed, the leader can help get it in the open by introducing physical struggle. If the issue is affectional or sexual, then perhaps it's time for the group to express who is physically attracted to whom and see what evolves. Obviously the theory will not always be correct, but it provides a set of guesses for the leader to work on as he tries to help the group to clarify itself and discover its own reality.

Responsibility

Doesn't a group obliterate individuality and reduce the group members to mindless conformity? My view is simple. In order for a man to develop his potential most fully he must take responsibility for himself. And a properly run open encounter group is one of the most effective ways I know to develop individuality and individual creativity.

Treating someone as if he were capable of being responsible for himself brings out his most responsible parts. If he is treated as if he can't be trusted, then his most untrustworthy sides will appear. This is somewhat oversimplified, but not much. Being responsible for one's self usually increases one's motivation to perform better. No one else is responsible, no one else is to blame. This holds for all levels of functioning. I'm making the radical assumption that I am responsible for myself at every level. I make myself ill, I make myself nearsighted, I bore myself, I achieve popularity. If I used to say, "I can't come because I have the flu." I now say, "I won't come and I gave myself the flu," or, "Perhaps I even gave myself the flu in order to have an excuse not to come." This is a very different statement. I suspect that this assumption of total responsibility is almost always right and that it is extremely valuable, even if fallible. For once I make this assumption I find that I start to get in touch with myself more.

I recalled breaking my wrist in a football game several years ago. A broken arm is surely not something I would give myself, I thought, when just beginning to entertain this idea of responsibility. As I thought about it, I remembered the hour on the analyst's couch the same morning, looking at my left arm and hand and rejecting them because they looked feminine. Then I remembered the moment of falling in the ball game, having a brief moment of disgust and anger at myself and my arm, and, not wanting to protect it, just jamming it down on the ground to stop my fall.

When I gave my last few encounter workshops at Esalen, I noticed that I was getting a cold before each one. When I asked myself why was I giving myself a cold, the answer came back quickly. The cold meant, "Don't judge me too harshly." I didn't have much energy for those workshops and people were expecting a great deal from me. If I had a cold perhaps they would forgive my anticipated mediocre performance.

More and more people feel that many ailments—indeed, the whole psychosomatic realm—are induced. Taking responsibility for one's behavior at all levels—physical, interpersonal, and spiritual—leads to new self-understanding.

A clue to what are probably the chief body correlates of responsibility is given by two terms often used to discuss the topic: "stand on your own two feet," and "be self-supporting." Both focus on the feet and legs. A person not ready to take responsibility may disown his legs, not have much sensation in them, and not feel them connected to the rest of his body. The energy does not flow from his legs to the other parts of his body; they feel wobbly and incapable of supporting his body weight. A willingness to "support" oneself is accompanied by allowing more awareness into the legs and feet and accepting them as part of the body.

Taking responsibility for myself in no way precludes taking responsibility for others. That is a separate decision for which

I am also responsible. I can be as responsible for other people as I choose to be. There are consequences to my choice and weighing them is my problem. If I decide not to be responsible for others, people may not like me, or may not allow me to live with them. A group of people with like views that people should be responsible for each other may get together and exclude others who don't share this view. Or at least they may exclude people who won't comply with some minimum requirement, like not physically harming each other. These conventions become more complex, become codified, and, finally, exclusion from this society is enforced by laws.

Along with assuming individual responsibility goes the freedom for a person to behave as he wishes until it impinges on someone else's freedom. When that happens in the encounter culture, an accommodation is made through an encounter. But strict recognition of personal responsibility allows personal freedom, hence laws should apply only to situations of conflict. Any individual's behavior that doesn't impinge on the freedom of others is not a fit subject of regulation. This means the usual subjects included under the title of morality, such as sexual behavior, abortion, and length of hair. The omission of laws in these areas would put more emphasis on individual responsibility. Conversely, it seems to me that the presence of an external law or coercion tends to reduce individual responsibility.

Whenever someone takes over for me and tells me what to do, I find myself back as a little boy, in a dependent state. When I went to San Francisco with a friend, she told me where to turn because she knew the streets better. I became very dependent on her, even asking for obvious directions. Actually, when she wasn't along, I got places quite well by myself.

Obviously there are complications when some people don't accept this responsibility and their behavior begins to impinge on others. However, the attitude toward laws from the encounter point of view is clear. It begins with the assumption that each person is responsible for himself and makes laws only when absolutely necessary, when one man's actions curtail another man's freedom significantly. The burden of proof is on the person who wishes to make a law to demonstrate that it is necessary. This principle is not one born of considerations of jurisprudence, but rather of the experience of encounter groups, that such an orientation maximizes a person's likelihood of realizing his ability to be responsible for himself. It is very important that the group leader (society, or lawmakers) believe this orientation thoroughly because it won't always work well initially, but it must be administered with patience and faith. The members must live in the setting long enough to be convinced that such an orientation is indeed going to be followed, not just tried briefly and changed. Since this is a well-worked area of philosophy and jurisprudence, I won't labor it here. I just want to keep it close to the issues of the book.

The application of this theory to childrearing practices is clear. I know that when I was patient enough to let my children tie their own shoelaces rather than do it myself, they profited. They had the opportunity to experience their own competence and the feeling that I regarded them as capable. I'm certain that this strengthened their concept of themselves as competent people.

I believe that dealing with today's youth is subject to the same principle. It amazes me when a university refuses student offers to take over part of the decision-making apparatus of the institution. It seems that the administrators have gotten caught up in their own power needs and lost sight of effective educative procedures. To allow students an opportunity to exercise their own decision-making abilities seems to me a rare opportunity for a teaching institution, and it is fortunate that the students are willing to try. Refusal of this wish again has a two-sided detriment: it denies the students an opportunity to develop their competence, and it implies that the university does not regard students as capable people—both antieducative outcomes.

The treatment of mental patients is also subject to the same comments derived from the experience of encounter groups. I don't want to go too far. Some patients do need a certain amount of care. But I'm advocating that one should always start with the assumption of individual competence and only make as many inroads into it as necessary.

When I was working at the Albert Einstein School of Medicine in New York, a thoroughly respectable institution, I learned what to do with patients who freak out. Once a patient started acting crazy. He was immediately surrounded by three attendants, his arms were pinned back, and he was given a shot of tranquilizer, a standard procedure that seemed to me at the time very sensible. Shortly after I arrived at Esalen, a similar experience occurred. During an evening drum dance, a girl freaked out. She started screaming uncontrollably, threw herself onto the middle of the dance floor, and started pounding her fists into the floor. I could feel my reflexes starting to operate as I started to run toward her to grab her and somehow tranquilize her. After all, I certainly knew how to handle these matters more than the Big Sur mountain people. Before I could reach her, two of the Big Sur women were on the floor next to her, soothing her brow. One of the Big Sur drummers, Ron, was saying, "Let there be no fear on this floor," and kept drumming while the Big Sur women kept soothing. No one attempted to stop her, "She's doing her thing," they later explained, "that's what she has to do now. We're here, available if she needs us." Then Ron shouted out, "I'll be here thirty days and thirty nights if you need me," and the beat went on. People danced around her. Finally she stopped, and very shaken, started to walk over to a table, accompanied by the girls. She sat down and started a long process of collecting herself.

I was very taken with this whole scene, and very impressed.

The Big Sur community assumed that she was doing what she needed to do, no condescension, no infantilizing; simply, here is a girl whose life state requires her to freak out right now. She is responsible for her psychotic episode, she is choosing to do it. We choose to help her through it, with a very supportive attitude giving her acceptance and respect. Since that incident, I have become more familiar with the work of Laing with schizophrenics and others who regard psychosis as often a good thing, a positive disintegration, and I have had personal experiences leading me to believe that the assumption that a person is choosing to go crazy, and that he can within wide limits determine his own behavior, is both accurate and very helpful for encouraging the person to use his greatest abilities.

I was conducting a weekend workshop once in which a girl who had been in several of my groups suddenly started having a psychotic episode. She slid behind one of the chairs and wouldn't come out. I finally got her into the hallway but she rushed into the closet. She was convinced that she was in a dark, cold tunnel and I could see that she was shivering. I tried to talk her back to reality but to no avail. The tunnel was very important to her and she had things to do there. Finally I was able to talk her into going to bed. Chagrined, I returned to the group, unhappy that I couldn't handle the situation better, worried about my reputation, fearful of what this would do to the group. To my horror she reappeared in the group about a half hour later. My God, that really blows it, I thought. For a while she said nothing. What next? Then she made a statement that seemed very rational, even helpful. To my amazement, this continued. It became clear after a while that she had never been so coherent or well integrated in the other groups in which I had seen her. At the end of the workshop I drove her home and she confirmed what we had all seen. She said she had never felt so good, so serene, so centered into herself. She also had the feeling that she had more work to do someday back in that tunnel. About a year later I had her in another encounter group and it didn't help her. She reiterated the need to go back to the tunnel. Subsequently she had experiences at a similarly deep level and was able to further her growth.

It seems clear that the frequent accusation that encounter groups are like brainwashing or groupthink could hardly be more mistaken. On the contrary, the pressure of the group on one individual, operating under the assumption of individual responsibility, is a superb method for helping an individual develop his own autonomy. I have often held a firm belief, then gone to a group and, through the pressure of the group banding together against me, changed my mind. When I went home I discovered that I still held to my original view essentially. It is at this point that I have my choice of joining the rightwingers and agreeing that there is a strong brainwashing quality to these groups and that they are dangerous and that I was duped —in short, feel it's their fault I changed my mind. Or I can do what is in keeping with the encounter mode, consider why I changed my mind under this pressure. They didn't change my mind, I did. And why did I if I still believe my original thought? This line of pursuit turned out to be extremely fruitful. It revealed that I was conflicted; I wasn't sure of my belief; I wanted to be liked so much that I would allow their arguments to convince me even though I didn't believe them, or I didn't want to be seen as rigid; or I didn't have that much confidence in my own reasoning ability.

Other considerations came flooding in as I allowed myself to explore the consequences of being responsible for my own mind changing. The result is that I am forced to face all of these facets of myself and get much clearer about them, so that when I return to the group I am sufficiently centered that I can deal with the group's opposition. When I am centered I can hear the group's opposition, filter out what seem like good points and incorporate them, and reject the points I don't agree with. In

short, group pressure has forced me to be more certain of myself and where I stand and hence has added to my independence and autonomy. In open encounter a norm gets established that supports the development of this kind of autonomy.

Group opposition is often just a reflection of inner conflict.
When I arrived at Esalen I was playing a song by the Tijuana
Brass on my car stereo. There were some remarks to the effect
that that was pretty square, and that the Beatles' *Sergeant Pep-
per* album seemed to be in. This set me off on a well-formulated
criticism of the conformity among the anti-Establishment people and complaints that I'm not allowed to be what I am, like
what I want, and so on. However, it soon became apparent to
me that I did feel a little square, that I wasn't sure of the quality
of the Brass, and that maybe the Beatles were saying something
important. After I lived at Esalen for a while and felt clearer
about my taste in music, I found that no one objected to anything I played. My complaints about their intolerance were
primarily a projection of my own uncertainty. When I was clear
everyone accepted it, and there was no criticism.

The two main operating mechanisms of open encounter are
honesty and self-responsibility. I am assuming that man is far
more capable of coping with reality than he is usually given
credit for. If life in all of its manifestations is opened up through
honest interaction, exploration, and perception, man can accept responsibility for himself and can deal with the conse-
quénces. And if people are assumed to be competent, they
generally perform better than if they are assumed to be fragile,
weak, or sick.

I am a little suspicious of myself as I write this. I was brought
up to be tough. My body reflects this; it is built to take it.
Apparently I have internalized some of this forced toughness,
because it looks like I am asking others to be tough, too, tougher
than they usually are. I must be careful to be aware that some
people are more fragile than I would like them to be, but they

are nevertheless fragile and this factor must be taken into account. I do think people can take more than they think they can, but I must be careful not to overdo it.

Another self-suspicion is that I am assuming all people have the same needs that I have, that they need to let go in their bodies as a way of realizing their potential. I have a hell of a time letting go. I am still quite tight and constricted, my muscles are much too unyielding and resistant. On some occasions when I have taken psychedelic drugs I have experienced a release of muscle tension, and it is ecstatic. I'm sure that I'm taking my quest, which is rather extreme, as a goal for all, although probably most people don't need it as much as I do. Still, I feel most, no, *all* people could let go more. But I must be vigilant.

Bulletin: *Business Encounter Group*

September 1984, NEW YORK (Special to *The New York Times*) —A departmental encounter group in a government-industrial branch reported the following interaction. (Boss, two assistants, Charlie and Alvin; his secretary, Gloria; and group leader.)

Boss: This encounter group business can't work in this setting. You people all work for me. We have to be together every day. If you lose respect for me then I won't be able to do my job. The encounter method is all right for strangers but not for this situation.

Charlie: I understand your feeling but why should we lose respect for you if we know you better? It sounds like you're not confident that your real self is respectable.

Alvin: No I know what the boss means. I think he's right. If he's doing his job, I don't care what he's like as a person. We can't psychoanalyze each other all the time.

Boss: Well, I didn't mean to go that far. I am a person as well as a boss and I do care about you people as people and not just as workers, and that includes you, too, uh . . .

Alvin: Alvin.

Boss: Yes, you, too, Alvin.

Leader: You seem to have forgotten his name.

Boss: Just a temporary slip.

Ldr: Did you have any feeling about it, Alvin?

Alvin: About what?

Ldr: The boss forgetting your name.

Alvin: Oh, no. It was just an oversight. He's done that every once in a while for years.

Ldr: You mean you've been working for him for years and he still doesn't remember your name?

Alvin: He's a busy man.

Ldr: Boss, do you have a bad memory?

Boss: Not usually.

Ldr: Will you just assume for a moment that there was some reason that you don't remember Alvin's name in particular. Does anything come to you?

Boss: (Lights a cigarette, clears throat) Yes. But I certainly don't want to say it here. It isn't fair to Alvin. After all, I'm his boss. It would be taking advantage of my position.

Ldr: Alvin, would you like to hear it?

Alvin: It's up to you, boss. If you don't feel like saying it, I understand perfectly. I respect your right to . . .

Ldr: Don't you want to answer the question?

Alvin: Oh, I'm sorry, would you repeat the question?

Boss: Goddammit, Alvin, that's just what I'm thinking. It's that namby-pamby yes-man stuff that really pisses me off. You're always apologizing, and understanding and agreeing. You haven't taken a stand on anything in five years. That's why I forget your name. It wouldn't matter if you're here or not most of the time. There, I said it. I didn't want to—well, I guess I did. But I don't want to hurt you, Alvin. Goddammit, leader, now look what you've done! How am I going to work with Alvin anymore? Your goddamn encounter group is going to destroy this agency. You don't know anything about our business anyway. I'll bet you've never met a payroll. Just going around acting superior like you know it all.

Alvin: Boss, I want to say something. I've known all along that you felt like that.

Ldr: Alvin, would you stand up and look down on your boss while you talk to him.

Alvin: (Stands over boss) I'm glad you said it. I really feel good about it and I know better where I stand. Now may I tell you how I feel about you?

Ldr: You want his permission?

Alvin: No, darn it, I'll tell him anyway. You're always blaming everyone else for everything that happens. You're so defensive that I hate to bring up anything to you that isn't simply praise or support. I could contribute many things but I don't bother anymore, it's more trouble than it's worth. Look what you just did now. You told me what you thought of me and then blamed the leader for what *you* did . . . I may lose my job for this but it sure feels good to say it.

Boss: I don't like what's happening here. I don't have to take this from, uh, Alvin. I can get plenty of men to take your place, Alvin, who'll probably do a lot better than you will. I told you these encounter groups were kooky, they're just like brainwashing. Alvin and I have been getting along fine for five years without these groups. Isn't that right, Alvin?

Alvin: Well, I guess so.

Boss: (Angrily) Whadda you mean, you guess so?

Alvin: Well, I haven't been as happy as I would like to be, but I suppose it's not your fault, it's mainly my arthritis.

Boss: Look here, leader. Is there anything more? I'm a busy man and I could spend this time more profitably back in the office. (Gets up and starts for the door.)

Secretary: I don't think you're setting a very good example for us.

Boss: (Exploding) Good God! Now I have to take this crap from my own secretary.

Secretary: I'm just saying what I feel, Boss. I don't mean to be disrespectful. I think this is very valuable for us, and I don't like to leave Alvin feeling like he does.

Boss: All right, all right. I'm sorry if I made you feel bad, Alvin. I just get so stirred up.

Ldr: Boss, you seem much more frightened to me than anyone else here.

Boss: (Outraged) Frightened! What the hell are you talking about! Your goddamned psychology talk is bullshit. At least I'm not just sitting here like a dummy and saying "wise" things. Say, who are you anyway? Are you a doctor?

Ldr: Uh, I'd like you to make the statement behind your question.

Boss: Statement? I'll tell you my statement! I don't think you know what the hell you're doing. Is that a clear enough statement?

Ldr: You frighten the hell out of me. I'd be a nervous wreck if I worked for you. You don't listen, you just lurch around like a pin-stripe Captain Bligh. You just roll over your employees whenever they threaten you; you don't seem to give a shit how they feel. You can't stand the fact that I have some authority that you don't have. I've wanted to belt you a dozen times. I'd probably get arthritis too just holding back from hitting you.

Boss: (Sarcastically) Well, he talks.

Ldr: Sure I talk. But I doubt if many of your employees talk. You're a petty tyrant.

Secretary: Not always. He can be very sweet and gentle sometimes.

Boss: Never mind that, Gloria.

Secretary: But Harold, it's true. You've given a one-sided picture of yourself here. I don't know why you're acting this way.

Ldr: I'd like to see that side of you, Harold. What's so frightening about this situation?

(Long pause)

Harold: Now you're trying to act like you care.

Ldr: I do. I see a lot of similarities between us.

Harold: (Softly, head down) I don't know what you want to know. I've worked hard to get where I am. I have a good job, money, I'm successful.

Ldr: But . . .

Harold: But . . . whaddya mean but? I'm not happy, that's but. I've spent all this time trying to make it, and I can't enjoy it. I don't enjoy going to the office. I can't understand my kids anymore. My wife and I seem to have grown apart. Oh shit, what do you care about my personal problems?

Alvin: Boss, that's the first time I've ever heard you talk like that. I'm very thrilled. I really like you.

Harold: Oh, shut up Alvin. No, I'm sorry . . . Do you mean you didn't like me before?

Alvin: Frankly, no. I was afraid of you, and I didn't feel like you gave a damn about me, or about anyone. I never thought of you as a person. I guess I was too busy trying to stay alive myself.

Gloria: I love to see you like this, Harold. We've been very close in the past and I know this part of you. Whenever I see it I feel much closer to you.

Harold: Yes, but I'm afraid now that none of you will respect me or work for me anymore. You've seen my weaknesses and you won't . . .

Chorus: No.

Alvin: Look, Boss—no, I'll call you Harold.

Charlie: Thata boy, Alvin.

Alvin: I would work ten times as hard for you as a human being with problems of his own, and who cares about me, than I would for some tyrant who scares me all day. What I do most of the time—yes, I'll tell you—is spend my energy trying to do as little as possible without getting you mad. Most of the time, I'm working against you. It's gotten to be a game to see how much I can get away with. Hey, my arthritis feels a little better.

Gloria: And Harold, I know that Alvin is a very creative man and it never comes out in his work. He's always getting tired or sick.

Ldr: Alvin, would you and Harold sit in the middle of the floor facing each other and do whatever you want to do, nonverbally.

(They look at each other, Harold looks down. Alvin raises Harold's head up. Harold smiles and offers a handshake, Alvin takes the hand in both of his. Harold heaves a deep sigh and his eyes start to water. Gloria goes over and puts her arms around both. They all embrace. The other group members gather round Harold in one big hug. After a while, they stop. Harold looks up with tears in his eyes, smiles, and says, "Oh, shit!" Harold pulls leader over and hugs him around neck. Leader blushes. All laugh.)

THE OPEN
ENCOUNTER GROUP

A Typical Workshop

Groups using the open encounter model typically meet in a workshop setting. A workshop is usually a 5-day session, although some are designed to last for weekends, 7 days, 4 weeks, or 4 months' duration. The workshops are residential in that all participants live in the same location during the workshop.

I used to offer once-a-week groups, daily groups, individual sessions, and a wide variety of patterns anywhere from two days to three years in length. These experiences led me to the conclusion that the depth that could be reached in a concentrated workshop was so remarkable compared to the other approaches that I have virtually abandoned all other patterns. I now feel that an intensive workshop experience combined with the constant availability of workshops, such as at Esalen, is the most effective path to realizing the human potential. This approach requires that an individual plan his own growth experiences and therefore applies the principle of individual responsibility to selecting what one needs in order to grow.

Some people take many intense workshops successively and then stay away for long intervals to give themselves a chance to integrate their experiences. Some attend workshops infrequently but regularly. Others shift the type of experience from, say, encounter to sensory awareness to meditation to massage and perhaps back to encounter. But I've found, along with others who have reported similar conclusions (Rogers, Maslow, Perls), that one intensive week is equivalent to two or three years of periodic therapy sessions, and that groups are much more effective than individual sessions.

The open encounter workshops given at Esalen (formerly called *More Joy* workshops) typically start at 9 P.M. on Sunday night and meet each day from 10 A.M. to lunch and from 9 P.M. to about midnight. The afternoon is free until 4, when there is often a general session for all groups. A workshop typically has 40 to 60 people in it, broken down into 4 or 5 groups of 10 to 12 people each. Occasionally a group wants to go all night. It's up to the group leader to decide how long he wants to meet with the group. Often Wednesday night is free, and there is a drum dance where local Big Sur drummers play, a marvelous opportunity for spontaneous physical expression. The week ends Friday at noon with a general session.

Lately Esalen has been exploring month-long workshops in which participants work at maintenance tasks, such as dishwashing, gardening, and cabin cleaning as part of the workshop experience. This is a pattern that appears promising. The general principle is that a total concentrated experience permits breakthroughs and intensity difficult to attain in longer, drawn-out patterns. There are, however, advantages to the regular meetings over time, and it remains for each group leader and member to experiment to find the best tempo for himself.

The past years have seen the growth in popularity of marathons, meeting continuously anywhere from 12 to 48 hours without a break, or with very few breaks, and sleeping right in the meeting room. The point of these marathons is to break down defenses through lack of sleep in order to get to deeper material faster. Although I have run several of these marathons, I'm not inclined toward them. I very much like the idea of a great deal of meeting time, and often in 5-day workshops I would meet on Thursday night for up to 9 hours if there was still work to be done. But exhaustion does not seem to me to be an effective or necessary way to break down defenses.

Several of the methods described here and in *Joy* are much more effective for defense penetration. In marathons, it often happens that very important group events happen when many group members are asleep so that the integrity of the group is somewhat eroded. I have found that allowing people a break for sleep can be extremely valuable. Group members often seek out a few people with whom they have unfinished business and work on it; or they sleep and have important dreams; or they have time alone to assimilate what has happened and often come up with important insights and integrations. As a group leader I find my effectiveness greatly diminished if I'm too tired, and the rest rejuvenates me. These advantages seem to outweigh the virtues of staying awake. My preference, therefore, is to have long meetings to take advantage of the intensive build-up, but to stop whenever the group's work seems to be done and the members have had all they can assimilate. Then they can sleep and return refreshed.

After all of this rational analysis of the effective lengths of workshops, I would like to insert a personal note that should invite you to be a bit skeptical of the results of my logic. One of my personal characteristics is the tendency to gather up all of my machinery, focus it in one direction, and devote all of my energy to it in a huge burst until I've done with it. For example,

the rough draft of *Joy* was all written in one weekend. On the
physical level it is reflected in my aberrant breathing pattern.
I've never learned to breathe properly when I swim, so I can
only take a deep breath, put my head in the water, and go until
I run out of air. My breathing has too much inhale and too little
exhale. I think that this characteristic means that I am a more
effective group leader when I point myself for one big effort,
like a weekend or a 5-day workshop, than if I have to put out
a smaller amount of energy over longer intervals, like one hour
each week. It is quite possible that other group leaders with
different tempos function better in a different pattern, and also
that group members with different patterns would profit more
from other types of group experiences. Taking all this into account, I feel that there is still a great advantage to the concentrated experience.

Much of what follows was worked out with the Flying Circus,
a group that I originally trained and worked with over the past
few years. They deserve credit for many of the ideas and much
of the inspiration.

Openers

Sunday night is devoted to an "opener" designed to prepare
participants for what is to come. It tries to encourage and sanc-
tion behavior that goes beyond everyday acceptable behavior
so that ordinary limitations can be transcended. Further, an
experience that can rouse deepseated feelings and bring them
closer to the surface makes for a greater likelihood that important feelings will be dealt with during the week. The "opener"
is aimed at introducing the ideas that the body is important,
touching is possible, and that fantasy is encouraged.

Perhaps the best method for accomplishing these purposes is

the open encounter microlab. Actually, we usually vary the
openers a great deal from one workshop to another, a desirable
feature since it perpetuates experimentation with methods and
makes the workshop more interesting for the group leaders.
The microlab is also an excellent device for introducing people
to the idea of an encounter group because it involves everyone's total participation. I almost always use a microlab format
when I make a one-night presentation to a large group, or even
to a small one. This decision evolved after I had made presentations in many different forms, starting with lectures, then lec-
ture-demonstrations, and finally the microlab. One virtue of
this procedure is that with the proper physical setting—a large
room with no furniture, a rug if possible, and a microphone—
it can be done with very large groups, even a thousand or more.
The microlab format also ties in with some new theatrical forms
involving more audience participation.

The microlab takes from one to two hours and consists of a
warm-up, several short meetings of about five minutes each in
which many of the open encounter techniques are used, and a
discussion if appropriate. The types of experiences that can be
introduced into a microlab are unlimited. Which experiences
are used in a given microlab vary with the circumstances under
which they are given. I usually have very little planned when
I begin, simply jotting down beforehand a number of possible
activities that seem appropriate and that I'd enjoy doing, but as
it proceeds I take my cues from the way the groups are progressing to determine whether or not I'll use each activity,
whether or not another one would be better, and in what order
to use them. There are always many changes during the hour
or two, depending upon the readiness of the groups for certain
activities. For example, a microlab I did for a group of Catho-
lic nuns who had never had any experience in encounter was
quite different from one conducted at Esalen for experienced
people.

A Sample Microlab

The opening is very important. Most people on the first night of a workshop, or at a one-night presentation, are not fully *present.* Parts of each person are still on the road worrying about the traffic, wondering if they turned off the gas, worrying if the children are alright, etc. And they have very little connection with one another. The other participants seem like strangers, probably a little funny-looking, and possibly somewhat threatening. It is important in starting to allow for a discharge of their initial tension and to provide an opportunity for a common group experience. Such an experience brings everyone into the here and now and allows them to be more fully present. When I fail to take care of this inclusion issue, my presentations are much flatter and take much longer to get started. I now do this for every presentation anywhere.

There are several techniques for accomplishing this. First, in accord with the "rules of encounter" I ask everyone to take off everything other than minimal clothing. (Suggesting casual clothes in advance is helpful.) Then participants are asked to sit on the floor, hopefully on a rug, and I talk for a few minutes to introduce the event and perhaps mention some of the rules of encounter and whatever else seems valuable in terms of the situation.

I state at this point the principle of individual responsibility. "If you want to resist instructions or group pressure, that is up to you. If you want to bow to pressure, it's your decision. If you want to be physically injured or go crazy, that, too, is up to you. You are responsible for yourself." I then introduce the microlab. If someone doesn't want to participate, he simply stands aside and watches. If someone objects to this, the conflict becomes an issue. There are then several possibilities for opening. (I'll name each meeting for ease of reference. Names usually aren't used during the microlab.)

Breathing. *Everyone shut his eyes and breathe* (about 1 to 2 minutes). *Breathe deeply and concentrate on your breathing.* (This helps get feeling going through the body.)

Sound. *Now, open your throat, put your tongue on the floor of your mouth, and let a sound out, any sound that's in there . . . slowly rise to your feet.*

Pounding and screaming. *Make a fist and start pounding your arms up and down like you're pounding on a table; let the pounding get harder and harder.* (Can also be done by facing a partner and pounding and screaming while looking at him, or can be done both ways.) *Now let the sound get louder and louder until it's as loud as you can get it; hold it there for a long time and then gradually let it get softer and softer.*
An alternate or supplement to this is the following:
Moving meditation. *Take any position that's comfortable— sitting, standing or lying. Relax and breathe. Open your throat and let any sound that's in you come out, and continue to let it out through this whole experience. Now get in touch with how your body is feeling. Let your body move you. Without thinking about it just let your body move wherever it wants to go. Keep this up, too, throughout the whole exercise; let the sound and the movement go wherever they want to go.*

This should go on from ten to twenty minutes. It's often very good for discharging surface tension and getting the feelings just beneath them.

Reflection. *Now complete silence. Continue to breathe and go inside yourself and note how you're feeling.*

Sinking. *Now gradually sink to the floor and lie on your back. Keep breathing deeply.*

OM. *softly form the syllable OM and keep saying it. Let it also rise in volume, hold, and come down . . . feel the energy in the room go through your body.*

Breathing. *Again, complete silence. Breathe and rest.*

Some such sequence as this is usually effective in discharging old tensions, bringing people into the present, starting feeling flowing, rousing some deep feelings like anger, loneliness, closeness, and beginning to give feelings of security in the setting. Group members are now ready for another step toward making contact with each other.

Blind milling. *Slowly rise, keeping your eyes closed; put your hands out in front of you and silently mill around. If you contact another person, do what you feel like doing. Keep milling.*

Looking. *Stop, open your eyes and look around, still silently . . . now shut your eyes and continue milling.*

Face touching. *Stop, open your eyes, face a partner and just look in his eyes. Now both touch the other's face, explore it with your hands and eyes, try to see into the face . . . when you feel finished, move onto other faces.*

So far, the microlab has taken the person out of his past tensions, pumped up his feeling, brought him into the present, and touched on feelings of belonging and loneliness—inclusion; anger and hostility—control; and intimacy and touch—affection.

If the competitive feelings of control are desired, another activity can be inserted, probably before blind milling. Divide the number of people by ten and ask that number to spread themselves around the edges of the room facing inward. Then ask about ten people to form a straight line in front of each of them.

Dominance. *If you feel you are a dominant person, go to the front of the line right in front of the anchor person. If you feel you are submissive, go to the back. Place yourself wherever you feel you belong. If there's anyone where you want to be, get him out of there any way you can.*

This usually introduces physical combat at the level of scuffling, and raises the energy level in the room with much the feeling of an essentially friendly group of children roughhousing.

If more feelings of inclusion are to be roused, the blind milling can be altered slightly by saying:

Space feel. *Put your arms straight out and feel all around you. This is your space. Now walk around in your space. If anyone comes into it do whatever you wish.*

This gives more of the feeling of being alone and together and puts the person in touch with how much he wants and how strongly he feels about each one.

If it is desirable to arouse more feelings around affection, the high school dance is very effective. It is also very potent and time should be allowed in subsequent activities to work out the feelings it elicits. I generally do not do this one in a one-evening demonstration, but only in the preliminary session to a 5-day workshop. I'd probably do it after Dominance.

High school dance. *All the men line up on that side of the room and all the women on this side. Look across the room at each other and select the one person you find most attractive. At some point walk across the room and nonverbally ask him or her to come with you as a couple and sit at the end of the room. The person you ask then responds yes or no, nonverbally, making sure to do exactly what he or she wants. If the answer is no, walk back across the floor to where you are and decide on your second choice. If the person you have selected has already been chosen but you still want to try for him or her, go over to the couple of which he or she is a part and see if he or she will give up his partner and come with you. I'd like you to do your selecting one at a time, so please raise your hand when you are ready to select and I'll call on you. The next person won't go until the first one is finished.*

Feelings of rejection, competition, fear, embarrassment, and many others, often reminiscent of adolescent days, are very common. Tension increases as the activity progresses because the wallflower phenomenon gets close. One decision each person faces is whether to risk early to get the person he wants, or to wait, perhaps lessening the risk of rejection, but risk losing the person he wanted. I try to pick from alternate sides so as not to get into the social amenity of men always initiating.

I want to stress again the flexibility of a microlab. I have just given one example of a preliminary session that I have found effective, with a number of alternatives. It is quite possible to make up new activities, often on the spot, if they seem appropriate.

By this point in the evening a great deal of feeling should be aroused. Now I'll break the group into smaller ones for most of the remaining activities in order to get into more intense encounter.

Microgroup. *Arrange yourselves on the floor in groups of 5 in a circle. Try to divide it evenly between men and women* (bad

joke; occasionally laughter) *and get with people you don't know*
(or *know least well* in a better-acquainted group).

Five is a good number because it is small enough for the
time allotted for people to know each other and also for the activities where everyone goes around to everyone else so that it
isn't too long. Six is also a good number, especially if there are
several physical activities requiring group strength; it also provides an even number for pairing off. The sex division is useful
for generating a broader range of feeling, like sexual ones. The
stranger requirement allows the group to start fresh with no
history. An exception to the stranger suggestion is when two
people want to be together, either to work things out or for
protection. I generally discourage that in a microlab, but not
strongly.

The choice of activities at this point depends on how well
things have gone. If the groups seem involved in what has
happened, I might continue with several more nonverbal activities. If not, I'll introduce an encounter group.

Encounter group. *Trying to remember the rules of encounter
that I read to you earlier (or at least repeat three rules: be open
and honest, talk about feelings, concentrate on the here and
now), have an encounter.*

The encounter seems to go better if I stop everyone after
three to five minutes with a general session.

General session. *Now let's have a one-minute general session.
How did the groups go? Were you able to be honest and stay
with feelings in the here and now, or did you wander off into
anecdotes and bullshit* (light laughter)? (Answers usually
mixed.) *All right, now have another encounter group, and this
time try to do a little better* (or *try to be more honest*).

If the preliminary activities were being responded to well, continuing the nonverbal is valuable.

Nonverbal encounter. *Now have an encounter group; remember the rules I mentioned earlier, but make no sounds.*

From now on the groups vary greatly and the sequence of activities accordingly. I like to keep a balance between physical and verbal activities and between interpersonal and individual experiences. The physical activities generate a great deal of energy and keep feelings and excitement high. The verbal activities are most useful following here-and-now feelings generated within the microlab, usually by the nonverbal activities. Too many nonverbal activities together generally leads to excitement that gets dissipated and not assimilated. Too much verbalizing gets dull and defensive and gradually energyless. Thus, I usually follow each nonverbal activity with a verbal one, usually an encounter group to explore and consolidate the feelings generated. Whenever the energy level starts to lag, a nonverbal activity can usually revitalize it.

The interpersonal activities profit greatly from being balanced by individual activities like shutting eyes, and sometimes ears, and looking inside, then expressing those feelings to the group; and some of the fantasy methods are good for self-exploration. These methods help each person stay centered, in touch with his own feelings and not carried away by the group. Here are some of the better ones.

Breaking in. *Take a few minutes to decide which member feels most out of the group and put him at the outside of the group. Now, everyone rise and make a circle with that person outside. Get the circle tightly together and have him try to physically break into the group. People in the circle try to do every-*

thing you can to keep him out. Make as much noise as you wish.

This is an excellent inclusion activity. It puts graphically the problem of breaking into a group, allows everyone's feelings about it to come out, and helps the process of group formation by incorporating the outsider. Often someone else will want to break in. That's fine. Breaking in is usually good near the beginning, but not necessarily, and profits from being followed directly by an encounter group to discuss the feelings generated.

The next activity also deals primarily with inclusion, and is an excellent indicator of how much trust has been generated in the group.

Falling back. *Pair off. One person stand with his back to another person who stands several feet back. The first put his arms out from his sides slightly, and fall back, hoping to be caught by the person in back . . . the back person may catch or not, as he chooses. Watch closely for feelings in the stomach and chest as you fall, note if your feet move at all—they shouldn't if you trust fully—and notice how you feel as you are descending.*

This exercise is good for illustrating how truth is in the body. Verbalizing about how much people trust each other in the group could continue indefinitely, but once the falling back is tried, the situation is greatly clarified.

One verbal technique involving the issue of loneliness joins inclusion in terms of the content of the topic, and joins affection in the sense that group members are revealing something of great importance to each other. This is good for deepening relations once group members start getting comfortable with each other.

Loneliness. *Think of the time you were most lonely in your life.*

Try to get back the feelings you had then (about 2 minutes). *Now exchange with each other these times.*

The effect of openness and honesty on group relations is very easy to demonstrate in the following two exercises. The lesson to be learned from them has extraordinary application to all human relations, work groups, and nations.

Impressions. *I would like you to give your impressions of each other, your main feelings. One of you move over in front of the person next to you, look him in the eye, touch him in whatever way you feel like touching him while you talk, and then tell him briefly how you feel about him, including both positive and negative feelings. When you finish, go on to the next person until you have completed the circle. Then have the next person do the same thing until everyone has given his impression of everyone else. Do not respond, just hear. And be sure everyone can hear when each person speaks.*

Impressions usually brings the group closer because the feelings are said openly. If, on the other hand, there is a desire to have the group experience edginess and irritation with each other, an opposite activity can be given, based on withholding rather than on openness. I devised this for a workshop on conflict management when the objective was to generate some conflict.

Withholding. *One person choose the group member you feel most distant from and send him to the far corner of the room. After he is gone, tell the others why you feel distance. When finished, invite him back but don't tell him anything that was said. Then a second person pick the one he feels most distant from, send him out and repeat the process. Do this until all members have sent someone out.*

Nothing illustrates so strikingly the insidious quality of with-holding feelings. The group members usually feel very prickly when this is over. The office group that complains about some-one, but never to him directly, has the same destructive effect. It is desirable to have a meeting later where group members can tell what they said directly to the target of their remarks. This helps restore good feeling in the group.

In introducing each of these activities, I find it useful to mix three types of presentation. Most sessions are introduced simply by saying the instructions approximately as they are written here. Some are more quickly understood if demonstrated. This is especially true of falling back, arm wrestling, and even break-ing in and breaking out. For demonstrations, I usually look for a lively group or pair of people who seem to be interacting with high energy, and ask them if they would be willing to help me demonstrate the next session. I don't tell them what it is so that they will be more spontaneous. I explain while they demon-strate, and then ask each group to follow. A third type of presen-tation involves participation by several people in front of the whole group. Sometimes this method is used to present fanta-sies. I'll ask the whole group to fantasize something, and then ask for volunteers to tell or act out what they saw in front of the whole group. This tends to bring the whole group together for a few moments before they return to their small groups.

Another activity that is presented well by this method is High Noon. It is a way of helping pairs of people in each group who are having trouble communicating.

High Noon. *Each group take a few minutes to decide which two people in the group are most distant from each other . . . decide this as a group* (about 3 minutes). *Now, would a pair from one group volunteer to do this next activity* (I select one pair, then pick a central place in the group). *Would one of you stand on*

*that side of the room and the other stand on this side, facing
each other? Please clear a path between them. Without words,
look each other in the eye and start walking slowly toward each
other. When you get close enough, do whatever you want to do.
Let your body lead. And do it until you feel finished. Make sure
you don't plan anything ahead of time. It is important that
everyone else be silent as you watch.*

This can end in a struggle, an embrace, a dance, a play, or in
almost anything. The inhibition from the large watching audience is usually overcome after a short time, especially if the
principals are reminded a few times to make sure to do whatever they want to do. When they are finished, I ask the audience
what they saw and encourage an exchange of perceptions, especially around the issue of how real the action appeared. If it
seems to be going well, I'll ask for one or two more pairs of
volunteers. Several examples gives a better sense of the variety
of responses to this relatively simply instruction. After these
large group demonstrations are finished, each group is asked to
do the same thing with two people in their group. Afterward,
they are given a group meeting to discuss their feelings about
the whole experience. Sometimes other pairs want to do this
also. That's fine.

For getting at competitive and energy feelings, physical con-
tests, such as arm wrestling, are very good. They not only mobilize competitive feelings, they also bring out problems of how
to focus all of one's energy in one direction, and result in creating great involvement. They also increase breathing and circulation. The ties between group members are strengthened
because each person puts a great deal of his energy into each
other person. And it often leads to heightened gaiety in the
group.

Arm wrestling. *In pairs within each group, lie on the floor facing each other, forming a straight line. Put up your right forearms and lock thumbs. Place your left hand around your opponent's elbow to keep it stationary. Now look him in the eye and make enormously loud grunts, groans, or noises of any kind and try to push his arm down toward your left. Do this for every pair of people in the group. Remember to make lots of noise.*

The high level of noise in the room is exhilarating and energizing. Arm wrestling with the left arm is also good from a Rolfing standpoint to balance the exertion.

In order to build a strong group feeling, helping an uptight member is important, and can be done well by breaking out. This again allows for the physical statement of a feeling to be acted out with the advantages of total body participation. It also mobilizes energy and helps the body to lose its tightness.

Breaking out. *Each group take a few minutes to select the one person in the group who is most uptight, the one who feels the most uncomfortable, the least free to be spontaneous and express himself, and put him in the center* (about 3 minutes). *Now stand up and form a circle with him in the center. His job is to break out of the tightness he feels represented by the circle. Members of the circle close ranks and try as hard as possible to keep him in.*

When a group is going well, they are often ready to go to a deeper level of understanding with each other and themselves. The fantasy methods provide a good opportunity to let unconscious factors appear. The fantasies should be chosen so they do not get into material too deep to handle in the available time. One of the simplest and most satisfying is the wise man. It demonstrates what some current personal problems are, and that within each person is the ability to answer more questions than he thinks he can.

Wise man. *Shut your eyes, breathe and relax. Picture in your mind a meadow . . . at the end of the meadow is a wise man who will answer any question you ask him. See yourself going up to him, ask him any question you wish, and hear his answer. On a tree behind him is a calendar . . . read the date on the calendar.*

Having each person assume the date is significant, and having them associate to it enlarges the fantasy and the richness of its meaning. Having each member tell the others of his fantasy helps to get the group closer through sharing some deeper feelings.

Another technique for increasing closeness and also for bringing in the body feelings is the body image. This works well only if the group is feeling good and beginning to trust each other. If it is given prematurely, it usually is very shallow and superficial.

Body image. *Shut your eyes and imagine you have no clothes on. What part of your body would you least like to have people look at? Put your hand over that part. Now open your eyes and tell the other group members how you feel about that part. Keep your hand over the part during this whole session.*

Sometimes it is possible to help people come to terms a little with that part by using a little gestalt therapy next.

Body talk. *Now shut your eyes again and carry on a conversation with that body part. Play both roles, you and the body part, and see if you can reach a point of greater acceptance.*

One fantasy that can be very powerful and that I only use, therefore, at the beginning of a group I'll have for a while, is the future fantasy.

Future fantasy. *Shut your eyes, breathe and relax. Imagine yourself ten years from now. Let a picture come into your head of yourself as you'll be then.*

If people are sympathetic to mysticism, this can be preceded by rubbing between the eyebrows to stimulate the third eye before starting. Sometimes people don't see anything, or see themselves as dead, and this is why it's important to have an opportunity to follow up this experience.

Toward the end of the microlab, a number of affection activities fit well, allowing warm feelings to emerge, and helping to end on a pleasant note. One of the best allows the group to get closer by communicating on a more unconscious level through the use of fantasy.

Group child. *Each group lie on the floor with your heads together like spokes on a wheel. Breathe and relax . . . each person imagine the whole group as children. Let a picture come into your head of all of you as children. As soon as one person has a picture, tell it to the others, and everyone try to get into the same fantasy. After that, any time a group member sees anything, report it to the others.*

This is a way of clarifying perceptions of each other. It is also often a great deal of fun, and again the energy in the room builds up. Some groups are laughing, some yelling, some occasionally crying, and others very intent.

Another way of relating closely is through singing.

Singing. *Starting with the person closest to me, turn to your left and sing a song to that person, any one that comes into your head. When you are through, he sings one to the person on his left, and so on around the circle. Sing loud.*

If the microgroups will eventually form one group, as when they all come from the same organization, there is a danger that each microgroup will become isolated from the others. Variations that make sure that the group remains whole involve more interaction between groups. While this decreases the intensity within each group, it aids the overall closeness. One method for accomplishing this is moving, used after each significant event, usually a nonverbal activity followed by talking it through.

Moving. *Choose one member to move to the group to your left. Choose him on whatever basis you wish.*

Using this method, when the microlab is finished, each person has been with many others and there is less divisiveness. Another way to avoid divisiveness is to have the groups observe or compete with each other. Arm wrestling can be converted into a total group experience by having a championship consisting of nominated champions from each group. This can be a group-wide event, with cheering and booing encouraged. Or in the singing, one group can choose one of their songs and sing it to the group on their left, which then reciprocates. Or one group can observe another group encountering and tell them their observations. Then it's reciprocated. These interactions and group member exchanges can be designed for almost all activities.

Two techniques are very good for including people who, toward the end, still do not feel comfortable in the group.

Roll and rock. *Take a moment to select the one person who still seems to be least at ease in the group and put him in the center* (about 3 minutes). *Stand up, form a circle, and put him in the center. He is to shut his eyes, relax entirely and fall to-*

ward the circle. Members of the circle catch him and roll him around the circle. After a few moments, lift him up and rock him back and forth, then slowly rock him down to the ground.

It is usually more comfortable to put his hands on his chest and let his head fall back supported, only taking the tension out of his neck. There are many variations. He can be rolled from side to side, lifted over the heads, and rocked very slowly. Saying OM or humming while he's rocking is very effective.

Affection. *Have the person who is most uneasy stand in the middle of a circle and shut his eyes. Everyone who has a positive feeling for him advance at once and express these feelings nonverbally.*

In finishing a microlab, I like to tie up loose ends.

Last meeting. *This is your last meeting. Think of all the things you will think of when you leave here, things you wish that you had said or done, but didn't. Say them now. Now continue saying goodbye, but without any sound.*

When the microlab is over, I will often ask everyone to make a sound indicating how he feels. This gives a good sense of the community of feeling and closes off the experience by releasing any tensions. Usually, we then talk a little about everyone's experience so that it can be shared. But there is a timing danger. If the talk goes on too long, it gets too intellectual, and the feeling that has been generated begins to fade. If it's important to discuss the experience intellectually, my preference is to do it later, like on the next day.

Often, if the microlab is held at Esalen, and it is the first activity of a week's workshop, everyone will then be invited to come to the natural hot baths. The issue of nudity is thereby opened up, and most of the workshop members are provided with a very enjoyable experience.

Group members are usually highly stimulated after the first meeting. They often have vivid dreams, an inability to sleep, long talks with each other, self-reflection, periods of fear, excited anticipation, euphoria, and countless other feelings. The following morning the larger groups of 10 to 12 are formed with a group leader, usually of their own choosing. They typically remain with that group for the entire week. The daily routine outlined earlier is followed through Thursday, with Wednesday night free for a drum dance, often preceded by a fantasy trip to help release the group members so that they can move their bodies freely to the music. The workshop concludes Friday morning with a short group meeting followed by a general summing-up session with the total group, including all the leaders and me. I generally rotate among the groups and conduct the beginning and closing sessions and one general session during the week. My predilection for the Friday final includes corny music that seems to fit in with the prevailing mood—*The Impossible Dream,* Aretha Franklin's *You Make Me Feel Like a Natural Woman, Camelot, Zorba,* and so forth.

The week usually follows an amazingly predictable emotional evolution. Sunday night: great energy and excitement. Monday: grim, earnest, a little disappointment because the larger groups don't go as well as the microgroups. Monday night and Tuesday morning: beginning of depression and anguish as problems and negative feelings are opened up. Tuesday night: very bad, anger, hostility, and sometimes several people almost leave, which they report on Wednesday morning. Wednesday: the gloom starts to lift as problems start yielding to work; dance is a relief and many find it a great catharsis and are proud that they can

feel so free. Thursday: good feelings start to rise and positive
feelings emerge; joy comes about noon Thursday, and continues
to grow. Friday: euphoria and tears, difficulty in leaving, sadness, joy, and ecstasy.

Of course, this is not invariable, nor does it happen for each
person this way, but the general trend seems quite pronounced.
It is very valuable for a group leader to know, especially on
Tuesday night, when people often turn on him. Actually, however, my personal anxiety never was totally allayed by this
theoretical knowledge. Every Tuesday a part of me still felt that
this would be the workshop that wouldn't work out.

The Rules of Open Encounter

The philosophy and theory underlying open encounter lead to
very specific ways of conducting a group and their consequences can be expressed as a set of rules for group interaction.
As these rules are described, please note their general applica-
bility to all human interaction, not only to encounter groups.

Encounter does designate a specific mode and philosophy of
relating, and it should be conveyed to the group members in
order to alter their interaction from a familiar method to the
encounter method. It is very important for the group leader to
be clear about what this mode is and not to have deluded himself that he is totally open to anything that happens in the
group, or that he is objective.

The method by which these rules are conveyed varies with
the setting. Any or all of the rules can be stated, modeled, or
conveyed by reinforcing or punishing spontaneous group
behavior that conforms to or violates the rules. In an engineering group I worked with several times, I had great difficulty in
getting them to follow the encounter group model. They appeared at the group meetings with notebooks and clipboards

and expected to hear a lecture on human relations. After fighting this I decided to capitulate and take them from where they were. I proceeded to write five rules on the blackboard: talk only about feelings, be open and honest, and so on. This worked beautifully. They copied these rules eagerly and had a great deal of fun following them and conscientiously calling each other on rule violations. Other groups don't react as well to this structuring of the group. For them more gradual methods can be used, including reading the rules, letting the rules be known gradually, making a rule clear whenever something comes up in the group that is relevant to it, or however.

The first set of rules establishes open and honest communication.

1. All communication in the group should be as open and honest as it's possible to be, and everything that happens outside the group must be available to the group on the same basis. If there is lying, evasion, or duplicity, the whole group effort gets clogged up. One objective is to learn how to be more open with everyone, including yourself.

2. Pay close attention to your body. With some practice, you can learn when it's telling you you're lying, either to someone else or to yourself. My stomach gets knotted when I withhold. Use your signals regularly to keep yourself straight.

3. Concentrate on feelings rather than ideas. Ideas are often used to hide feelings. Keep trying to stay in touch with the feeling—the body helps here, too—rather than the rationalized thought that follows it. Thoughts are good mainly to explore a feeling already experienced.

4. Stay with the here and now as much as possible. This helps staying with feelings and avoids going off into safer areas invested with much less real emotional energy. The uniqueness of the group is best used by concentrating on the joint experience of group members, those events that occurred while they

were all present. "Dear Abby" accounts of outside experiences usually can elicit nothing more than a round of advice-giving, something that does not require an encounter group. However, outside events are valuable when they derive from the here and now. For example, if a woman is told in the group that she is domineering, it may remind her that the same comment was made by her husband. She can continue to learn more about her marital situation and utilize the value of the group by finding out, for example, how the men in the group would react to her if they were her husband. In this case, the men are responding to her marital situation in terms of their own firsthand experience with her rather than, as in the "Dear Abby" case, responding to her one-sided report of an outside event.

5. No one may wear wristwatches except for the leader if there is a compelling practical reason, but it must be compelling. This helps to stay in the now and substitutes subjective time for chronological time.

The next set of rules focuses on the body, integrating it into the group activity.

6. Meeting areas should be without chairs or tables, without encumbering clothing like jackets, purses, or shoes, and in a room with only a rug on the floor. Padded walls and no sharp or excessively hard objects like radiators are desirable. This provides a safe surrounding for maximum physical mobility. Chairs anchor people and tables place barriers between them, both undesirable factors.

7. All members should sit or stand in such a position that they can move toward any other person easily, creating conditions conducive to movement and physical contact. Sitting in distant locations, like against opposite walls, loses this advantage.

8. Coffee or food is never allowed during a meeting. It serves as a marvelous diversion and dissipates almost all the energy a group has generated.

9. Whenever there is an opportunity to express something physically rather than verbally, do it physically. If it's a push or a hug or a fight, try to use your whole body to express the feelings rather than just talk about it. Tears, bruises, scratches, sore muscles are very possible and almost never very serious.

10. If there is a fight, the group should be trained to spring into action to stand in front of windows, sharp or hard objects, or anything in the room that might cause damage, and fend off the principals. Usually I don't allow men to use their fists; I restrict them to wrestling in some form, and it is a little safer if both start in a kneeling position. But these limits are open to negotiation. If both want to use fists or start upright that may be alright. Remember, everyone is responsible for himself and what happens to him. The risk of physical injury has proven very small in my experience and, compared to the very important feelings that are generated by fights, like fighting unfought fights, facing physical fear, testing strength, I've found it greatly worthwhile.

11. An attempt should be made to accept taking off clothes whenever it is valuable to the activity of the group, such as for working on body image or body acceptance. There is a great taboo on nudity in our culture. Overcoming that taboo, like the one on physical combat, has proven so extraordinarily valuable that I don't hesitate to underline its importance. (That's not true. I find as I write this that I feel concerned that this is the part of the book that critics will take out of context to attack. But, so be it. Nudity has led to marvelous breakthroughs, and bodies turn out to be much more beautiful than most imagine.)

12. Smoking is strongly discouraged, sometimes even prohibited. It reduces tensions that would be more useful if they were brought out and worked on in the group. It should be noted when a cigarette is desired, and that desire used as a signal of anxiety.

13. The same remarks hold for aspirin. Bring the headache to

the group. Alcohol, marijuana, tranquilizers, or any drugs designed to alleviate anxiety or pain, except, of course, in extreme
cases, should be avoided. With the bodymind orientation, all of
those body cues are being done by the person and should be
worked with, not masked.

14. Glasses, including contact lenses, are discouraged. Very
often during the course of a week-long workshop a glasses-
wearer will have a brief moment of perfect vision. If he objects
that he cannot see people if he takes off his glasses, give him the
alternative of moving near enough to people so that he can see
them. This often helps him to begin finding out what function
is being served by his not letting himself see better. Removal
of glasses also removes a physical barrier and eliminates a time-
consuming delay in physical confrontations.

In order to establish each person's identity and encourage his
taking responsibility for himself, several other rules are helpful.

15. I always announce at the very outset of the group that
everyone is responsible for himself and whatever happens to
him is very important. "You have your choice, if you want to
bow to pressure or resist it, go crazy, get physically injured, stay
or leave, or whatever, it's up to you." Frequent reminders are
helpful until the realization sinks in. This also applies to "accidents," unconscious behavior, body attitudes, and many other
individual productions.

16. Questions are discouraged in favor of the statements that
are almost inevitably behind them. Most questions are statements made without the questioner taking the responsibility
for the statement. For example, "Are we supposed to be talking
about . . . ?" often means, "I am bored with what the last speaker
is saying," or "You are a rotten leader." The questioner is encouraged to state the latter, and to say it directly to the boring
person. There are some legitimate questions, but not many. A
teeny exception is made for the leader at the beginning of the

group when he's trying to convey the structure of the group. But if he keeps it up too long, he's defending.

17. Word habits reflect the failure of many people to take the responsibility for their own feelings and behavior. "Can't" is discouraged, to be replaced by "won't." The statement, "I can't make it to the meeting today," or its variation, "I'm too busy to be able to meet with you today," is almost never true. What is more true is, "I choose to do something else rather than meet with you." The use of "can't" implies a force beyond the control of the actor, whereas in fact he is in complete control of his actions. By the using the word "can't" he is not taking responsibility for what he is choosing to do, and he is not recognizing that he has a hierarchy of values in which the present activity is not on top.

18. "I don't know" is also discouraged. This phrase usually means "I don't want to think about it anymore," or "I don't like what I might find if I pursue it further" (a frequent reason behind "no comment" in press conferences or law courts). One example is when "I don't know" is given as an answer to a question like, "Why don't you invite your boss to dinner?" Probing often reveals that the respondent does indeed know and that the answer, "I don't like him" or "I'm afraid of him" or "I'm afraid he'll turn me down and think less of me," reveals a situation that he can avoid facing by saying "I don't know." Group members are urged to think more and give another answer ("If you did know, what would it be?" or "If you had to give two answers and the first was 'I don't know,' what would the second be?").

19. Avoid general phrases that imply popular support for a personal feeling. Such phrases include, "People always . . . ," "Whenever you are in a situation you. . . . ," "We feel . . . ," "It's only human nature to . . . ," "The group feels. . . ." These are all phrases that attempt to say "*I* feel" without taking responsibility for the feeling. By saying "people" or "we" the implica-

tion is that yours is a common response and certainly not unique to you. There's safety in numbers. Usually you have no idea how "we" or "people" or "the group" feels. All you know is your own feeling. Interviews after big events are full of these general phrases, e.g., "How did you feel making that last putt, Clyde?" "Well, when you've come a long way in a tournament like this you are bound to feel nervous. It's natural for people to get a little tense." It helps to take personal responsibility by saying "I feel . . ." and speak for yourself.

20. Talk directly to the person addressed. Too frequently group members will say, "Frank doesn't seem to be too happy to me," when Frank is sitting right there. The communication is much more direct and meaningful if the subject of the remark is faced and talked to directly rather than being talked about as if he weren't present.

21. Globalisms are discouraged. These are statements so broad that they make any action relevant to them very difficult. Examples are: "I just want to be me," or "I have trouble with interpersonal relations," or "I have a father complex," or "I can't communicate with people," or "I want to be real." The broad statement does not allow for anything specific to follow and, further, it usually hides a much simpler and more workable feeling. For example, "I can't communicate with people" has sometimes meant "I am attracted to that man, but he doesn't seem to respond to me." The latter statement is much more valuable and direct. Another example, "Sometimes people find it hard to adjust to a new frame of reference," may be saying "I don't understand what's going on and I'm afraid you will think I'm stupid, and it's not my fault."

22. No-feeling words are discouraged. Several words sound like they convey meaning but most of the feeling is hidden. Such words include "interested," "surprised," "curious," "different," "strange," and "funny." For example, if someone says "You sure are different," very little is communicated unless it

is stated how he saw you before and how he sees you now.

23. If something is happening that you don't like, you are responsible for doing something about it. If you're bored and you don't want to be, do something so you won't be bored. The same holds for any feeling you don't want to have. It is up to you to change it.

24. If you find yourself bored or with any other negative feeling, try to find out what it is you do that brings out the boring (or irritating, or dominating, or self-pitying, or whatever feeling is bothering you) parts of people. Someone in a group complained about how another person talked too much at one time. Observation showed that whenever the second person started talking the first just looked blank and totally unresponsive. The result was that the second just kept talking, trying desperately to get some response. Clearly the unresponsive reaction of the listener was eliciting the overtalking he complained of. Searching for your own eliciting behavior is always a valuable exercise.

The use of body energy to help expand the limits of the self-concept gives rise to two important rules.

25. If you are saying something about yourself that you have said before, stop and say something else. The feeling of cold potatoes becomes increasingly easy to pick up because the feeling behind the account is often hollow and without much energy. It's pretty certain that if this is a recounted tale, like something told to a psychoanalyst, then it's probably hiding something else of greater importance. The speaker himself can become familiar with whether or not his language has any energy behind it.

26. Whatever you are most afraid of is the thing it is most valuable to do. If it's combatting a strong man, or professing your attraction to a girl, or challenging the leader, or making a fool of yourself before the group, or taking your clothes off, or

singing publically, or whatever, the fact of being afraid is the signal that you feel that your self-concept limit has been reached. Going beyond this limit frequently results in a euphoric feeling of expansion and of freedom. The more things that you are able to do or not as *you* choose, the freer you are. This is a frightening rule and a valuable one.

The final rule has to do with a combination of the life flow and responsibility.

27. As all aspects of the group are voluntary, including entering, staying, participating, and leaving, part of taking responsibility involves presence. Other members, including the leaders, pressure you to stay or go, but the ultimate decision rests with you. I feel strongly that it is usually unfortunate if someone leaves in the middle because the energy cycle is incomplete. I sometimes also put a lot of pressure on someone to stay if I feel that withdrawal is their common defense and a part of them wants to be forced to stay. And I also urge anyone planning to leave to tell the group directly instead of stealing away. But these are just pressures I exert. The responsibility is still ultimately with the group member.

. These rules describe the kind of interaction desired in an open encounter group. They are based directly on the theoretical ideas presented earlier. As I read them over they sound tough and demanding, just as I frequently am with myself and others, so again I suggest that you take into account what may be my own idiosyncrasies in reading and applying them. I also think that on the whole they work very well, fast, and deep, so that much bullshit is cut through and the group time is used extremely effectively.

Bulletin: *The Encounter Politician*

September 1983, GUALLALA, CALIFORNIA (on the campaign trail) (Special to *The New York Times*)—Interview with the Encounter candidate.

The man running for governor on the Encounter party ticket seemed very pleased at the reaction to his off-beat campaign. He explained his philosophy simply.

"Political campaigns take enormous amounts of time and energy and are largely wasted. I'd like to make my campaign itself valuable to the people. I want them to experience the things I'm talking about rather than just hear me talk about them endlessly."

Q: How can they experience them?

A: Well, one of the main objects of my candidacy, indeed of all Encounter candidates, is to improve the quality of life for all people. So a large part of each appearance I make is devoted to an encounter microlab. With the help of my assistants I just divide the crowd, no matter how large, into groups of five strangers. The size of the crowd doesn't matter as long as there's enough room and I have a microphone so they can hear me. Then we go through several small encounter meetings for maybe an hour.

Q: Does everyone participate?

A: No, there are always some who stand and watch but that's alright. No pressure. People come in when they're ready.

Q: What's been the general reaction to the microlabs?

A: Overwhelming. Almost everywhere people end the microlab with feelings of anywhere from pleasure to ecstasy. They often yell and applaud. Then they talk about how sad it is that they can't feel this close to people always.

Q: Isn't there a danger here?

A: Not really. They have experienced how fulfilling relations with people can be if they'll just open up, be honest, not be afraid of physical contact, and be willing to encounter. And this fulfillment, of course, is what I'm trying to demonstrate.

Q: I understand that your crowds are being swelled by people coming just to meet other people, often of the opposite sex.

A: I think that's wonderful. We talk so much of alienation in our modern, impersonal, industrialized society. Here people are actually not only meeting other people, but they have an opportunity to start meeting them at an important level, not just superficially like at a cocktail party. I've had so many people, especially older ones, tell me afterwards with tears in their eyes how wonderful it is not to feel lonely.

Q: Do many old people come?

A: Yes. As the word of what we're doing is spreading, we're getting people of all ages and types. And because we encourage each person to meet with strangers, many dialogues are beginning between groups that never spoke to each other before.

Q: Is that how your Hyde Park groups started?

A: Yes. Some of these small groups would stay together after the microlab when we took a break, and get into important issues. Blacks and whites, older and younger people, Mexicans and whites, radicals and middle Americans. Sometimes I'd invite them up on the stage to continue and maybe I'd get in it. When there were several of these talks, we'd just let everyone stay where they were and groups would gather around each. We would wander around and get involved in them. For me it was a great way to get a feel for the issues.

Q: Is this really any different than any other discussion of the issues by citizens, say like at a city council meeting?

A: I think so, because it comes after the microlab so the whole atmosphere is different. People relate to each other basically as people, and it seems to me there's more attempt at understanding. I don't want to exaggerate the difference but I think it's there.

Q: You use music a lot in your campaign appearances. That's not entirely new but you seem to do it differently.

A: It started when many musicians offered to help in my campaign. Since the Encounter platform emphasizes a richer life with more pleasure, and since music serves that purpose, it seemed like a natural. The result is that after the microlab and the discussions we usually have music for listening or dancing. Dancing usually goes well, because the microlabs include many physical activities designed at releasing muscle tensions, so people feel freer.

Q: What's Big Rock?

A: That's one of the fascinating creative developments that emerged from this campaign. I received many musical offers not only from some Rock stars but also from many musicians that used to play in the Big Bands of the forties. These Bands, of course, delighted the older people at these meetings. But another thing happened. In the receptive mood stimulated by encountering, the young people started listening to the Big Bands and the older people started to try to understand Rock. Most of each group liked what they heard. Then one night when I was down in Morro Bay two groups got together. The

Big Band instruments started backing up the Rock groups and the groups started improvising with the Bands. Some of them have started working together combining all the instruments with all the voices. Some of the numbers are great. Someone named their music Big Rock.

Q: What happens to the people who don't want to dance or listen to the music?

A: That emerged, too. Many people didn't want to dance but they seemed to be enjoying themselves, so they started to just stand around and talk. Pretty soon some of them started bringing things they wanted other people to know about, preserves, or collections, or paintings. And—one thing that delighted me —there were many ethnic contributions. Greeks and Irish and Jews and others would bring objects for rituals and show them to others.

Q: Doesn't that operate against integration by emphasizing ethnic differences?

A: I think not. I'm strongly for integration but I also want to retain subcultures. There are some marvelous qualities and traditions among our ethnic groups, and it would be a pity to see them lost. No. These people, many for the first time, were getting acquainted with people different from themselves, people they formerly had prejudices against.

Q: Haven't you had some trouble with the police?

A: Some. We have had occasional troubles in our crowds, though nothing serious, and the troubles are diminishing rapidly. I had difficulty with the police because I said that the only police I wanted were those that came without arms and that would be there to help, not punish, more along the lines of the London bobbies. Gradually, some policemen have accepted the condition, and the crowd loves it.

Q: You frequently tell people that you don't know about some important issues. Won't that lose you votes?

A: Probably. But a major purpose of our party is to bring honesty into politics. There are many issues I don't know about; I'm especially weak in economics. I also have occasional doubts about wanting to win and having this heavy burden. It's important for me to tell people just where I stand and how I'm feeling. I also tell them that I think I'm smart and can learn about those issues and that I'm good at finding people who compensate for my deficiencies. But I do have weaknesses and I don't want to hide them.

Q: What do you do about people and groups you don't agree with or don't like?

A: I tell them. I don't like everyone who could vote for me and I certainly don't agree with all of them. If I try to satisfy everybody I won't stand for much of anything. So I tell them what I feel. Probably some won't vote for me, but that's the lesser evil.

Q: Lately you've been introducing a spiritual element into your campaign appearances. How did that emerge?

A: I think it was always there but it's coming to the fore lately. Generally toward the end of the appearance people are still feeling good. I then often ask them to shut their eyes and hold the hands of the person on either side of them. Then as the silence settles I ask everyone to breathe together. When the energy starts building up we'll all start to hum, or say OM, or make some appropriate sound. The effect is often indeed spiritual. I like this ending because it produces the feeling that I think it's possible to achieve in daily living, and most people leave deep in that very experience.

Q: I've been to a few of your meetings and I think they're beautiful. I go away uplifted. But is this kind of thing really related to the concrete issues of the governor's office?

A: I think so. Our main approach is aimed at the most basic issue, the quality of a man's relation to himself and to his neighbor. If that's self-deceptive and dishonest there will be trouble with every issue. If we can establish a close, trustful feeling

among men both in the government and among the people,
then we can enlist the very best talent we have available to
solve any problem. My campaign is aimed at demonstrating to
the people that such trusting feelings can be experienced and
that I'm capable of creating the circumstances in which they
can to exist.

Q: Do you think you'll win?

A: No . . . but I might be wrong.

The Techniques of Open Encounter

Since the term "open" refers to a never-ending accumulation of techniques and methods, any description I can give must simply be as of a given moment. Methods are constantly being added to the arsenal of the encounter group leader. They come from anywhere: psychotherapy, the theater, the dance, art, physical education, Oriental religion, party games, children's games. The only criterion for inclusion is that they be effective in some circumstances. The more proficient an encounter group leader is with a larger number of methods, the more he will be able to have an effective method available for any given situation. It seems clear by now that no single method is universally applicable, or more precisely, better than any other method for every situation. This is, alas, also true for open encounter no matter how valiantly it strives to encompass all.

These techniques are presented for three reasons. First, they'll give you a more specific idea of exactly what goes on in an open encounter group workshop. The methods are the ways in which the theoretical ideas are put into practice. Second, for

163

those who wish to pursue the developments I'm writing about, this will tell you whose workshops I recommend and which books to read to pursue your interest. In addition, many of the following approaches provide more intense work in specific techniques used in open encounter. And finally, I want to lay the basis for a training program for open encounter group leaders.

Some of these methods are normally done as a total unit and included in an open encounter workshop, but not within the encounter group itself. Examples of this are Hatha Yoga and Tai Chi. Various valuable techniques have been borrowed from other approaches and integrated into the group interaction itself, like the guided daydream and some bioenergetic techniques.

One frequent criticism of encounter techniques is that they are gimmicks and mechanical or forced. Techniques can indeed become gimmicky if they are applied mechanically, hence it is important that they emerge organically from the group interaction. Each method has a particular set of circumstances in which it is effective. The skill of the leader is in recognizing when those circumstances have arisen and in knowing how to apply the appropriate method. When this is done well the method aids the energy flow and usually quickens and deepens the phenomenon being explored. If the method is applied inappropriately it is usually simply ineffective.

That the exercises are artificial is true. Ordinarily most of the techniques are not done in everyday life. We don't usually touch the faces of strangers or pound on pillows and scream. But these methods get at deeper feelings quickly, often feelings that our conventional behavior is designed to hide. In most cases, although the doer might initially feel unnatural, once he gets into the situation his feelings become very real.

Many other methods are described fully in *Joy*. These methods are proliferating rapidly. Once the major breakthrough was made—that it's desirable to do a large variety of things in an encounter group, not just one—the latent creativity of group people and others has burst forth. I'm sure I've not kept up with all of these and I prefer to only present those I've used and found valuable. I'll outline the techniques in groups and try to describe the optimal circumstances for their application.

BODY METHODS

The body is becoming more and more central in encounter. It is the source of truth; it is the place to find one's identity; it is the place where one's whole life history is located. It is the place where alterations must be made if permanent psychological changes are to be expected. All experiences are recorded in the body and all are available for recall—in the nervous system, in the muscles, in the way the body is held and moved, in the expression on the face, the chronic muscle tension, restrictions of breathing, aberrations of circulation, digestion, and excretion, the patterns of illness, and the acuteness of the senses.

The body has a central function in the open encounter group. If a person doesn't know how he feels, he is asked to attend to his body to see where his feelings are. If there is a tension, he is asked to do whatever it takes to rid himself of the tension. It is assumed that the tension is caused by the body both wanting to do something and holding itself back from doing it. For example, a person frequently will discover a tension in his forearm. Swinging it about usually reveals that smashing something (like a pillow) relieves the tension. Upper arm tension is often relieved by embracing someone. Knee strain is helped by kicking, upper leg tightness by running away. Stomach pains often go away when a person reveals something he has been withholding, or vomits.

These symptoms, of course, do not inevitably go with these interpretations any more than dream symbols always mean the same thing. But experience has led to the conclusion that the meanings given occur with considerable frequency. Attention to these body phenomena often give insight into the person's present feeling state, and it is very helpful for breaking through impasses.

Another use of the body involves observing postures. If a person is physically blocking himself off from other people, it is often futile to try to contact him without unblocking his body. For example, a person will often lock himself up by crossing his arms and legs and bowing his neck and making his breathing shallow. Asking him to breathe and to unlock his arms and legs, and even massaging his neck to help him relax, usually makes him much more receptive to taking in communication that others direct toward him. Locking up is a tough resistance to any type of penetration.

Another type of blockage characterizes a person who is extremely anxious and tense. His high level of tension prevents him from being present, and some of this excess tension must be discharged before he can relax enough to be in the here and now. Letting him pound pillows, run, scream, or whatever he needs, allows him to relax enough to be able to pay attention.

Artificial tensions, like girdles, tight shoes, tight belts, tight ties, also restrict the free flow of feeling through the body by tightening muscles and restricting breathing, the physical equivalent of feeling. This becomes clear when someone removes one of these constricting garments. The first reaction is usually a great sigh of relief, as when a woman removes her girdle. The sigh, of course, is a large breath resulting from the release of the constricted breathing. Encounter group members are encouraged to note the presence of tight garments as a signal of what parts of their body they want to restrict, and then to loosen them for the group interaction so that their feelings can flow more freely.

The concept of body image is of central significance. Everyone has a conception of his body, usually not very positive, and often arrested in adolescence. Negative body images have profound negative effects on feelings of attractiveness, masculinity or femininity, sexual ability, physical strength, phoniness, and general acceptability as a person. Dealing directly with a person's feelings about his body is essential. At least one meeting and often more of the open encounter group is held in the nude. Each person presents his body, talks about how he feels about it, and hears how others react to it. It is especially important to explore feelings about physical defects and unliked characteristics, such as excess fat or skinniness. Particular attention is given to breasts and genitals, and penis size is compared. Most men have very definite feelings about how they compare and seldom allow their concern to come to consciousness. (We find that about three-quarters of all men feel their penises are too small and are greatly relieved to find that about 90 per cent of the women are seldom aware of the differences.)

There often emerges a sense of living in one's body. This can happen on such a simple level as shaving off a beard. I did this recently and found myself very uncomfortable with the lower part of my face. It was as if it weren't part of me, it embarrassed me, it looked funny, and I didn't know what to do with it. It took several weeks before I felt like I was settling into my face, relaxing it, and feeling as if it were actually me. This is similar to meeting an old friend who has changed a great deal. It takes a while to get integrated with him again. In fact, my facial appearance changed. At first I held my chin tight and assumed peculiar, strained expressions. My chin looked too small. As I got comfortable my chin actually relaxed and dropped so that my facial balance was restored.

This same phenomenon occurs with other parts of the body. Body parts that are alien or unwanted or sources of shame are often treated very badly. Women who feel their breasts are too large have often rounded their shoulders, restricted their breathing, and cut down the circulation to the pectoral area so that their breasts look pale, neglected, and unloved. Men who are uncomfortable with their penises have frequently retracted them, pulling them up into their body. A great deal of the difference in penis length is accounted for by the difference in ability to relax and let it fall into its natural position. Often the lower back is bowed and the pelvis pulled back as if to make the penis disappear. Similar things are happening in other parts of the body—hanging stomachs, big hips, thin or fat legs, bony chests. The pattern of alienation from these parts begins to emerge as the neglect or hiding of these parts becomes clear in their tone and general well-being.

As a person is able to face his real feelings about his body and deal with them, the reality of his body is almost always far better than his private image and he begins to accept his body more. This is reflected in holding the body more proudly, relaxing formerly unwanted parts, breathing more deeply, and often feeling so much better about his body that better dieting and exercising result as a sign of caring. This type of experience integrates well with a technique such as Rolfing, in that despising a body part probably leads to its being held very tightly and making it difficult to Rolf. Accepting it can make it easier to relax and "let it all hang out." Conversely, Rolfing helps a person begin to feel those parts that he has denied or rejected and begin to integrate them into the rest of the body.

When people are nude, the more openness they show toward each other the better. If some woman has rejected her fatness and is afraid it is repellent, it helps to invite other people to feel her fat or do whatever she most fears. When a group gets advanced and comfortable and trusting with each other, even deeper body concerns can be dealt with. In groups for couples we will often ask them to use a speculum to examine the interior of the vagina. The husband will use this instrument, used by a gynecologist, to explore the reality of his fantasies. A very common feeling is that vaginas are filled with tar, or soot, or bugs, or teeth, from very early childhood experiences, and to actually look and see can be a very rewarding and delightful experience. Similarly, examining her husband's penis very thoroughly is something few wives have done. This intimate contact can help break down many deep-seated unconscious barriers and often leads to a much more satisfactory sex life.

I found as I was writing this last part that I was debating whether or not to include it on the basis of offending some people or giving fuel to critics. Then I wondered if I was just projecting my own uncertainties and hang-ups in this area. Probably the personal motives behind this very sober, excruciatingly rational justification of nudity in a group are many. I do like to look at beautiful, shapely women, and justified nudity gives me a good rationale; it even allows me to touch them. (Since we have the baths at Esalen this doesn't seem to be a compelling motive.) Then, too, it's helped me. I was, and still am deep down, one of those men who felt his penis was too small and I very much enjoyed looking at other penises, especially big ones. Over the years I have really gotten a much more comfortable, confident feeling about the size and beauty of my penis and I think it has made a big positive difference in my life. And, oh yes, I do think I have a pretty good body and I like to show it off and have it admired, especially by women. So my main conclusion is that there is a titillation to nudity for me; claims that it is sensual and not sexual I think are bullshit. It is both. And there are possibly many personal gratifications in nudity for any group leader. It is therefore important for the leader to stay closely in touch with his own personal gratifications while in the nude group. But also, these considerations should not mask the fact that the nude experience is of the greatest value and importance; indeed, I would say that body acceptance, which is so greatly aided by a well-conducted nude experience, is an absolute requirement for getting the most from an open encounter group.

The social status of nudity as one of society's major taboos, though being eroded lately, has three major effects on encounter. It often prevents a leader or organization from using nudity for public relations reasons. This, of course, is a personal decision for that leader or organization. What is unfortunate, I believe, is when either the leader or organization attempts to justify this omission of nudity on the basis that it is theoretically undesirable. A second outcome is that several journalistic write-ups of encounter can't resist the added titillation for their stories of a photograph of a nude group, especially if they want a more sensational story (*Life* and *Newsweek* are two examples). This seems unfortunate, too, for although nudity has an important role, it can hardly be elevated to center stage of the encounter group, but since nudity is so titillating, it usually overwhelms the reader and leaves a distorted picture. The final effect of the social taboo on groups, however, is very useful. If a group can go through a nude session comfortably, then barriers to opening up in other areas are usually dissolved. Being secretive in other areas seems pointless after having taken off all your clothes in front of someone.

From the most immediate feelings revealed through body postures and tensions to the most deep-seated feelings seen from the body structure, the body is central. If the group experience is successful, the body is more released, lighter, smoother functioning, more relaxed, healthier, and more personally acceptable.

A man's concept of himself is viewed as a total body pattern, not only as an intellectual idea. If a person feels immobilized, unable to express himself, perhaps due to a fear of rejection or ridicule implanted early in life, this feeling includes tense and immobile muscles, shallow breathing, a tight voice, watery legs, a knotted stomach, bowed head, and averted eyes. He can be made aware of this body pattern by simply directing his attention to the feelings in his body. It follows that the most effective therapeutic method for dealing with his blocked feelings involves physical action through which these feelings can be contacted. Simply talking about the feeling usually just begins to relax all the places that the person is tensing. To the person experiencing it, immobilization is a complex feeling involving intellectual, emotional, and physical elements in response to a stimulus. His self-concept tells him that when he is confronted by a certain type of situation his body feels helpless and incapable of coping. The best corrective experience is one in which he confronts the same difficult situation, but then copes with it and has an entirely different physical feeling, one of relaxed muscles, full breathing, stable legs, relaxed stomach, etc. In this way he has experienced himself emotionally, intellectually, and physically as coping with a situation he previously could not handle, and his self-concept is thereby expanded.

A common method for dealing with this situation is to transform the feeling of being immobilized into a physical action. One possibility is to ask the person to break out of his tied-up feeling in such a way that his whole body is required, by doing the breaking out. One girl confronted with this situation tried very hard to break out for about ten minutes, then fell exhausted in the center of the circle. It was very important at that point not to let her out. Up to that point she had simply recapitulated her life style of trying once, and if she failed, giving up. So she was then faced with a new situation that she had always felt she couldn't cope with. She finally mobilized herself for a huge effort and did finally break through. Her exhilaration was beautiful. She went skipping and dancing about. She had had a total body experience of doing something she had assumed she was incapable of. This was over two years ago and the positive effects of this are still apparent and obviously now a part of her (see *Joy,* p. 170).

This technique is similar to but different than behavior therapy. In this case, the behavior therapists would recondition the person by having him relive in fantasy, in a graded, step-by-step manner, immobilizing situations and associate them with relaxation rather than anxiety. The present approach is to act out the event in reality rather than in fantasy, and reassociate it with the act of successfully overcoming the anxiety with the whole body rather than through relaxation.

The principle of action is central. Whenever an activity can be put into action terms, it is preferable to talking. This is in contrast to the psychoanalytic concept of "acting out (in the transference)," which implies an advantage to delaying action in favor of talking through. Taking action in the group context, and then experiencing the feeling and perhaps talking it through, is preferred in open encounter.

Virtually any feeling has a physical counterpart. If a person is "so mad I could shake you," have him shake you; if he doesn't feel any contact with people, have him go around and touch each one; if he feels isolated from the group, have him go to the corner or out of the room and really be isolated; if he feels so frustrated he could scream, have him scream; if he feels that women are always holding him down, have him pick four or five women and let them hold him down on the floor and have him try to get up. Similarly, if he has a feeling that he doesn't like, he is responsible for changing it. If he's bored, he should do something that will make him interested. In short, it is very important to take feelings literally and convert them into physical action so as to involve as much of the person as possible.

The emphasis on body action alters the traditional psycho-therapeutic role of the psychological interpretation of the meaning of group members' feelings and actions. In open encounter the use of interpretation and insight is becoming less and less important, for they can be used to avoid body feelings and to get back to thinking. Early in my career as a group leader I found that interpretation was an ego game for me. I liked the impact of a dazzling interpretation on the group. Participants were very impressed and I felt very competent and admirable. However I began to notice two things. One was that I was often technically correct, but the person who was the object of my interpretation was not helped. For example, I would say to a man, "The reason you lost interest in this girl that you were attracted to last night is that you identify her with your mother and you cannot yet combine sex and love. In his collected papers, Freud cites this as the second most frequent problem." He was concerned with the details of their interaction last night, and would gratefully acknowledge what I said, but it became obvious that he had several levels to go before my comment could have any relevance for him. The other thing I noted was that these interpretations were rarely remembered. They were almost like lectures in that someone would recall what I had said only if he remembered to bring his notes.

On the other hand, if I asked someone to report what happened at the last meeting I found that he would know everything that he participated in, especially his physical interaction. This was another corroboration that the more lasting experiences were those with the most physical involvement.

This is not to say that interpretation is never valuable. If it is brought in after an experience is finished and the full feelings have been dissipated, then an interpretation at the level where the person is can be helpful for consolidating his experience and helping to prepare him for the next one.

Another instance of patient experience replacing therapist interpretation occurs in the handling of dreams or other fantasy material. The method of preference derives from Fritz Perls' technique. It assumes that all parts of the dream, animate and inanimate, are parts of the self, and the meaning of the dream for that person is revealed by a psychodramatic technique in which the dreamer acts out the parts of the dream and carries on conversations, which can become nonverbal, between these parts, finally substituting "I" for each part. For example, a man had a dream in which an airport appeared. At one point, speaking for the airport, he said, "I have people constantly coming to me and leaving but none stay." This turned out to be a very significant feeling for him.

Minimizing therapist interpretation has the advantage of making the patient work more to understand himself; it gives him more personal experience, and keeps him feeling rather than intellectualizing. It also avoids therapist projection.

I feel a little suspicious of myself as I write this. I seem to be overelaborating. My desire to make open encounter unique and therefore a major contribution, and my desire to show the psychoanalysts (and in particular my own) that I was right all the time, might be leading me to minimize the importance of interpretation. I notice that three paragraphs above I made a rather weak attempt to be balanced in the presentation. I remember also wanting to act out in my own analysis, to philander, for example, to see what it felt like, but my analyst forbade it. I can feel that part of what I'm now saying theoretically—it's better to act out than just to talk—is to some extent still working out my anger at being frustrated by him, and doing it in a most respectable way, theoretically. Maybe interpretation is somewhat more important than it's presented here, and perhaps acting out is not always as valuable as I've stated it. I'm going to try again to discuss insight and interpretation.

The significance of insight or interpretation, that is, the intellectual understanding of the psychological situation to therapeutic effectiveness, is called into question when the body and fantasy methods seem to work so well with minimal interpretation. It often happens at both the body and the fantasy levels that important experiences and significant changes occur without any intellectual understanding.

Following the idea of the unified man, it would seem that maximum change would occur when the body, the feelings, and the intellect have all undergone the same alterations. One without the others is incomplete. In addition, I feel that the deepest level of change is in the body, the next deepest is with the feelings, and the least so in the intellect. Put another way, if a body change is not accompanied by parallel changes in the feelings and thoughts, the change is still real, but there is the danger that the body will eventually return to its former condition because the original cause of the body aberration still exists. However, intellectual insight not accompanied by emotional and body changes is really not a true insight and will lead to minimal change if any at all. On a simple level, this is frequently seen in a group when a person working on a problem finally gets an insight but doesn't look happy. He still has tension in his body, tension that indicates he hasn't really uncovered the basic issue.

Another example of how intellectual insight can be confirmed by the body happened to me many years ago when I was in college. I had just broken up with a girl and was very depressed for reasons unknown to me. I went to several friends, many of them therapists, to try to get to the bottom of the problem. I would say, "I don't know why I'm unhappy. It's not because she's now with Stan. We really were broken up long ago. I think it has to do with my status in the psychology department. She's the brightest and prettiest girl there and my prestige depends a lot on having won her, the belle of the department. Without her I'll lose my importance." I would then feel sad and my friends would confirm my insight and reassure me that I really wouldn't lose status. Then I'd feel better. Except I noticed that the next morning I felt very bad, my body felt heavy and dark. In other words the intellectual insight was not being accompanied by appropriate emotions and physical feelings. Then I went to another friend and started, "I know it's not because she's with Stan because—" He interrupted.

"Do the other fellows think she left you for Stan?"

"No."

"Do the girls?"

"No."

"Then who are you trying to convince?"

"Huh?"

Of course, I was trying to convince myself. I didn't believe what I had said. We explored in some detail my feelings of being left, of losing the competition to Stan, and so forth. This time when I woke up I felt very good and my body was light and energetic. The accuracy of my insight was confirmed by my body and feelings. By constant reference to the body, insights can be discriminated as valid or intellectualized. If the latter, they are not very helpful.

An example of a physical change without intellectual insight comes from Rolfing. One man has been Rolfed many times and one area of difficulty is a rounded back. On several occasions his back muscles have been released and his back begins to straighten. And, indeed, it is now much straighter than it has ever been. But the emotional feelings and intellectual insight about the meaning of that conformation have not been worked through. It apparently has to do with a sense of being weighted down with responsibility, a concept he continues to resist in therapeutic contexts. The lack of ability to break through therapeutically is accompanied by a continuing resistance to a physical change and a tendency for the back to incline toward its old pattern. Perhaps a reason why the body change is more enduring is that the tissue takes many years to reach a certain condition. If the condition can be altered physically it will take another long time to get back to its original condition. But lack of understanding at levels other than the body prevents complete release.

Many critics have described encounter as anti-intellectual. It is, in fact, anti-intellectualizing. So many ostensibly sensible arguments are simply ways of rationalizing and justifying personal needs or fears that staying at the level of the words is irrelevant and tiresome. If the arguer or presenter is aware of the depth of his own truth and speaks when it is clear that his is a deeply felt conviction and not an intellectual argument attempting to compensate for an unwanted body feeling, then the intellectual discourse can be growing and creative. If one summons up arguments because he wants to triumph and is oblivious to the fact that he doesn't believe them deeply, the argument is misleading and sophistic.

Yes. I like that discussion of interpretation better.

In my experience, the body techniques listed here all work well for some people at certain times. The first few are more vigorous and strenuous physically, while the later ones stress body awareness and subtlety.

Rolfing. This is a technique developed by Ida Rolf of deep body manipulation aimed at restructuring and realigning the body back to its normal position. The body has strayed from this position through muscle tensions and subsequent body compensations to accommodate the misalignments. The tensions are assumed to be caused by emotional and physical trauma. I regard Rolfing as the most detailed treatment of the body and all of its parts, and the fastest way to uncover emotional problems.

Dr. Rolf is in the process of writing a book. It has been a long time in process, partly due to the common difficulty of pioneer practitioners taking time out to write down their methods. It should be excellent.

Bioenergetic exercises. This is a series of methods of pounding, stretching, kicking, screaming, pleading, and so on, to help the body to recover and work through feelings. For example, a person may lie on his back, put his hands in the air, and say "Mama" over and over. Often a rush of feeling going back to infancy returns. The method derives from Wilhelm Reich and psychotherapy and is much more directly aimed at uniting emotions and the body.

The principles of bioenergetic analysis, especially the unity of mind and body, are very similar to those written here; in fact, I have borrowed many of their ideas copiously. Several bioenergetic techniques have also been borrowed and integrated into the open encounter group (see *Joy*).

Hatha Yoga. Hatha is the physical yoga, the one with the asanas, or postures. A good balanced set of yogic exercises can lead to a greatly energized body through improved breathing, stimulation of the endocrine glands, and muscle stretching. A feeling of flexibility and lightness frequently results from following a yogic discipline. Yoga, like Rolfing, also involves an opportunity to understand and deal with pain. The experience of feeling pain and staying with it until it changes into something else is very illuminating. Also, the view that "pain is an opinion," as Fritz Perls used to say, can be explored in the yoga experience as well as in interpersonal and emotional situations. In Rolfing and yoga, two aspects of pain soon become evident: the part due to physical pressure and the part due to emotionality, leading to a tightening of the muscle. When it is possible to relax a muscle and deal with the emotional aspect of pain, the painful feeling is greatly reduced.

This illuminates the whole question of hypochondria and the function served by feeling pain strongly. The differences between people's reactions to pain both in yoga and Rolfing are usually related to their ease of complaining about pain in emotional situations. Some people feel pain easily so as to evoke sympathy and avoid being criticized or judged harshly. Others block out pain so as to appear "manly" and not weak. People who feel pain easily also frequently tend to get harried because they have so much to do that they are overwhelmed, therefore short-tempered, and so forth. Their choosing to be overbusy is often a way of gaining sympathy, justifying keeping people away, and legitimizing abrupt, thoughtless behavior.

Yoga also makes an important contribution to the art of

breathing, a central concept in the method, and to the art of meditation and getting in touch with body feelings. Western culture does not stress meditation and internal sensitivity, so the yogic discipline is a good balance.

Some of the yoga postures, like the lotus position, are not consistent with the Rolf conception of helpful body exercise. Some people are now working on a reconciliation of these two approaches.

Yoga is often done regularly during an open encounter workshop but outside of the encounter groups. In the morning before the first group meeting is a good time for yoga since it is a good energizer. Also, in good weather, doing yoga at sunset is a very uplifting experience. A yoga teacher is very important in learning the discipline.

Massage. At Esalen massage has been developed in the direction of a meditation and an energy exchange, consistent with the Rolf body concept. Using massage as a supplement to the encounter group enhances the physical experience and sharpens the feelings about giving and taking. It is also a very effective way of giving affection and learning how to make someone feel good, to give pleasure. It is often taught early in the workshop and group members can then give massages to each other. It is especially effective in couples groups, where issues of giving and taking are particularly pertinent.

Tai-Chi Chuan. This is a Chinese moving meditation. It is very slow and deliberate and focuses on very subtle body movements. The entire discipline is consistent with Rolfing. It enhances calmness, psychological centering, and body awareness. Classes in Tai Chi are often given in the morning, accompanying an open encounter workshop. I have personally never done Tai Chi because it appears too slow and unvigorous. But I suspect that is due to my body armor, and probably it's an excellent thing for a mesomorph like me to do. I do know that many people find Tai Chi very valuable.

Body awareness. During the past several years a variety of approaches to increasing body awareness have been developed and used in various workshops. One of the most profound is that practiced by Charlotte Selver. Her method involves the utmost subtlety in appreciating the nuances of body structure and movement, requiring a quiet and deep concentration. One of her students, Bernard Gunther, has developed her method in his own direction and published it in a book called *Sense Awakening*. Unfortunately, Charlotte Selver, like Ida Rolf and other pioneer practitioners, has not yet put her method in book form herself.

A method based on increasing sensitivity to and awareness of body movement is the Alexander technique. This is a form of individual treatment in which the practitioner deals with the ability of the body to let go and experience itself in the most careful and detailed way. The Alexander technique is a valuable adjunct to Rolfing in that it helps a person to feel when his body is out of alignment so that he can begin to control his own physical destiny. Both the Selver and Alexander techniques are best done in conjunction with the open encounter workshop. Selver and Gunther methods have been integrated into the group experience, especially as a beginning experience to open up a group.

Word blocking. Methods that prohibit words are remarkably effective. Words are so often used to block feeling that feeling often erupts as soon as words cease. Many nonverbal methods are described in *Joy*. One illustration will give their flavor. A back-slapping public relations man from the East was criticized by the group for being too nice. He seemed phony to many. I asked him to sit in front of each person and say something negative. After doing this to two people, he turned to me and said plaintively how difficult it was for him. In front of the third person he was stuck. He just rocked back and forth, looked at her, and couldn't say a word. I asked him not to talk but to keep rocking. He immediately started to cry and remembered a cradle scene in which he was never rocked enough by his mother. I asked him if there was someone in the group that he would like to have hold him and rock him. There was. She rocked him and he sobbed for a long time. After this experience, it became clear to him that his overly nice come-on was literally an attempt to get people to rock him. His behavior was markedly changed. He could see what he wanted from people clearer and could come on straighter to them.

The nonverbal behaviors are often communicating something more basic about the person than their verbalizations and are extraordinarily helpful in breaking through to more meaningful levels.

Diet and Fasting. As body awareness increases, so does awareness of food and how it makes one feel. Purer and lighter foods taste better and lead to a more pleasurable emotional condition as body sensitivity increases. Successful encounters often lead to desires to improve one's body appearance, especially after accepting its appearance more and coming to own it. Accompanying the encounter with attention to diet is a more complete approach to realizing the human potential. Although in our open encounter workshops in the past we have only approximated this ideal, it is desirable to accompany a workshop with a balanced diet, preferably organic foods, and to encourage group members to concentrate on their feelings while eating, to chew their food slowly, and to try to follow its path down the digestive tract so that the act of eating can take on new dimensions of pleasure and awareness. As his body awareness increases, a person becomes much more sensitive to which foods his body needs and wants and makes his body feel satisfied and pleasurable and which foods are alien and leave him unsatisfied, feeling physically bad, and usually with an accompanying bad emotional feeling. Combining this sensitivity with being responsible for one's self helps a person become aware of how food can be used to reward or punish the body depending on how he is feeling about his body. For example, if I feel my body is too weak and frail I may cram food into it in the attempt to make it stronger, although at some level I know that my body is rebelling and the food is doing harm. But if I am angry with my body for not being different I take some pleasure in its discomfort. It is a deserved punishment. My body is treated as a stranger, an alien entity.

Fasting is a time-honored ritual, having appeared prominently in numerous cultures. Many authorities feel that periodic fasting is of great value for giving body functions a rest and cleaning out body toxins. I don't have any expertise in this area, but I'll tell you the thoughts and experiences that are most compelling to me. Fasting seems to slow down the digestive processes, which does indeed rest the body. If there is an enema or equivalent preceding the fasting, then prolonged digestive rest allows the excretory system to work better and begin removing toxins. According to Shelton, when the body finishes digesting and eliminating all the food from the last meal it then goes to the reserves stored in the cells, then the stored adipose tissue or fat so that weight loss begins. After the fatty tissue is eliminated, the poisons also stored in the cells are released, so that several days into a fast, poisons begin emerging, the urine gets dark, and the breath and skin smell foul. When that process is completed the breath sweetens and the urine lightens, and eating should begin again because the body has only its vital parts remaining. The total process usually takes from two weeks to 30 days of fasting. Naturally I'd only recommend it under expert guidance. The idea of cleaning out accumulated poisons, along with the notion of unblocking energy and realigning the body through Rolfing, revives an old childhood wish of mine to have a second chance.

Another frequent consequence of fasting is a lightheaded feeling and an easier access to unconscious material, or, in modern argot, "tripping out." A heightened sensitivity to feelings and sensations is very common. Within a five-day workshop I have occasionally invited people to fast for as long as they wish and the results are generally very good. Perhaps a more practical way to start is to adopt the practice of some religions of fasting one day a week to help the body by giving it one day to rest and catch up on its excretory functions. It's important to note that any dieting or fasting aimed at physical improvement is very difficult to maintain unless preceded by work aimed at improving the body image. There must be a liking and acceptance of the body before a person is willing to do what seems like sacrifice to improve body feeling and appearance. Once this occurs, then the body becomes integrated with the rest of a person, and "my body" becomes "me."

In addition to these specific body methods, most activities in the open encounter group are geared to the body, such as wrestling, touching, and hugging, and some others have body components, like chanting, a vibrating column of air that can be felt throughout the body.

METHODS OF INNER IMAGERY

Methods of inner imagery are of the utmost value. Like the body methods, they get through the conscious verbal behavior that we are all so familiar with and allow other levels of consciousness to take over.

These methods help release creativity. The inability to allow oneself to relax sufficiently to let fantasy material into awareness seriously restricts the creative imagination. A resistance to being able to relax and allow this material to come to consciousness is often related to specific feelings of which the person is ashamed or afraid. Feelings of hatred, lust, or other unacceptable emotions are often dealt with by vigorous denial. For example, denied violent feelings can be dealt with by becoming an excessive advocate of law and order or a militant proponent of peace. Denied feelings of sexuality and lust are sometimes dealt with through becoming an extreme opponent of pornography and sex education. Taking these extreme positions has the effect of a public denial of one's own feelings, usually reinforced by righteous indignation, while at the same time allowing the person vicarious gratification by always being near the violence or being "forced" into violence, as in the case of a law officer, for example, or by always being near the pornographic material, as in the case of someone who gets on a review board and is "forced" to look at all those pictures. This, of course, is not the psychological picture for all people who adopt these views, only those for whom it is of excessive importance. Accompanying this public denial of feelings of violence and lust is a resistance to looking inward and discovering one's own actual psychological make-up. This in part explains some of the opposition to encounter, psychotherapy, sex education, or anything that threatens to reveal underlying feelings and motives.

It also keeps people from delving deeply into humanity and curtails their creative ability to understand human motivation. If a writer knows only that a husband's reaction to his wife's infidelity is anger, and doesn't allow himself to understand the deeper feelings of hurt, inadequacy, fear of loneliness, and dependence, he will be a very shallow writer indeed. Unless the writer has access to his own feelings, it will be difficult for him to express much depth in his art form, and the same holds true for other artistic endeavors.

Access to the unconscious when exhibited in a group is what brings the group close together. If all group members are operating at the level of their defenses, there is usually very little close feeling in the group. It's more like the feeling at a cocktail party. But when members start letting their deeper feelings out, the group gets closer, people become more human, and the similarity of all people takes prominence over their differences.

Guided daydream. Briefly, this method allows a fantasy to be created at any time on any topic, and allows it to be entered into by the guide, usually the group leader. It is extraordinarily powerful for deeply repressed material and permits close working together on a symbolic level. This technique greatly expands the values derived from dream analysis. The subject is first relaxed and then usually given a symbol relevant to the issue most salient for him. For example, an organization head was concerned about his competence to hold his present job. He was asked to picture a mountain and see himself climbing it, since a mountain usually symbolizes achievement. The aim of the guided daydream, then, was to help him to climb to the top. On his way up he came across a huge boulder, and the main work of the dream was to overcome the boulder and get to the top. Overcoming a fantasied obstacle constitutes another method of expanding the self-concept, since symbolically the fantasizer accomplishes something that he didn't feel he was capable of at the beginning of the guided daydream. During the experience, the subject goes through many real body changes: squirming, sweating, crying, tension, anger, fear, and, finally, relaxation and pleasure.

A new development that appears very promising is a combination of the guided daydream with Rolfing, and perhaps both with encounter. This unites very powerful methods for investigating the levels of the body, the self, and the interpersonal. The combination of Rolfing and fantasy arose almost accidentally in the last residential program, when I was demonstrating the fantasy method and one resident had just returned from her fifth Rolfing session, the one dealing with the stomach area and often related to aggression. As I was demonstrating, it became clear that she was becoming very emotionally involved. I stopped the demonstration and worked with her. The Rolfing session had released tension, primarily in the large muscle in front of her stomach (rectus abdominus) and the internal muscles behind that attach to the spine (psoas and iliacus). One limitation of the Rolfing is that it does not provide any method for dealing with the feelings released when muscle tensions are released. This seemed like an opportunity to supplement the Rolfing.

I asked Helen to make herself very small, to enter her body, and to go to those muscles that were just worked on. This symbolic method would help her see all of the feelings and events just liberated. She then proceeded through a remarkably lengthy and deep fantasy, focusing on her feelings around the recent death of her husband that she had been trying to work through for the last two years. This time she was able to reach her real anger and hatred for him and express it fully. Before, she had been aware only of the love feelings and the loss and grief. After she had expressed these feelings—including anger, grief, loneliness, and hatred—she confronted her husband. Now she was aware of the whole spectrum of her feelings about him, ranging from love to hate, and in the fantasy was able to see their relation for what it was, to part with him warmly, lovingly, and realistically, and let him go.

This so impressed me that I tried it deliberately a few more times with similar results. This I see as a future development uniting the power of Rolfing to break loose the stored memories and fantasy to deal with them and work them through. It seems an ideal combination for reaching great depth in an unusually short time.

The following fantasy took place recently in a group in London. It demonstrates the close tie between fantasy and the physical. Bobbi was a very quiet girl who had said very little all week; then at one meeting she suddenly started crying. Following is her account of the incident.

Anne was talking about feeling pushed away from her mother too early. My tears came, my heart hesitated, it was like I'd never been held and accepted enough even to be rejected.

Helen came and prompted me to keep breathing, this made me aware of my terror of the suggested idea that we should lunch with the person we had the most negative relationship with. I didn't feel able to do this; I felt I needed more time with the people I developed positive feelings to before risking myself with someone I felt negative about. I had worn eye make-up that morning because I wanted to leave the group feeling grown up; I was afraid to cry (mascara stings like hell with tears, so it's one added defense against them) because I felt I'd still have to deal with it next week (after the group) and I didn't feel I had anything inside me to do it with, I thought I'd just crumble again. I was encouraged to tell people how afraid I was by shouting. *I'm frightened, I'm afraid, I'm really frightened, I feel so frightened.* Bill asked me to lie down and imagine myself very small inside my body. I felt very small inside a big cave with black tunnels leading off, I felt like Alice in Wonderland —there was a feeling of awe and excitement at being allowed in. I was trying to breathe deeply with help, my jaw was moving a lot and I was still crying.

(Bill) Where do you want to go?

I'm going down my leg.

How does it feel?

It's a bit difficult.

Do you need any help?

No. I want to do it alone, I want to be able to help myself.

Where are you now?

I'm in my feet coming out of my toes.

Is there anything under your toes?

There seems to be sand under my feet, it feels good.

Are you on the sand?

No, I'm going toward the sea.

Are you going to go in?

I don't know yet.

Have you decided yet?

Yes, I'm going in. I'm swimming slowly, I don't get very far but I'm OK. It's calm and warm and feels good.

Are you going to stay there?

No, I'm coming out now. I'm going back to my feet. I'm inside my legs and travelling upwards.

Have you brought anything with you?

Yes, I've got a sack on my back.

What's inside?

I don't know yet.

Where are you going to?

I'm about here (hand on my stomach) in between the front and the back. I'd like to fill up the space and stop feeling backless.

Can you do it alone?

I'm not sure.

Can you use what's in the sack?

It's full of sea, it's filling up the space.

Can you feel your back?

I can from the outside—someone is pressing it on the left side but I can't from the inside. (Bill was.)

Can you try and feel it from inside now?

I'm beginning to, it feels warm and the front and back are together.

Do you want to come out of your body yet?

No, not yet. I can feel tingling down my legs, my knees feel strange.

Can you open your eyes and look around? (I felt at this time that she wasn't strong enough to finish. Climbing up helps give ego strength.—WCS) Go back into your body again. There's a mountain—can you see it?

Yes, it's here (hand on stomach).

Can you climb it?

Yes, it gets more difficult near the top. I have to breathe more.

That's OK, the air is thinner there, do you want to stay there?

No, I'm coming halfway down, it's too far to fall.

Is there something there?

Yes, there's a soft shelf where I can stay.

Can you see a lock to hold in the air?

Yes, it's here (hand just above the mountain).

Can you come out of your body now?

Yes.

Do you think you can stand up?

I think I need help the first time—my knees feel uncertain.

I was helped up and was supported till I felt my knees were able to support me. I had a lot of sensation in my legs, specially in my knees, around the vagina, and in my hands—my body was extremely hot.

Will you look at each person?

I then met each member of the group in a way that felt very different for me, I mean that I did not feel my whole being was threatened by them. That is except for Alex who was similar in stature to my father and held the combined identity of my mother and father; I still felt very afraid of him.

After further contact with Helen I gained strength.

Would you lie down and now see if you can get up by yourself.

I got up by myself. Then I returned to Alex and felt unafraid. I hugged him briefly.

I was very aware of the increased body sensation and change in breathing, I felt I had come to life.

After she had completed this experience the group put me on the floor and expressed affection toward me. When they were finished, Bobbi came over while I was still lying on my back and offered to help me up. I accepted. The cycle was complete. Bobbi went from having to be helped up physically, to getting up by herself, to helping someone else up. Following is how she completed her report.

I am writing this a week later and my body is still feeling the change. I've laid my foundations, which feel like firm ones at last. The change in breathing still amazes me in the way that it really helps me to know myself. I feel very much to be at the beginning of living with myself, which means I am facing my adult self with a child's experience. This excites me rather than displeases me.

Gestalt Therapy. The technique developed by Fritz Perls is based, among other things, on a dogged insistence on the here and now and on personifying the many parts of the self so that conflicts can be clarified. He also was a strong one for asserting individual responsibility; "wipe your own ass" was his pithy phrase. Fritz's insistence influenced me strongly, and, hence, the ideas on responsibility in this book. The gestalt method of dream analysis is the most effective I have experienced. Since the guided daydream is a type of dream, the Perls method may be used to deal with that, too. The gestalt method that I find most useful is that of carrying on dialogues between significant parts of one's psychological life, whether they be parts of a dream, or a hand held over a mouth, or whatever. If someone dreams of seeing a ship on an ocean, as did one man, for example, a gestaltist might say: Be the ship and be the ocean and carry on a dialogue. "I am the ocean and I have a dead body within me," is the utterance that came out. Assuming that each part of the dream is a part of the self, this opens up the area of the young man's feeling that he has someone dead inside him. But you can read this in more detail in Fritz's own books.

I'd like to tell now of a more recent use, combining Rolfing with gestalt therapy. I know that Fritz was trying this out, but due to a benign falling out between us toward the end of his life, I never found out exactly what he was up to. Independently, while Rolfing, I discovered one way to combine the two. I was working on a man who had great tension in his right foot and left calf. They were both extraordinarily tight, so I asked him to have a dialogue between the two. The calf started:

"You don't step out enough."

"What do you mean?"

"You don't carry your own weight. You just stay there all cramped up, passive, and I have to support your weight."

This opened up a whole area of passivity and conflict over masculinity. Fritz felt that the right side is the masculine one. Also, note that, again, the phrases in common usage in the culture are physically accurate: "carry your own weight" and "step out." I suspect that in the future, this combination of Rolfing and gestalt will also prove very valuable.

To my surprise, I find as I write this that I have very warm feelings toward Fritz. We had difficulties the last year of his life at Esalen, but apparently they weren't as important as deeper feelings.

Goodbye, Fritz, rest well. To paraphrase *A Thousand Clowns*, you were the best Fritz Perls you could be, and you affected many of us, including me, profoundly. You wanted to be a real person and you came as close as anyone I know. I want to, too.

Absurd statements. Another method of generating material from below the verbal, conscious level is to ask the group to divide into pairs and make absurd statements to each other. This gives permission to make statements without having to take responsibility for them and sometimes frees people from their internal censors. The statements are then pursued like a fantasy or a dream. One statement made recently was, "Hiawatha was the mother of hieroglyphics." The person was asked to be both Hiawatha and hieroglyphics and carry on a conversation. What emerged was that this man felt that he and his mother started out the same (*hi* in each word) but then became very different, and, furthermore, he became a mystery to her; she couldn't understand him, he was like hieroglyphics to her. This can then be pursued further. The point here is that just from an absurd statement significant content can sometimes be reached quickly.

Hypnosis. Direct hypnotic techniques are used when appropriate. The state induced is similar to that in the guided daydreams, but some people respond better to the hypnotic method. This should only be done by someone skilled in this technique.

Meditation. The ancient and honorable methods of meditation often, prove to be just right for discovering aspects of some people that are ordinarily blocked. Sitting meditation, and a type in which inner originating noise and movement is allowed, have proved the most effective. Meditation is offered outside meeting time, usually following yoga, although sometimes it is helpful for a short time during meetings and in microlabs.

Alone time. Inner awareness is often blocked by keeping oneself always busy as a way of not having to look inward. Simply giving people a specified time when they must be alone —perhaps walking in the hills, by the water, along the road, sitting and looking at the ocean, or however they wish—awakens them to feelings they ordinarily don't allow themselves to have.

Silent day. To enhance the elimination of words and noises of all types, sometimes the workshop will go through an entire day of silence. All activities will be nonverbal. Some are alone; some are to enhance getting in touch with the self. One of the latter that has proved effective is to have each person stand alone, naked, in front of a mirror for a half-hour, just looking, touching himself, and exploring in detail what he is like. So few of us have ever spent a silent day voluntarily that there are often remarkable results. Many people report a calming and sorting out of the confusion of life. Also, enhancing the going-inside quality can be accomplished by using ear plugs so that sounds heard come from the inside rather than from the outside.

BLOCK DISSOLVERS

The next set of methods concentrates on the problem of breaking through blocks, which are assumed to have both a psychological and a physical expression.

Breathing. Fundamental to almost all blockages in the body is breathing. Cutting off feeling is accomplished through cutting off breathing. Breathing is how one enters the world, takes what he feels he deserves, lets people in, gives out his feelings and whatever else is inside him, and exchanges feeling with others. Physical aberrations occur by not breathing deeply, constricting the chest, constricting the throat, and using the tongue to block full breathing. Because of the immensely important emotional meaning of breathing, the aberrations are many. I'll describe the ideal breathing pattern, the types of breathing aberrations and their psychological meaning, and some methods for trying to overcome the breathing blocks and release the feeling beneath. I'm not sufficiently familiar with either the physiology or psychology of breathing, so I will be quoting a number of people whose views seem consistent with my experience and who seem authoritative.

The centrality of breathing is recognized by Reich and Lowen in bioenergetics, and in yoga. In yoga, the breath, called prana (not an exact translation, but close), is the key to both physical and spiritual activity. Pranayama is the science of breath control. The importance of prana, also known as universal energy, is given by the great sage Vasishta, in his *Yoga Vasishta,* on the relation between the mind, the body, and the prana.

O Rama! For the motion of the chariot which is the physical body, the God has created the mind and *prana* (vital breath) without which the body cannot function. When the prana departs, the mechanism of the body ceases and when the mind works *prana* or vital breath moves. The relation between the mind and prana is like that between the driver and the chariot. Both exert motion one upon the other. Therefore, the wise should study regulation of *prana* or vital breath if they desire to suspend the restless activity of the mind and concentrate. The regulation of breath brings all happiness, material and spiritual, from the acquisition of Kingdoms to Supreme Bliss. Therefore, O Rama! Study the Science of Breath.

Different accounts of normal breathing vary, but following is the best one I have been able to put together. The mechanism of breathing involves the body from the shoulders and collar bone down to the bottom of the pelvis. Total breathing in should begin at the abdomen, and in a flowing wave come all the way up to the collar bone. Breathing out reverses this wave. Breathing in (inspiration) begins with the diaphragm, a large, dome-shaped muscle under the lower ribs that divides the lungs and rib cage (thoracic cavity) from the abdominal cavity. As the diaphragm contracts, it pushes down on the abdominal viscera (stomach, liver, intestines), pushing them outward as far as the abdominal muscles will allow. At the same time, the contraction of the diaphragm forces the ribs upward and outward. This leads to four motions of the ribs. They expand from side to side, front to back, up and down, and each rib turns upward like a Venetian blind. The movement of the ribs and diaphragm expands the two elastic lungs. When the lungs are expanded, a vacuum is created in the lungs and the air from outside rushes in.

These movements occur in chest breathing. For the total breath, the shoulders and collar bones must be raised. In yoga breathing, all three types of breathing are combined. The abdominal or deep breathing fills the lower and middle regions of the lungs, the chest breathing fills the middle and lower portion of the upper regions, and the shoulder or high breathing fills the upper portions of the lungs. Further, yoga breathing stresses exhalation, breathing out. Cleaning out the old foul air is essential in breathing, so exhaling should be twice as long as inhaling.

When this ratio is mastered, yogis try to learn to hold the breath properly by which they mean a ratio of 1:4:2 for inhaling:holding:exhaling. (This ratio varies somewhat with different yogis.)

Hence ideal breathing, in which the entire capacity of the lungs is utilized, in which the full benefits of the breath can be obtained, and in which used air is fully expelled, involves beginning with the diaphragm forcing the abdominal viscera out, then chest breathing to expand the ribs in four ways, raising the shoulders to complete filling the lungs, holding the breath, and then expelling it in a wave from the collar bone down to the abdominal area, taking about twice as long as the inhalation. Probably the best instruction on this type of breathing is from a yoga teacher. The process is described in the yoga book by Vishundevananda.

Any muscle tensions will throw off this breathing pattern. In order to breathe this rhythmically and deeply, a large number of muscles from the lower abdomen to the neck must all function together without restriction. Tension in any one of them will interrupt the breathing flow in a specific way. Various breathing blocks are described well by Lowen in *Betrayal of the Body,* and I will draw generously from him in the following account.

One feeling many people have is that their energy supply is inadequate. If a man's self-concept includes this idea, then increased demands of living can lead to a panic feeling, panic closely related to the inability to breathe. These increased demands can center around any area of energy, such as work output, emotional responsiveness, or sexual activity.

To some people, inhaling has several negative connotations. It sometimes means taking in one's environment, including the odors of other people, or perhaps the foul air. Perhaps, at a deeper level, it is the fear of being invaded by others. Some people feel that the sound accompanying deep breathing is animallike or uncivilized and associated with the sexual act or with severe anger, so that unresolved problems in that area can be expressed through holding back deep breathing. Breathing in deeply is often related to taking what you deserve. If you feel worthy of your fair share, you can take all the air you need. If you have internalized the notion that you are selfish or greedy or that taking your share will deprive others, you may be reluctant to breathe deeply. Another feeling that prevents a full inspiration is that of wanting to be invisible. A person whose childhood involved a fear of punishment may have found survival through "playing dead," through trying to be as inconspicuous as possible, hoping that no one would notice, and, therefore, punish him. Or, what may have been more threatening, he simply wanted to avoid someone watching and paying attention to him. The physical pattern of playing dead (think of hiding in a closet) is holding the breath, tightening the muscles, and not moving. Strong feelings of not wanting to be observed would also lead to very shallow, quiet breathing.

I have awakened several times lately during the writing of this book with a soreness in the roof of my mouth. This soreness inevitably goes away when I start to breathe deeply. My association to this is that I don't want anyone to bother me or make demands on my time because I am absorbed in writing. Perhaps if I don't breathe heavily they won't notice me, a reversion to a common childhood pattern of mine. A failure to recognize this would probably leave me with much soreness around the upper respiratory tract, and continuous feelings of this type would lead to some chronic respiratory ailment.

Problems of full exhalation generally revolve around not wanting to reveal oneself, not wanting to express feelings, or not wanting to give. Letting the things inside of you out can be very frightening if a great deal of energy has gone into holding them in. Internal hostility or poisonous feelings might come out in body odors and bad breath. Holding something in tight control involves not breathing out freely, as demonstrated by the fact that when something has been held in and finally does come out, it is often followed by a sigh of relief, that is a large, uncontrolled expiration. A feeling of psychological deprivation is sometimes played out by hanging onto all of one's possessions, including air, and letting go very reluctantly. There is a feeling of not wanting to spend much time giving out, but concentrating on taking in, thus another reason for too short an expiration.

Another major reason for diminished respiration is the need to cut off unwanted body sensations. This is especially true for feelings in the lower part of the body. The stomach and genitals, as we've seen above, hold feelings of anger, fear, hostility, and lust and sexuality. Shallow breathing prevents feelings from developing in the stomach or genital area and being connected with the upper part of the body. This would mean bringing them to consciousness and expressing them publically. Having a blocked person relax his abdomen and breathe more deeply usually leads to feelings of anxiety, or sadness, or emptiness. The story of the man following his fifth Rolfing session, the one that opens the stomach area, gives a good account of some of these feelings. The aberrations of breathing take many other forms and I refer you to Lowen's book for further discussion.

Since breathing is so central and since blocks of such enormous variety occur in this system, it is particularly valuable if breathing blocks can be overcome. Recalling the therapeutic model used in Rolfing is helpful here. There are some blocks that can be gotten through by simply providing a person with support and direction. This is sufficient to allow the person to consciously relax his tension and, in the case of the respiratory muscles, his breathing will be freer. At the other extreme are blocks that represent such deeply repressed and frightening material that a long and intense course of therapy, both physical and psychological, is required before the tension can be let go. In the middle are those blocks that may yield to a combination of direction and outside pressure in the context of a supportive environment, like a workshop. Steve Stroud and John Heider have worked on a method for physically breaking through breathing blocks in this middle range that is in a very experimental stage, but it shows much promise and has resulted in several dramatic breakthroughs. It also has sufficient dangers that I definitely don't recommend that you try it.

Steve and John bring a group to a six-foot square tub at our natural hot baths and ask a person to start breathing deeply while in the tub until he is hyperventilating. To intensify the experience, the person is often asked to then get into the cold tub, and perhaps go back and forth from the hot tub to the cold. Very often there is an involuntary outburst of feelings of sadness, crying, laughter, mixed laughter and crying, screaming, feelings of terror, involuntary vibrations in various parts of the body, and immobilization of the mouth. Probably the vibrations occur at those points in the body that have been chronically held. The responses are similar to those of Rolfing the whole respiratory system at once. Although feelings of terror, fear, and upset occur during the experience, there is almost as uniform a feeling of release and euphoria when it is over. A person is worked with while he is in this state or, if that is not feasible, the material that came up is used in later meetings of the group. This is one advantage of a workshop setting.

Obviously such a method could not be used if a person were not to be seen for a whole week after having this hyperventilation experience. By letting him break through and encouraging him to let the full play of his feelings flow without stopping and with the knowledge that there is someone competent there to depend on, a person can often make great strides in working through areas of blockage. Of course, the support and follow-through is vital. I notice I'm starting to repeat myself in order to reassure you, and me, that this method is alright. Actually, we must know more about it, especially the physiology of it, before I'll feel completely safe with it. But I don't want my fear and timidity to discourage Steve and John from pursuing it. It's an instance of how a rebel (me) becomes the Establishment as I begin to be more acceptable, then becoming the reactionary and stopping further development.

In addition to this rather radical approach to breaking blocks, breathing is used in several other ways in the encounter group. In open meetings, as mentioned earlier, starting with breathing is valuable for getting feelings going. For large groups, tremendous energy can also be built up by having a room full of people breathing together. In a small group, when a person is working on some issue, attention to his breathing is an important signal. When it stops, it indicates an area of anxiety and defensiveness. Keeping the breathing going makes sure that the feeling is still present. Also, people can be taught to be aware of their breathing so that they can learn to breathe deeper and to be aware of the onset of anxiety. It is an excellent self-indicator of the organism.

Eruptions. Just as respiration is the site of much blockage, so are other physical systems. Often the block is in digestion, usually related to the mother and problems around feeding. Sometimes having a person vomit is a great relief to his whole digestive tract and can be a symbolic expulsion of the undesired part of the mother. Frequently an oversoft voice and a strangled tight throat are signs of throat blocks. If the person can be made to scream it often aids breaking through the block. Bobbi's fantasy, reported above, could probably not have happened if she hadn't been able to scream earlier in the week in order to break through her throat block. Similarly, muscle tensions can frequently be expressed and relieved with strong pounding, kicking, throwing, choking with hands, or stomping. Props are provided in the group room to allow for these expressions, like pillows, mattresses, small cardboard milk containers to throw, towels to wring, styrofoam bats to hit each other with, and so on. Such a release allows a person to get in touch with these feelings, sometimes break through blocks, and work on them. These methods are used prominently in bioenergetic analysis and in psychomotor therapy.

Attack. The methods of Synanon, especially attack therapy, are also useful for moderately repressed material. In this technique all members attack one person on an apparent weakness. The accusations don't have to be true, although they usually are. This helps the person face something he has been evading by bringing the entire pressure of the group to bear upon him. This method seems to work well on certain people, but not on others, perhaps those with strong masochistic tendencies. I am also not in favor of the part of this game that encourages lying. It is often not made clear later what part is a lie and what part not, either to the target or the attacker. This is against the central encounter principle of honesty and seems to forfeit too many values for its worth. On the other hand, the attack game does provide the opportunity for building autonomy by constructing a situation in which a person must be able to face himself, what he's done and what he is, and take responsibility for it. In well-run games, there is a great deal of support underlying the attack. I like the method when used judiciously within the encounter context.

Support. The simple blocks that are primarily suppressions and that remain out of fear are often amenable to breakthrough through a warm, supportive atmosphere that rewards effort. This cannot be achieved by simply wishing it, but usually takes a long development within the group to achieve. As the group gets deeper and closer, support is more likely to occur. The whole theoretical area of positive reinforcement is relevant here.

Drama. There is a discussion in *Joy* of the methods of psychodrama devised primarily by J. L. Moreno for making situations more real in the same way that body and fantasy methods often seem to work. They basically involve acting out situations rather than talking about them.

Somehow the mention of Moreno always brings to my mind the question of priority. When I first met Moreno a few years ago, we had a pleasant lunch in which he told me he was very pleased with *Joy,* it seems partly because I was carrying on approaches and methods in which he had pioneered. I had heard this claim before from some of his followers and had investigated it prior to my meeting him. To my dismay, he was almost entirely justified. Virtually all of the methods that I had proudly compiled or invented he had more or less anticipated, in some cases forty years earlier—all except the fantasy methods that I had adapted from Leuner and Desoille. So when he alluded to his priority, I confronted him with my ace in the hole. What about fantasy? You didn't invent that. Ha! He patiently pointed out that Leuner's original articles had appeared in his journal in about 1932, and he had been using the method periodically since. Foiled again! So I invite you to investigate Moreno's work. It is probably not sufficiently acknowledged in this country. Perls' gestalt therapy owes a great deal to it. It is imaginative and worth exploring.

Physical interventions. When the group is going well, more unconventional methods can be used. One example of a method that has been successful is one used for highly constricted "tight-ass" people who have anal retentive characteristics, sexual problems, and a generally tight, bound-up personality. Utilizing the close tie between body and emotions while in the hot baths, I once asked a tight-assed man to put his finger up his anus and try to relax the two sphincters he would find there. It took a while, but he was able to relax them. He then had a feeling different than he'd ever experienced before. All of the muscles around the pelvis, genitals, and often upper legs seemed much more relaxed than they'd ever been, and he felt new sensations, usually very pleasant. The fact that tensions were built into his body that he didn't even recognize was made very clear. He now knows how he could feel if he could let go of some of his body tensions. The phenomenon of having a glimpse of the possible, whether through this method, fantasy, or another, is a very strong motivator to release the tension voluntarily.

Stop it! Some people haven't cried in thirty years, and having them cry is a very important event. However others cry easily, or they can explain their problems glibly, or they play games easily, like "poor me." Whenever a person seems to have already worked through some problem area, but continually persists in the same behavior—it's usually perceptible because it's boring and he's said it many times before—he's told to "Stop it!" —just like that. For certain persons this is much more effective than getting caught in the verbal web. They often use psychotherapy jargon and methods defensively.

These are some of the techniques to get through resistance and personal blocks. The ones described earlier (body and imagery) are also used. The most effective methods emerging from our work are those that combine some of the above techniques. For example, it is useful to follow Rolfing, which opens up tremendous amounts of feeling locked in the body, with a fantasy in which the person is asked to imagine himself going into his body and looking at the part that's tense. Or, I can use imagery to increase body awareness, and then use some of the physical bioenergetic methods. Or, pyschodrama can be followed by nonverbal behavior by the group; for example, if a person emerges from the pyschodrama in a sad state, the group picks him up and rocks him. These combinations seem to be the most promising newer methods for quickly, surely, and deeply getting to crucial problems and working them through.

I want to repeat that these are only *some* of the methods that are available. I hope this stimulates a would-be encounter group leader to seek out or devise his own, and suggest to a traditional group therapist that there are indeed a world full of methods.

Bulletin: *Education Encounter Group*

May 1984 (Special to *The New York Times*)—Following is a transcript ented with comments by the group leader of an educational group. This group comprised the president of the university, two members of the Board of Regents, two faculty representatives, and three students chosen by the student body, one black and two white. The group had met for one full day when the following transpired.

President: (Shouting) I'm sick of being pushed around by all of you. If you regents aren't on my neck, the students and faculty are after me. I can't . . .

Black student: Man, you chose the job. If you don't want it, don't take it. We're not responsible for you.

Regent 1: I wouldn't trust any of you students to run the university. All you know about is burning and objecting. I don't hear anything positive coming from you.

Faculty 1: Look, we've been through this for two days and we're getting nowhere. It's gotten so I can predict everything everyone is going to say.

Leader: I agree. Let's see if we can get below this. Would you, white student, and the president reverse roles. You try to be the president and say what you think he's really feeling, and you try to be the student and say what you think he's really feeling.

White student: (As president) Actually, I agree with most of your position. If I were a student now I'd probably be doing what you're doing. But I'm afraid I'll lose my job. The regents are so damned conservative that if I go along with the students at all, I might get fired. Then what would I do? I'm 58 years old, I've got a family and a beautiful house here and I don't have a lot of money saved. Trying to get another job —especially after getting fired—selling this house, moving my family, taking the kids out of school again—it's such an enormous effort. Besides, the regents aren't all wrong. Some of you kids are really destructive. But I realize that it's easy to use those few to condemn all of you. I'm really caught.

President: (As student) I understand your dilemma, but I want you to have guts. I still have the idealism of youth and I want to believe someone like you can live by your principles. I'm not as strong and independent as I sometimes act. Underneath, I have some admiration for you. You're not really a bad guy and you do have a tough job. I wouldn't want it, but goddammit, stand up for what you believe. I'm not always sure of what I'm doing, either. I like rebelling just for the hell of it. This whole movement allows me to aggress against authority like I never could alone. I always wanted to tell my father to go fuck himself and leave me alone but I didn't have the guts. Now I can. But also I feel exhilarated about what we're doing. I know we're right. The system should have been attacked long ago, by your generation.

White student: (As himself) I'm amazed. You're right on. I didn't realize you understood me so well.

President: (As himself) I hate to face it, but you were too. Jesus, I'm ashamed that these practical, material things mean so much.

Leader: Now, president, would you stand up and have the regents make a circle around you so that you can't get out. This will represent the safety that you feel being with them. If you want to maintain that safety, stay there. I'll ask the students to be on the outside of the circle and try to get you out. The regents will try to hold you in. If you want to break out of the safety of the regents and take your chances with the students, then try to get out with the students' help.

(At first, president stands immobile. Regents treat exercise as a joke. Then the black student reaches in a hand and grabs the president's wrist. Regents respond by closing tight around the president. He looks puzzled, also feels smothered. All three students grab the president and pull and strain, regents get mobilized, start pushing students away with their feet. Whole group careens around room finally falling in a heap. They get up huffing and sweating and grim. The president is being dragged both ways, apparently hasn't decided which way to go. White student 2 grabs one regent from the back and pulls him backward to give the president room to escape. President, still puzzled, doesn't take the opportunity. Looks very dark and depressed. Finally, with a great burst of energy he shouts "Let go" and frees his wrists from students, "I'll do it myself." Then, with superhuman effort accompanied by loud primitive noises, he smashes through circle of regents. But he doesn't go to students, he finds a place free of both groups, looks angrily at everyone. Breathing very hard, he sinks down and sobs quietly. Others gather nearby and circle him on the floor. He looks up briefly and smiles. There is a moment of empathy from almost all for a man in a dilemma, a moment that transcends their differences and unites them as men struggling. Except that one regent has wandered over to the corner by himself and sits, apparently unmoved by the scene. A minute passes while everyone catches his breath.)

Regent 1: This is a bunch of psychological hocus-pocus. The simple fact is that we run the school because we're more experienced and practical. You kids are running wild without discipline and we can't let you get away with it.

Black student: Look, dad, you cats are so far behind the times, all you can see is your pretty world slipping away. You don't have the first idea of what's happening.

Leader: Would you two, regent and black student, do something to test how much you trust each other.

Regent 1: Oh, christ. I'm getting tired of your silly games. Look, we've got some very serious problems and sitting around here all day acting like kids isn't going to help.

Regent 2: I was impressed with what happened to the president, weren't you, Harold?

Regent 1: Well, maybe. All right, what do you want me to do? I don't want you to think I'm uncooperative.

Leader: Just turn around and fall back and hope that the student catches you before you hit the ground.

Regent 1: What do you mean fall backward? What if he drops me?

Leader: That's the chance you take.

Regent 1: Let him do it first.

(Black student falls backward easily. Regent catches him.)

Black student: I'll be damned. I did trust you. That was easy. Far out.

(Regent tries to fall backward but stumbles. Tries again but breaks fall by putting foot back.)

Regent 1: Get a little closer. Sure you'll catch me?
Black student: Man, you've just got to trust. Like we've been telling you all along.

(Regent 1 tries again, falls about a foot and is caught. Black student backs up; Regent 1 won't fall again.)

Regent 1: Well, I don't know what that means. I'm heavier than you, you may not be able to hold me.
Black student: (Calmly) I can hold you.
Regent 1: I really don't trust you. I don't usually trust many people, even when I know them. If you'd been in business as long as I have, you wouldn't be so trusting either.
Leader: Would you two change roles and try to say what you think the other one is feeling?
Black student: (As Regent 1) I don't like what's going on here. I wish I could have fallen back. Maybe I am a little too suspicious. These kids don't seem so bad once I see what they're like. They're different from the others.
Regent 1: (As black student) Well, I really showed the old bastard that time. But it sure surprised me to find that I trusted him. I guess underneath all his bluster there is something solid that I can rely on. Never expected to feel that.
Black student: (As Regent 1) It makes me feel good to hear that. You are right, I do feel that I'm out of date. I don't understand what's happening today and it frightens me. It's not really the wildness. Hell, I was a wilder kid than any of you guys. Sometimes I think I'm dumb. I wish I'd gone to school more. I made it in the business world, but these kids seem to know

so much more than I do, it makes me feel small. That's when I want to squash them and show them who's boss. Then I still feel superior. (As himself) Hey, I want to stop playing you and say something for myself. I really understand what I just said. I don't know if you agree or not that you feel the way I said you feel.

Regent 1: (Grudgingly) Sometimes I might feel a little that way.

Black student: Well, baby, I know what it's like to feel inferior. I just realized you're doing the same thing I am. Look, I went to school in Texas, and every day for 12 years I had to ride my bicycle through a white neighborhood to get to my school. And every day for 12 years they called me names and threw things at me and I couldn't do a fucking thing about it. Can you feel how much hate I have in me? Every day for 12 years. And when I can get back at you, man, it's gonna be violent. I don't want to reason with you, not now. I want revenge. I want to be violent, or at least make unreasonable demands that you have to knuckle under to just because I say so, not because it's logical. Those things they threw at me weren't logical. Maybe I'll get over the feeling. But man, you can't beat me to a bloody pulp and then offer your hand and say let's forget it all and be equal. Not yet.

Faculty 1: I see what he's saying. Harold, you are reacting much like he is. You're threatened so you lash out irrationally. Tear gas, guns, killing. Just like he's being irrational.

Leader: Would you two regents stand next to each other, and the two students face you. Now shout and yell and scream at each other right in the face for as long as you feel like it.

(Students start first, then gradually regents pick it up. Finally they're shouting, sometimes words, most often screams; their faces contort. Suddenly faculty members step up and start screaming, mostly at regents, sometimes at students. After a while president gets up and starts screaming louder than everyone at everyone. After a moment the screams turn to laughter, tentative embraces follow. Laughter subsides. Regent 1 looks very pensive. Long pause.)

Regent 1: (Holding back tears) I'd like to tell you about my son. Maybe you could help me.

Energy and the Group Leader

Throughout this theoretical and practical development one concept recurs constantly—energy. It seems to underlie most of the important phenomena of open encounter and it proves to be a pivotal concept for an open encounter group leader. He is still dependent in large part on his ability to detect and use the group and individual energy.

Energy is such a basic life force that it is not surprising that investigation into these various levels of human phenomena frequently comes to that concept. The difference between a living and a dead organism is the presence or absence of certain energy manifestations. The size, weight, and chemical constituents of a living body and one newly dead are virtually the same, but the energy is gone. Body energies include: flow of nerve currents, contraction of muscles, circulation of blood, generation of heat, movement of food through the alimentary system, movement of liquid through the urinary system, movement of air through the respiratory system, and production of matter to repair cellular structures. Illness can be seen as a disturbance of the energy processes. There are also group energies and perhaps cosmic or spiritual energies, more difficult to measure.

One of the primary skills a group leader acquires is the reading of energies. In any group each person has a certain amount of energy ready to erupt, for he can be seen as a complex series of energy cycles. These cycles have four phases: motivation, preparation, performance, and consummation (they are similar to those described by George Herbert Mead in *The Philosophy of the Act*). A need arises and energy is mobilized. It begins to arise in the muscles, preparing for discharge. If it is not discharged, it remains in small unsatisfying movements like a foot jiggle, jaw clench, eyebrow furrow, tiredness, nervousness, stomach tension, dizziness, or headache. If it is discharged, the person goes through a series of activities that lead to a return to the original state accompanied by the feeling generated by completing the energy cycle.

A good example of an energy cycle is the running of a race. The athletes go from a relaxed state before they start thinking about the race to a state of preparation just before the race. The preparation is often accompanied by great physical activity—running up and down, nervous talking, grim set of jaw, jiggling, butterflies in stomach, sweaty palms. This feeling increases on the starting line, often resulting in false starts, that is, nonproductive discharges of energy. The race begins and the body preparations come to fruition and the muscles go into action until the race is finished. Usually after the race there is a need for some consolidation of the experience. The breath returns, and sometimes vomiting is needed to discharge the final energy. Finally the athlete returns to his original state, perhaps depressed if he lost, often euphoric if he did well, and feeling good because of the exertion. If for some reason he doesn't complete the race, the feeling of relaxation doesn't occur. These phases of an energy cycle are recognized by the familiar manner in which numerous events are started: On your mark, get set, go. This almost states: Get yourself motivated, perpare your body, perform. The outcome of the activity is its consummation.

All of these principles apply in a group. A look around the group will reveal people in very different states. Some are in a relaxed state, where there is no pressing issue trying to be worked through. If these people are focused on by the group, the result is a dull, lifeless interchange, because there is no feeling, no energy behind it. This is almost always boring to group members. The person may be talking about apparently important things, but the talk is not attached to any feelings. These people are frequently repeating things they've said before, like people who have been in psychoanalysis a long time and who use their technical knowledge as a way of avoiding feeling. When people do this I find myself bored, which I take as a cue that probably others are bored, too. Physical observation of these people usually reveals a lack of physical activity, either because they are in fact relaxed or because their defense is to hold their bodies rigid so as not to allow the feeling to come through. If it is the first type, I find it useful to cut them off and go on to something else and wait until more energy is mobilized. Often cutting them off will help to mobilize their energy because it will help them face their lack of feeling.

If a person is holding himself tight, I would either move on to someone else and count on the group interaction to loosen him up so that he can work better later, or perhaps choose to try to help him break through that defense. The body is a good place to begin. It is usually locked up. Feeling is blocked by tightening muscles, making breathing more shallow. If you recall a time when you were afraid, it's likely that you tensed up and gasped, trying to stop breathing. A first step is to ask the person to relax by unlocking his arms and legs if he has them crossed, perhaps to stand up and shake himself loose, jiggle, and breathe very deeply for several minutes. If he seems tight in a particular place, the leader or a group member might massage him there. From then on, as the leader, I pay strict attention to how his body responds as he talks or acts. When there is a tightening or jiggling or any action, I use that as a focus. That's where the feeling is and that's where the most value comes from working.

Sometimes a person is wound up too tight to be able to function. In these cases I encourage a large physical discharge, like simply beating on some pillows and screaming. This seems to drain off enough energy so that he can begin working with the real problem. When there's a lot of holding but it's being denied, a physical activity is also helpful. If the issue seems to be competition—and the leader is always making hypotheses about what the issue is—a wrestling match, or at least an arm wrestle, can help mobilize and focus the energy. Frequently the strength of anger, jealousy, or competition becomes clear when the whole body is involved in combat, whereas sitting and talking allows the person to hide this feeling from himself.

Retreat from feeling is often revealed in the other behavioral extreme, excessive lassitude and tiredness. In a recent couples group at Esalen, one couple had just driven to Big Sur from Los Angeles, about 300 miles, and arrived for the 9 P.M. meeting. We began by asking the couples to think of three secrets that they had kept from each other that would jeopardize their relationship if the other knew. The husband said he felt it was important—though he himself had no such secrets—and he would try in the morning, but after working all day the drive had left him exhausted, whereupon he lay down on the rug. His wife felt that it would probably be helpful to try to tell the secrets. But he remained exhausted. Experience with these situations led me to speculate that she had had one affair, and he had had several, probably one current. His lassitude was overdone; it revealed his defensiveness and reluctance. I received a letter from him after the workshop confirming my speculation and expressing how much better it was to have worked through this secret. (I mention this hero story because I was very proud of my insight, and I want you to overcome my statements in another part of the book that group leaders are not omniscient by thinking that I do have magical powers—a good example of the ambivalence of a group leader over his power. Ha, caught me!)

When there is undischarged energy anywhere in the body it blocks a person from being totally present in the now. In the last example much of the husband's energy was being utilized in keeping his secret. His muscles were tense, his energy low, he was listless and tired easily. And very little of his energy was available to his wife.

Often a person is all ready to work in a group, but he needs support. Clearing the throat sometimes means that a person wants to say something but an inhibition stops him. The throat-clearing invites attention and inquiry that can help to bring him out. Or a person may ask for support by looking depressed, or by crying, or by withdrawing, or by making sarcastic comments, or by any number of things that call attention to himself. Frequently interest and initiative by the group leader will be sufficient to help the member come out and start dealing with his unresolved energy.

Once a person starts working, that is, talking or acting on an issue, I keep an eye on his energy. Frequently he will start working and then switch into intellectualizing, at which time there will be a change in his voice tone from an emotion-filled to a casual, controlled, speaking voice. Some of his body tension will disappear or go elsewhere, frequently deeper into his body. My tendency is to allow some of this changed action—bullshit is the technical term—but to keep coming back to where the body is. Bullshit is frequently a good fertilizer and makes the other material grow more fully. Some of the members of the Flying Circus are more intolerant of the bullshit and so was

Fritz Perls, but I tend to allow it more. It seems to permit a more full-blown working through, and also gives me clues for where to go next with the material coming out. But the focus on the energy must be maintained or else the defenses take over and the value of the work is dissipated.

A frequent failing of an inexperienced leader is the Green Apples phenomenon. A new leader eager to try out his abilities will often grab at the first feeling presented in the group and start working on it with great flourish and virtuosity. The only trouble is that he frequently has chosen a very shallow feeling not attached to much energy, so that after the first interchange the feeling is gone and the action is all verbal. The choice to pursue a given line is better made after getting a sense that the apple is ripe, that the feelings being expressed are deep and backed by significant energy. Dull groups result from the pursuit of energyless issues.

As a leader gets more skilled, more happens in his groups with less effort on his part. If he is sensitive to where the energy and feeling are in the group he can help them to focus on these; then every group event is meaningful and valuable. Other advantages of working with energy is that it helps observer members get ready and gets the group functioning as a group quicker. If a member with great fear sees people working ineffectually and with less feeling than he knows he has inside himself, the group is not a safe place for him, since his feelings are deep and he has no reassurance that feelings of such depth can be dealt with in this group. However, if important feelings are revealed and dealt with effectively, then it is safer for him.

The energy concept is also the key to when a person is finished working on a problem. If he has really resolved the issue, his energy is discharged and his body is relaxed. If a sequence of work appears to be finished I always check with the person's body. Does it look relaxed or are there still some parts that are tight? Is he still jiggling or picking at the carpet? Is his voice tight or relaxed? Does his face look relaxed or is it still tight? Is his breathing full or shallow? These and other clues tell when the issue is resolved, and the indicators are usually quite clear. It is important to follow through until the relaxed place is attained. If a person doesn't seem relaxed even though he appears finished, encouraging him to continue usually will reveal greater depths of the problem and prove especially valuable.

The energy concept also explains why such things as cigarettes, aspirin, and alcohol impede the group progress. These substances dissipate energy and therefore preclude its use in a profitable way in the group. When people desire these substances, it is a valuable indicator that their anxiety is aroused, but their use flattens feeling. In one demonstration I was giving recently, one girl started to light up a cigarette after a group meeting. I asked her what she might be anxious about. "Nothing," she replied. "I always light up when I feel relaxed. I've been smoking for years. It's just a habit."

"Anything happen in the group that might have upset you?"

"No, it was a very nice group."

"Were you attracted to anyone in the group?" When observing her group I thought I detected a flirtation.

"Well, yes, one young man."

"Was he attracted back?"

"I don't know." Her voice dropped.

"Which one is it?"

She pointed to a young man who was just lighting up a cigarette.

As this vignette unfolded, the anxiety around the possible unrequited situation became obvious and the role of the cigarette as an indicator crucial. If she were to just have finished her cigarette, her anxiety might have been alleviated sufficiently so that she need not have dealt with the situation of the unresolved attraction, and perhaps she would have been able to keep her concern out of her awareness. When I walk into a group enshrouded in cigarette smoke, I feel that nothing of much significance is happening. The usable energy of the group is hanging in the smoke cloud.

Similar remarks apply to headaches or other physical symptoms. Following the thoroughgoing bodymind unity described earlier, every physical symptom is usable and revealing, and any outside substance that dissipates it is a loss to the group's work.

The group leader can judge where to go next by observing responses in the group as one energy cycle is completed. This cycle has usually affected many people. Picking up on the people with the most energy preparatory to working in the same way as described above continues the group along the lines of the most pertinent, energy-filled activity.

An extension of this energy concept to the group level is seen in a group decision-making situation. If the group is regarded as going through an energy cycle when it is making a decision, then the decision is only completed when there is bodily relaxation in each group member. When this is not achieved, then the group is not fully ready to implement the decision and retrogression may occur, just as the situation of an individual failure to complete the cycle may result in a reversion to the earlier behavior. Completion of an energy cycle should make a permanent change in a person, and in a group.

A group leader can detect quite readily whether or not the group members are ready to go along with a decision by asking the members individually and noting their reactions. If there is any response other than a clear yes it almost always means that the person is saying, "No, I'm not yet ready to go along with the decision." In my very first group as a member a beautiful example of this occurred. We were trying to decide on admitting a new member. Finally a vote was taken resulting in "Yes, yes, yes, yes, yes, yes, yes, OK." Semrad asked the last man, "Do you mean yes?"

"OK. It's OK with me."

"Can you say yes?"

"If you want to let him in, it's all right with me."

This repartee continued for a few more rounds until it became clear that OK meant no. He wasn't up to opposing the group so his conflict was expressed as agreement, but an inability to state total agreement. Further discussion opened up the issue and his objections were aired. When he had the feeling that his position was understood and saw that the group still opposed him he said yes. He was willing to go along, even though he still personally disagreed. The group energy cycle was completed and each member was ready to comply. This is the condition known as consensus. Airing the differing view doesn't mean that the decision will remain unchanged. The movie *Twelve Angry Men* provided an excellent portrayal of this when one juror who held out gradually convinced all other eleven jurors to switch.

A nonreadiness to go along can be indicated by verbal differences or by anything that prevents an easy flow of the decision-making process. For example, a question like, "Would you repeat the decision again?" "Shouldn't we take up another matter first," or "It's time for lunch," or nonverbal cues of discomfort as described above can all be indicators of nonreadiness, or of an incomplete energy cycle. Ignoring these phenomena may lead to a quicker decision, but usually to a far slower compliance with the decision, so that the speed is illusory.

A chief cause of clogged communication is the failure to recognize the first feeling that occurs in response to some action, and then to interact in terms of the second feeling, usually a defense. For example, a man said to another group member, "I think what you just did was phony," to which the second replied, "Well, if you didn't like it why didn't you stop me?"

"I didn't stop you because it's not up to me to teach you how to behave."

The first feeling was omitted from each statement, so their

verbalizing grows more and more irrelevant. If they were in touch with their first feelings, the interchange might have gone more like this:

"I think what you did was phony."

"It hurts me when you say that, and then I feel angry."

"I'm sad that it hurts you. I don't want you to dislike me." And so on.

The next interchange might have gone like this:

"Well, if you didn't like it, why didn't you stop me?"

"I feel guilty when you say that. You're right. It makes me sad and despondent, because I think I never speak up when I should."

The overlooked feelings of hurt in the first case and of guilt and sadness in the second are the first feelings. The anger and debating that is the original manifest behavior just represents defensive reactions to hide those feelings. As long as the interchange continues at this defensive level it remains relatively unproductive. If the focus can be redirected, each person is hooked into his real feelings so that the words and the feelings are congruent. This is productive verbalizing. The first kind is that referred to as bullshit.

The use of nonverbal methods often robs the defender of his verbal defense and restores the energy back to its origin. When the talk seems to be making things less and less clear, it is very useful to ask the principals to continue communicating, but without words. Sometimes, if the anger is high, this will result in physical struggle, like wrestling, until the anger is diminished. Then, keeping the two interacting usually gets them back to the first feelings.

Another way in which this defensive behavior arises before the first feeling is recognized is in fixed expressions. In a recent group, a man was being criticized and he smiled back, attempting to understand and like his critics. The smile had an automatic quality to it. The lines seemed etched into his face as if the expression were always present, or ready to be present. I asked him to stop smiling in order to see what was behind the smile. Immediately his face dropped, revealing almost desperate sadness. This look of sadness was reflected back to him and he acknowledged feeling that sad if he weren't smiling. The talk then focused on the understanding, smiling front he presented. On one side of his relaxed face was also a look of tremendous hate, a kind of snarl. Much of his energy was going into a facial expression, smiling, designed to mask his true feelings.

Bypassing the first feeling is usually indicated by a phony, wheel-spinning quality. The general technique for refocusing onto the first feeling is to stay with nonverbal aspects, such as facial expressions, postures, or nonverbal communicating. The problem of skipping first feelings is the source of many marital difficulties. One husband would always come home at night and make an offhand remark to his wife, who would then start nagging. When this situation was examined, it turned out that she felt he often belittled her intelligence, about which she was very sensitive, not having gone to college. Her response was deep hurt, which she didn't acknowledge and mostly wasn't aware of. Her defense was to fight back and get revenge by attacking him and trying to put him down at every opportunity. When he became aware that he was hurting her, his whole attitude toward her changed, and then hers toward him. They were able to turn a fighting situation into a mutual exploration.

The remarkable thing that happens when the energy is redirected back to the first feeling is that there is frequently an exchange of human warmth that is not felt when defenses are being exchanged. When the man had on his fixed smile he was very irritating to virtually everyone. He was phony, unreachable, saccharine, and many people were simply withdrawing from him. When his smile dropped and his sadness became so obvious, there was a feeling of moving together in the air, moving both emotionally and physically. He relaxed and started to

confide some of his fears about the present situation. Others
were empathizing; these were feelings they could recognize
personally, and they began to feel closer to him.

As feelings get deeper, the unity of man becomes clearer. If
a group is allowed to stay at the level of defenses where energy
is phony, the amount of human exchange is minimal and superficial, like at a cocktail party. Mutual identification is minimal, both because there are many defenses not all alike and
because common defenses do not provide contact with deeper
feelings. When defenses are penetrated there is the dawning
recognition of the universality of the human condition, the
same needs, fears, and hopes; then criticism of others becomes
irrelevant, and the search for a mutual accommodation takes
over. Deep hatred is very difficult to maintain toward anyone
very long if you are encountering each other. This doesn't mean
that everyone who encounters likes everyone at this deep level.
It means that understanding is greatly increased and threat
reduced. It is for this reason that deeper groups are safer
groups, I believe, though it seems paradoxical. When a group
has shared deep feelings, the close feeling that results gives
each person a place to go if he gets into emotional difficulty—
a friend, a roommate, a group member. In a more superficial
group, a person in emotional difficulty does not have a refuge
and problems may ensue. The sharing of humanity, the energy
coming from the center of each person, very often gives this
phase of a group a mystical or spiritual quality. The feeling of
the brotherhood of man becomes a reality as people who look
so strange, alien, and undesirable unfold into people with the
same underlying structure. The spiritual dimension emerges.

The phenomenon of energy has entered into the writing of
this book at several points. I started writing concentratedly for
several weeks. Then I stopped for about three months, content-
ing myself with the explanation that I was busy with other
things, etc., until one night I had a dream. This is what I wrote
the next morning.

Dreamt that someone like Milton was telling me that John Heider now knew as much as I did. Told him that Steve and Betty were better than him. Insight: my fear of the truth of this is what's holding up writing this book. I'm afraid John, Seymour, and Steve know more about energy and how to use it, and Betty has learned more varied methods so that what I write is old hat. It's like Arnold Palmer was no good once Jack Nicklaus started playing. I think the whole Circus is my Nicklaus. I can just acknowledge their contributions, then write the best I can. They can later write their own elaborations. I did start the energy concept by telling them to go where the feeling is, anyway— so there. I hope this insight springs me loose, because obviously I have a lot to say and I think it's still true that I have the sharpest eye in a group. Probably my attempts to go in the social and Rolfing directions are ways to get into something new so I can again be preeminent. Also, my being tired of running groups is related to a feeling of being overtaken. As I listen to the tapes of my lectures, I feel better. Most of the ideas of importance are all there. Yeh, I'm not so bad.

This led me to associations about tiredness, that is, lack of energy. The idea of losing interest or getting tired of something fascinates me. Once Fritz Perls told me that I must understand the meaning of tired when I told him I was getting tired of running groups. This cryptic remark infuriated me because of its pomposity, but I find I keep coming back to it. Once on an LSD trip I thought it meant I had cancer, but that alarm proved erroneous. But now the idea that it means that I feel footsteps behind me about to surpass me makes sense. I think immediately of examples from sports.

The Palmer-Nicklaus example seems clearest to me, although I've never seen anyone write about it. Arnold Palmer was the world's greatest golfer for several years and then began to decline. I mark the decline from the moment Jack Nicklaus turned pro. It seemed clear after a few tournaments that Nicklaus was better. Then Palmer had a series of injuries, like to his hip; he began busying himself in outside activities, and began eliciting from a number of sports writers the opinion that he'd do better if he cut down on his outside enterprises. I would project into Palmer the fear that if he did cut down, and did try his hardest, he still couldn't beat Nicklaus. Other examples come to mind that, of course, can be no more than speculation. Jim Ryun was our best miler for many years, then along came Martin Liquori who beat him once and raced him again; Ryun dropped out of the race, and then retired.

There have been several other cases where a preeminent person is supplanted and perhaps gets tired, preoccupied, finds other interests, changes fields, just as I did when I heard the thundering hooves of the Circus. I got tired of running groups, started popularizing encounter, trading on my reputation, and getting interested in a different field, the body, and having trouble writing down what I know about groups. I now fantasy Palmer a little reluctant to tell people how to play golf because of his image of Nicklaus over his shoulder shaking his head, "No, no, Arnold, not that way. That's why you don't win." As I write this Nicklaus has just beaten Palmer in a two-man playoff. Alec Guinness was the preeminent British comedian until Peter Sellers. Haven't seen a Guinness comedy in years. Jim Brown was football's greatest runner for years; then came Gale Sayers who might be better. Brown retired and is now an actor. Marlon Brando started retiring about the time Paul Newman attained stardom. Now comes Robert Redford, and what will happen to Newman? As I write this I feel how speculative and without foundation it is, but I have a feeling that my discovery applies to many, not all, who have a central place and then sense their imminent replacement. Oh hell, as long as it's just projection I'll list some others I'd like to know about: Liza Minelli is rising toward Barbra Streisand; Martin McGrady is starting to beat World's Champion quarter-miler Lee Evans; how did Willie Mays feel when Orlando Cepeda started sharing his glory, even occasionally eclipsing him?

It reminds me of a time in high school when I was easily the best student in biology until Milton Thaler transferred to my class. My response to the obvious fact that he knew much more than I did was to softpedal my knowledge of and interest in biology, not study much, and become good friends with Milton.

Writing this helps me to see the irrationality of it. Obviously Palmer is still a fine golfer even if Nicklaus is better. As I talk to the Circus members about this issue I find that they all have similar feelings to the ones I'm expressing. The reality seems to be that the Circus is made up of extraordinarily gifted people, each of whom has a unique strength and each of whom on occasion discovers and develops something very important, temporarily leaving the others behind. But we're all good and must continue to produce what we can, and it'll be good. All right, Schutz, are you convinced? Yeah. So let's get on with it.

The Group Leader As Human

The term "group leader" always sounded too stark and military and seemed not to convey the most participative, democratic elements of the process. I joined many others in the search for a better name: trainer—no, too much like Clyde Beatty; coordinator—no, sounds like a telephone operator; facilitator—well, true enough, but a little thin; how about just another group member? No, too hypocritical. Then, in thinking about my concept of a leader, it occurred to me that I felt that all leadership should be like encounter group leadership.

All leaders should be sensitive to the feelings of the group members; be able to create an atmosphere in which feelings are recognized and expressed easily; have self-awareness; be able to sense what the group needs and cause it to be provided— whether it be strong direction, passivity, more information, more energy, or the ability to express openly and honestly his humanity to the group; and be able to bring out of the group its best talents for decision-making. In short, any type of leader should have the qualities of an encounter group leader. So, I have returned to the original term, defining it as above.

The realization of the convergence of all types of leadership was another step in my realization of the generality of the encounter group to all other aspects of life. Leaders fail because some of the inabilities to lead are also present in an encounter group leader, such as lack of honesty, or sensitivity, or not sensing the needs of the group, or not functioning so as to bring out the best in the group members.

Once again a personal consideration enters into my view on leadership. I'm not terribly sure of many decisions I make in life and I feel much better about them if they are confirmed by others. I often have the feeling that I might be overlooking something, usually something obvious, and I try to have my decision checked by others as a safeguard. Thus professing a democratic ideal gives theoretical support to my weakness. Another side of me leans toward the authoritarian. I greatly admired General Patton, the epitome of the confident, authoritarian leader. Part of me longs to simply tell everyone what to do and be obeyed. But another part, usually stronger, is too uncertain of my own decision-making ability to risk an authoritarian role, thus I become a champion of participatory democracy. When I'm clear about these personal considerations and look at the situation with more objectivity, I see the democratic process as fundamental, but I can envision an authoritarian structure being desirable if it is agreed to by all those subjected to it. And I still see training as an encounter group leader as fundamental to all leadership training.

Each leader brings out different facets of each group member. This is due partly to the type of person he is, and partly to the attitudes and expectations he conveys to the group members. Knowing his common impact on group members is an essential trait for a group leader.

When I am a group leader I find that awe and aloofness is felt first by group members, due lately in part to my reputation, but more by the way I comport myself. I tend to convey a feeling of distance, and very tentatively, a little bit of warmth. My face tends toward being relatively frozen or emotionless though several pick-up feelings that are conveyed through my eyes. I'm seen as stern, tough, and unfeeling by some at the beginning, while I'm trying to convey the way of behaving I feel is most productive in an encounter group. I often do feel impatient with the group at this stage. I wish they'd hurry up and relate encounter style, since I like groups and the people better that way. The bullshit bores me. Then as the group develops I begin to be less rigid, more flexible, and enter in more as a person.

As time goes on I'm frequently seen as being more human and several people feel they've detected signs of caring. Indeed I do care more as the group develops. Usually if there's a girl in the group who attracts me I find more interest in the group as a whole, and must watch myself because I tend to find everything she says and does somehow much more fascinating than I do anyone else's contributions. Girls frequently find me sexually attractive, although I have an uneasy suspicion that their numbers are decreasing as the years go by. Men often see me as a competitive figure and, because of my mesomorphic build and authority role, many toy with the idea of physical combat, which usually—if they bring themselves to challenge and I overcome my fear of humiliation and physical injury and we then struggle—turns out to be an extremely valuable experience. At the end I am usually loved widely, sometimes seen as a guru but usually a little too human to be a guru, and often still kept distant from, because people aren't sure I like them or even give a damn about them. All I can say is that I vary a great deal, like all people. I'm usually keenly aware of everyone and can remember names remarkably well, but my caring is not terribly great except for selected members of the group.

My energy for group work was much greater at the beginning of my career than lately, and it is much greater when my personal life is bleak. When I'm not getting much personal gratification and home is not a desirable place to be, I spend much more time and energy in the group and with group members outside, often feeling sad when I have to leave them. My desire for women in the group is greater then as well as my attempts at rationalizing why it's alright for leaders and group members to have intimate relations, including intercourse. During periods of full personal gratification it is more desirable to go home, so I adhere more rigidly to the prescribed hours of group meeting and also start rationalizing about the importance of sticking to the promised times so as to encourage independence, etc. My response to criticism is generally good until it gets to be too much. Actually, it isn't that good because I tend not to get defensive or even give much feeling back.

One of my largest weaknesses as a group leader is my relative inability to initiate feelings. It's very hard for me, for example, to get angry first. With great effort I respond to anger, but I don't start it very effectively. Affection is easier for me to initiate, and I often have some trouble accepting it. Usually when I'm receiving adulation I love to hear it but don't quite know how to respond. One result is that I respond in such a way that it stops, and then I'm disappointed. I also feel still that people don't want to hear about me very much, a feeling that I know in my head isn't true. But even as I'm writing this—what I feel is an extended account of myself—I feel self-conscious, like it's going on too long, but then I start justifying its importance which I'm now impelled to write. It should be a good model of self-analysis to emulate for people trying to be group leaders.

If I sense variations in these perceptions it tells me of a possible projection on someone's part. I can expect to rouse the feelings I described. Other roles played by leaders—such as the benign father, older sister, younger brother—elicit different responses accordingly.

I fear being dull, repetitive, and disappointing to people. This leads me to sometimes overdo flamboyance or to be over-dramatic. I feel a desire to be always new, original, and to not do things like other group leaders, even including not doing things like in my own book *Joy*. This does have the virtue of impelling me onward toward new things, but there is a some-what compulsive quality about it that I find I must fight. It comes up when people are just talking in the group. Even though talking may be exactly the right thing to do at that point, I feel some push that must be suppressed to make the action more exciting. Often fantasies of the Flying Circus members intrude here, thoughts that they would be doing something more dramatic, and I'm just going back to my old, tired, T-group (yet) techniques.

The fear of boring affects my type of humor, which is typically the quick comment, darting in and out of the conversation. In this way my humor doesn't bore anyone as it might if I told long stories. Also, I usually say the funnies with a straight face, not initiating a laugh response in case others don't follow suit. So, the wry, fast comment doesn't bore anyone and doesn't embar-rass me too much if no one laughs.

It's also true that some *Joy* methods are appropriate for every group at some point, and even though they are now well known, it's still good to use them. Since they have become popular, I feel a different strain, the strain to now do something different. My projection is that people will say, "Is that all he knows?" Also, the more my reputation grows, the more likely I feel I may disappoint people. I often feel like "the fastest gun in the West" and that other people, especially male profession-als, will take great delight in revealing my weaknesses and showing that they are better than I am. "I shot Billy the Kid!" This leads me to feel competition from people, some of it, perhaps, even when it's not there, and some of it because, although it is something of a burden to be the target of these feelings, I love it. I would feel bad if anyone else were in this position. I want it to be me. So there is some sham in my protests; I even feel a little guilty as I write this because, as I now see it, I feel that under the guise of trying to make a profound point about group leadership I am presenting a hero story.

Another phenomenon that it is essential to be aware of is the tremendous influence of the leader on the course of the group. This became clear to me when I noticed a great coincidence in my groups. Whatever I was interested in at the moment turned out to be exactly what the group happened to focus on. If I was exploring nonpermanent relations, behold, they were exploring the limits of marriage. When I had just had an insight about the nature of competition, my groups were wrestling and competing an inordinate number of times. Of course this was no coincidence. If I were preoccupied with a topic I would be relatively placid in the group until something remotely connected with this topic arose. Then I would pluck it out of the group flow, enlarge it, reward those who responded to it, and generally make happen what I wanted to see. When I was happily involved in a close, committed relation with a woman, the issue of commitment loomed very large in my groups. When I started writing this book I found an extraordinary number of people interested in the theoretical side of groups and group leadership. I was just reading Rollo May's book *Love and Will* where he says he wrote it because he found all his patients started talking about love and will. Hmm.

It's important for me to be aware of where I am in my own life prior to doing a group and to keep that place in my awareness, often sharing it with the group. One thing I've been doing lately is telling a group when I don't really want to lead the group and when I'd rather be elsewhere. This gets me lots of hostility, but usually if I can say it I can get over the feeling and am more present. If I try to fake it, it's painful and not very productive for anyone.

Physical characteristics of the leader are always responded to, and references to the leader are often made by people who are not aware that they are preoccupied with him. In these instances unconscious references can sometimes be detected through physical allusions. I once shaved my head like Yul Brynner. References to crystal balls increased greatly after this act. This was precipitated by a combination of awe, manifested as a belief in my ability to see into the future, and hostility expressed by ridicule of my bald head. Such references also provide a clue as to what issues are central to group members.

A group leader profits from regularly examining his impact on the group, because it often changes. A good knowledge of the effect of the self on the object being observed helps the leader to understand better what's happening in a group. Again, this is a principle that far transcends encounter groups and encounter group leadership. When hawks go to Vietnam they find hawkish attitudes prevalent, just the opposite of what dove observers find. Pronouncements about "trends in the American public" always leave me skeptical. The trends I see are almost always what I want to be true or what I fear is true and want to prepare myself for. And I think that's true for most people. One advantage of public opinion polls is that they lend some objectivity to trend analysis.

In marriage the phenomenon of eliciting one's own preoccupation is a crucial experience. One example came to me forcefully when I noticed that my girl was constantly threatening to leave me whenever things got bad, and she made numerous trips to Monterey (50 miles away) before returning. I kept berating her for doing this: it made me want to go to other women, it damaged our relationship, it was a childish response, and so forth. One day it dawned on me that I was eliciting from her the very behavior I was criticizing. A characteristic of me was (I hope *was*) being a foul-weather friend. Whenever there was a crisis I was very present and helpful giving all of my energy and effort. But when things went smoothly I disappeared—my attention went elsewhere, my interest waned, I gave very little. So if she wanted me she had to create a crisis. I was subtly rewarding crises, like running away, while punishing serenity in the relationship. I was eliciting the very behavior I didn't want.

My suspicion is that this phenomenon occurs in street riots also. The cities that are prepared for rioting by having troops, street barriers, warnings, and tear gas ready seem to get riots with uncommon frequency. With all the troops, the probability of a short temper or of a small igniting incident is greatly enhanced, and sure enough, they get what they expected. Some militants do indeed have a desire to riot. But the eliciting behavior brings out the side of our targets that is presumably not desired.

That brings us to the next level of understanding of this phenomenon. There is a sense in which I did want my girl to create a crisis. I was concerned that I wasn't feeling much for her affectionately or sexually. The crisis brought back both feelings. Something inside of me, out of my awareness, knew that I needed some energizing, and it happened.

In life outside the encounter group it is not typical for people to have much insight into the way they influence or elicit the behaviors that they deal with. This makes most discussion of social issues peripheral. What effect does it have on China's trustworthiness to have much of the world not trust her? What effect does it have on youth to be treated as irresponsible? Assuming that someone is irresponsible tends to bring out his weaker, irresponsible side.

Related to this is the manner in which intellectual attitudes reflect personal predilections. Often great arguments are marshalled to support intellectual positions that are simply attempts to justify a personal predilection or support a personal need. From the realm of the exact sciences comes a splendid example. Several summers ago I was taking a course in mathematics for social scientists. Our instructors were two very competent mathematicians who constantly differed on one point. Pat felt that statistics using continuous distributions were more powerful and effective, while Bob felt that discrete distributions were superior. It was difficult for any of us in the class to see great differences; they both seemed to work, and it was puzzling that both men felt so strongly about it.

Then I got to musing about the men themselves. Pat, who preferred the continuous distribution—where there is always a point between any two points and there are no sudden differences—lived in the same area the students did, played baseball with us between meetings, had a beer with us, invited us to his house for dinner; in short, as a person he was continuous with the class, there was no sharp break personally between Pat and us. Bob, who preferred discrete distributions—where there is a break between one number and the next with nothing in between—lived twenty miles away, didn't play ball, went home right after class, and didn't invite us to his house; in short, home and work were distinct parts of his life and he wanted them that way. This observation made their mathematical preferences more understandable because it became increasingly clear that there was no mathematical way of deciding between the two types of distributions. It was simply a matter of choice. And the choice apparently was made on the basis of each man's life style. Their failure to recognize this led to several futile attempts at mathematical proofs of the relative values of continuous and discrete distributions.

Another example also supports the idea that the basic nature of intellectual styles has deep, traceable psychological roots. A friend and I were exploring why she was so much more oriented toward specific detailed knowledge and I toward large overviews. When we went to a movie she would almost always know the dialogue, often close to verbatim, while I wouldn't remember it at all but I would get the overall point and start relating it to other facets of life (much like this book).

Exploration revealed that both of our intellectual styles were defenses against our fathers. She recalled coming home one day when she was young and telling her father that she had learned how to make chicken fricassee. He responded with a series of detailed questions to test the truth of her statement. What are the ingredients? In what order do you use them? What's the temperature of the oven? How long do you cook it? Her defense against her father could only be to learn whatever she was learning in excruciating detail. What her father didn't require was a weighing of the relative importance of various events. Perhaps cooking fricassee wasn't worth all the time and effort to learn details. But her father's approach made details important and relative values secondary.

My childhood recollection concerned my hero, Lou Gehrig, the baseball player. I was explaining to my father what a magnificent batter he was. He hit .349, had 42 home runs, and 120 runs batted in. My father's response was not to pin me down or ask for details. On the contrary, he said, "Yes, but he can't field. He plays first base like a baby elephant." My God, I wasn't prepared for that. I was ready to present the merits of Lou Gehrig, the batsman, not the fielder. I had been caught off balance. I'd overlooked something that undermined my case, perhaps fatally. My only defense against this type of response was total knowledge. If I wanted to convince my father of the worth of Lou Gehrig, I had to know his batting, fielding, perhaps relations with his wife, leadership capabilities with his teammates, ability to hit in the clutch, and so forth. In short, I had to be prepared to discuss any aspect that my father could think of, or else I lost. The result is that I tend toward comprehensive theories that take into account all factors so that nothing significant is omitted. It makes me eclectic. The drawback is that whenever I'm concentrating on one element I must fight the nagging feeling that there's something somewhere else I should be paying attention to. It has applied even to women. I often have the feeling when I'm with one that there's a better one somewhere, a thought that prevents me from concentrating my full attention on the first.

Eclecticism also serves another purpose, I have recently learned. It helps me avoid threat and rejection. If someone tells me how much more he profited from a weekend gestalt therapy session than he did from a week-long encounter group of mine, I feel threatened that maybe mine isn't so good and rejected by this man who has chosen another over me. But if I can say, "Oh, yes. Gestalt therapy is very good. We use it in our encounter groups, you know," I have enveloped and incorporated the threat. Just like I did with Milton in biology.

The upshot of all this is not that there is no substance to intellectual arguments. Certainly there is. But much of it reveals personal needs and desires masquerading in the guise of objectivity and intellectuality. A failure to recognize the personal contribution makes much intellectual activity irrelevant and off target. This helps to explain the role of talking and of intellectual material in an encounter group. Talk in the guise of being rational is often a cover-up for personal feelings (e.g., "I think groups in a democratic society function more effectively with an agenda," instead of saying, "I feel very uncomfortable when I don't know what I'm supposed to do"). This type of verbalizing is definitely discouraged. It is misleading and unproductive. The second statement in the example is more accurate and helpful. The encounter effort is to help each person know the difference between intellectualizing as a defense against feeling and intellectuality as a legitimate enterprise.

Unacknowledged eliciting behavior also clouds understanding. Recently, I was giving a demonstration microlab for several hundred people. Afterward one person said she was disturbed because a woman in the group had gone away unhappy and hurt. I asked if that woman would be willing to identify herself. She was, and a discussion ensued, some people supporting her, some disagreeing, she responding. After about ten minutes of this she said, "I don't like to be put on the spot like this." This is a statement in which the eliciting behavior is not recognized and therefore the communication is misleading. She wasn't acknowledging her role in putting and keeping herself on the spot. She identified herself; she responded to people in such a way as to keep the discussion on her; she didn't ask at any point to stop.

This principle is simple but enormously pervasive. Most public discussions take on an attack-defend quality, with the object of assigning all blame to the opponent. An appreciation of these more subtle factors makes the discussion much sharper and more gratifying. In industry, schools, and hospitals, people often complain that there are too many meetings. I think the problem is that there is too much bullshit in each meeting. A meeting on the encounter model is usually very exhilarating, productive, and fun. Feelings are expressed, everyone says what he feels, and decisions are based on both the objective situation and the feelings of the people involved.

Sometimes a theoretical position is taken in order to compensate for a behavioral or emotional weakness. In one of my first workshops I ran one group, a colleague, Murray, ran another group, and a graduate student sat in on both as an observer. Murray and I had spirited arguments about the most effective way to run a group, my view being that the leader should be oriented toward individual group members, he asserting that the leader's proper role was to intervene at the level of the group as a whole. The debate continued over several days, each of us marshalling glittering, unanswerable arguments.

Finally the graduate student couldn't contain herself any

longer. "Look," she said patiently, "I go into Bill's group and he's talking about group phenomena, and I go into Murray's group and he's having a shouting match with one of the group members. What the hell are you two talking about; you act in just the opposite way from your theoretical positions." Of course she was right. As I reflected on it, it became clear that I was uncertain of my ability to make personal interventions and my vehement adherence to this view was partly to divert the observer from seeing my weakness.

In a similar instance, two architects were arguing the importance of including feelings in architectural design as opposed to limiting the structure to a rational solution to the design problem. "Of course feelings should not enter," screamed the fiery Latin architect, his veins bulging. "An architect's job is to make an effective structure, with sound engineering and aesthetic design," he concluded, sinking into his chair, spent. "I can't agree at all," said the other coolly. "Feelings are at the core of the design and their omission constitutes an architectural error of the first magnitude." He crossed his legs and puffed on his cigarette deliberately. The contrast between their bodies and personalities and their intellectual positions was striking. Again each was talking to a felt weakness in himself as in the case of Murray and me, as you can clearly see.

Again, let me underscore that I'm not saying that these arguments have no merit because a personal motive can be identified. It is simply that the strength of conviction and other elements can be understood better and the intellectual content assessed more rationally—yes, rationally—if both intellectual merits and personal involvements are understood.

This is another vital factor in assessing intellectual content. Politically, President Nixon seems to have a strong propensity toward this compensatory theorizing. Frequently he will come out with a stand directly contradictory to his critics, thus defusing them. The suspicion immediately arises in me that these words do not represent his true feelings but rather mask or attempt to compensate for a feeling he would like to have but doesn't. And many people now feel that his words are good ones but not followed by relevant actions. For example, the "credibility gap" was a major failing of the Johnson Administration, so Nixon promised that he would eliminate it. He would hold a news conference "every week or two," it was announced on January 29, 1969. One year later he had held nine conferences.

For most people, being a group leader is the realization of a childhood dream. He is in a central position, the object of attention, respect, and often affection. Great powers are attributed to him; people look to him for help and guidance; he is regarded with awe and wonder, and often seen as sexually attractive, potent, sensitive, gentle, masculine (if he is a man), and caring. Some of these attributions are true, some aren't. It is very easy to become seduced into the belief that they are all true. This makes it difficult for a group leader to open up and let his weaknesses show. (It is also a reason, a humble origin, of the sober therapeutic dictum that it is good therapist behavior to remain aloof and mysterious, so as to provide a projection screen. Among other things, it allows the myth of therapist omnipotence to go unchallenged, often a rewarding feeling for the therapist.) I feel that being able to let everything personal show enormously enhances the group leader's opportunities to be helpful. This requires self-awareness, so that what is expressed is close to what is really felt, all to the good of the group members.

The personality and needs of the leader, the relations between leaders as in a workshop or co-led group, and the progress of the group are intimately related at several points. In classical psychotherapy, one such relationship is discussed under the titles transference and countertransference. Transference means that a group member sees the leader in part as someone in his background with whom he has unresolved feelings. In other words, the group member's perception of the leader is in some proportion realistic, in that he sees the leader as the person he is and also, in some proportion, a projection from an unresolved infantile conflict. For example, if a woman had a deep-seated, unfulfilled desire to sleep with her father, and if the leader and his role give her the same feeling as her father did, then she may want to sleep with the group leader and vicariously fulfill her desire. Countertransference is the same phenomenon in reverse, that is, the leader's displacing feelings from his own early life onto group members.

The open encounter group provides for multiple transference objects and therefore makes it easier for many deep feelings to be aroused. This suggests some principles for group composition. Putting people of many ages into a group enhances the possibility of a parent-child transference. Hence it is much more likely that these feelings will be elicited in the group situation than when a person works only with one psychotherapist.

The phenomenon of transference toward the leader is one reason I believe that he should make his own reality known to the group. The valuable part of working with transference is that the person transferring can learn about his distorted perceptions and perhaps minimize them. The discrepancy between the way he sees the leader and the way the leader is is the degree to which the viewer is working out his unresolved infantile conflicts. For example, a female group member may perceive the leader as physically attracted to her and acting seductively. This may be because she always wanted her father to feel seductively toward her. If the leader is not willing and able to reveal his own feelings in this situation, great distortions can occur. Out of the leader's own failings, the group member can struggle over the problem of why she sees authority figures as trying to seduce her. Often the concept of transference is invoked as a justification for not revealing oneself as the leader.

Countertransference can be similarly distorting unless the leader is aware of his feeling and willing to express it. When he does have feelings of which he is ashamed—like sexual attraction or hostility to certain members—it is important that he reveal them to the group. Otherwise his behavior will seem very obtuse to group members. I've found in some groups that there were times when I didn't like a patient and had no desire whatever to help him. On the contrary, I had an urge to be sarcastic. One woman played directly into an unresolved prejudice of mine. She was a rigid, old, Irish-Catholic woman, very righteous, defended and self-deceptively destructive and hypocritical. Whenever she'd have an interchange with another patient I'd want to make her realize how stupid and evil she was. Soon my body tensions reminded me that I was in one of my own areas of difficulty and I had better be careful. I noticed that a nurse in the group had a more benign feeling about the woman, so I invited the nurse to take over and simply supported what she did with the woman. I have found on occasion that I spend more energy on girls I am attracted to; people who threatened me I perceive as saying irrelevant things that I find myself ignoring, putting down, or interrupting to get back to something else; people I want to impress will find me much more showy and preening. All of these trainer feelings can clutter up a group and being constantly aware of them is vital. When I detect such a feeling, I find the best thing is to tell the group and ask them to be aware of it. This often leads to the group putting a check on me, to my becoming more objective, or often to my confronting the person and working out my feelings.

The qualities that make a good group leader also make a good helper. In encounter groups the ability to help someone is very complex and requires far more than simply a soothing hug when someone is crying. A hug is sometimes the most unhelpful thing a person can do. In a professional group at a state hospital one social worker began to express great concern over her incompetence. A psychologist, abetted by several other group members, immediately reassured her that he felt she was unusually competent, that everyone liked her, and that she was doing wonderful work. Her tears stopped in a few minutes and she managed a brave smile of gratitude. At the next meeting she came in very angry. Her feelings had been cut off yesterday, she said. She still felt incompetent but hadn't had a chance to get out all her feelings. She felt that the reassurance came without knowing many things that she knew about herself and she didn't have a chance to express and explore them. She had allowed them to put a band-aid on a festering sore.

This phenomenon is often not very helpful because it is done reflexively, usually as an act that makes the helper feel good without much relevance to its effect on the helpee. Our foreign aid program has often been accused of the same failing. It is somehow satisfying to our government to be generous, but too often the recipient government is offended and apparently ungrateful. In fact, we often pay small attention to what really constitutes help from the standpoint of the recipient.

The encounter group and our foreign relations came together in an incident involving a member of Accion, a private Peace Corps operation in South America formerly run by Joe Blatchford. In addition to their training in the language, customs, and history of the country, in this case Venezuela, the volunteers were put into an encounter group for a week to become better acquainted with their own motives and feelings. About fifteen months later I met one of the girls who had been to Venezuela and back. The encounter group had been useful, she said, but more useful had been the experience she had had right afterward when her group of volunteers arrived in Venezuela. They had decided to continue the encounter, and she, as one of the most experienced, was selected to be a co-leader of the group. That experience was the most valuable aspect of her training. It helped her to be sensitive to the feelings of other people, to know where attention could be paid profitably, to know when someone had a feeling he wasn't expressing, to know when someone needed prodding and when he needed support, to sense when a group was ready to go along with a decision, and to feel when they required more time and exploration. In short, she could be more useful in terms of helping the natives to find out just what they needed and wanted and how it could be provided most effectively.

Her experience suggested to me that training as an encounter group leader would be good for anyone who is in a service profession, including nurses, social workers, ghetto workers, in fact, to absolutely anyone in any leadership role. Training to be an encounter group leader includes doing a great deal of work on one's own problems and achieving some self-awareness, and requires a great amount of attention to and understanding of other people. It is rare when anyone pays as much enlightened attention to anyone as an encounter group leader does to a group member.

Training Group Leaders

Frequent objections to encounter groups, especially from the medical and psychological professions, are that there are no standards for licensing and that innumerable quacks are roaming the land preying on innocent people. I am in complete accord with the objective of assuring the competence of group leaders, and I would be delighted if we had a way to certify those people who were effective encounter group leaders and eliminate those who were ineffective or dangerous. However, effective licensing assumes that we know how to evaluate group leaders, which in turn relies on our knowledge of how to train group leaders. I have only a vague idea of how to do this, and

I'm not convinced that other people know a great deal more. Actually, I'm convinced that they don't.

I've trained group leaders in three types of situations that gave me an opportunity to compare various types of preparation. While at Albert Einstein School of Medicine I helped to train group therapists and I regard this as the same as teaching encounter group leaders, except that for group therapists more emphasis is placed on the treatment of hospitalized patients. But the general leadership principles are the same, though the adaptations of the principles differ somewhat between therapy and encounter groups. These students were all M.D.s in their psychiatric residency. At about the same time I was a part of the training staff at NTL for training T-group interns in group leadership. These candidates were almost all Ph.D.s in psychology or a closely related field. And finally, when I arrived at Esalen, there was an opportunity to train anyone that gave promise of being a good leader.

Physicians have a trained incapacity for being good open encounter group leaders. The medical model teaches that the doctor possesses the required knowledge and functions most effectively if the patient maintains the belief that he is relatively infallible and that he, the patient, is the sick one who needs help. This is almost precisely the opposite philosophy of a good open encounter group leader. The first psychiatrists I observed leading therapy groups arrived for their groups with their ties, coats, usually glasses, often vests, and frequently pipes, and sat on a chair listening to the patients talk. At intervals, the psychiatrist would intervene and explain to the patient what the patient really meant, and what his problem actually was on a deeper level. Frequently he would prescribe what should be done. Sometimes he would explain an interaction between two members and how it should be understood. In almost all cases he would remain impersonal and not participate at all in terms of his own feelings. And he would certainly not touch a patient or allow any physical contact or leaving of chairs. His body was very tight and immobile, usually locked up in the sense of crossed legs and/or folded arms, and his face was generally expressionless.

This description certainly doesn't apply to all psychiatrists, but it does to many of them. This behavior follows logically from the medical model. And there is also organizational pressure not to deviate significantly from this model on pain of not gaining acceptance to a psychoanalytic institute. My impression of the therapy groups was that on the whole they were exceptionally dull. There is great emphasis in the psychiatric-medical setting on individual dynamics and diagnosis and relatively less on the process whereby the interaction among the therapist and the patients leads to growth in the patients. I know that this, too, is not true of all psychiatrists or even psychoanalysts (I feel my conscience saying don't go overboard here), since my original teacher was Semrad, a psychoanalyst, and he did not follow my description. But my suspicion is that the attitude I am describing is widespread in the medical profession. At any rate, I concluded that psychiatrists were very difficult to train because they were very tight and constricted and did not have the desire or training to open themselves up as people and use all of themselves to help the patients.

When I was at Albert Einstein, there was strong opposition from the senior people to having the psychiatrists be members of a group themselves, an experience I regarded as essential to their training. Also, the psychiatric tradition is very strong, and breaking away from purely verbal methods required a great deal of daring on the part of an intern. At one point, Otto Will, the head of Chestnut Lodge at that time, and one of the highly regarded men in the field, presented a case of 100 hours of individual therapy with a female patient. One of his chief conclusions was that possibly his most effective therapeutic step was when in the final hour he inadvertently placed his hand on the patient's shoulder. She responded more to this touch than to almost any other intervention he made, he said.

This was a rather radical conclusion, especially against the background of the psychiatric taboo against touch. These difficulties in training, philosophy, and tradition resulted in my finding about three promising psychiatrists for encounter group leading out of about 70 with whom I had contact. These three, incidentally, later turned out to be rather rebellious within the profession. On the positive side the knowledge of individual dynamics possessed by the psychiatrists is a valuable thing to have both for helping patients and for making the therapists more confident. Their knowledge of anatomy and physiology is also very useful. Unfortunately, in their approach to group therapy they made virtually no use of it whatever.

The NTL interns with their Ph.D.s offered a different picture. Being a group member was an accepted part of the training for group leadership and the medical model or psychiatric tradition did not weigh so heavily on the interns. The major problem with the Ph.D.s was one that I felt acutely since, being a Ph.D., I shared it with them, and that is skepticism and caution. Groups composed only of Ph.D.s were very constipated, everyone being wary of risking much in front of the other group members. There was much distrust, or at least skepticism, of the leaders and of the group methods. The risk-taking behavior so crucial in the group was scarce. The Ph.D. is a discipline in skepticism; it teaches how to doubt, weigh, evaluate, require evidence. It is, by definition, a research degree.

I found that my Ph.D. training, abetted I'm sure by the personality orientation that led me to research in the first place, stunted my growth as an encounter group leader. I was reluctant to use intuition at first, or to take chances on unsupported evidence, or to try hypotheses that might be wrong. If it appeared to me that someone was angry because of an earlier rejection, I was reluctant to use that speculation. I couldn't demonstrate it, I had no control group, there were other alternate hypotheses, etc. And so I did nothing, I was paralyzed.

A comment from Semrad helped me out of this. He suggested that if I wasn't sure whether or not to intervene in a group, to consult my stomach. If it felt relaxed, do it; if it was tight, don't. This was one of my first introductions to the importance of the body, and my first weaning away from reliance on the head to figure things out in favor of the body to get a feeling representing a consensus of all factors operating. The positive side of the Ph.D. training was that these interns probably knew more about individual dynamics and personality and less about pathology than the psychiatrists, and they knew a great deal about group dynamics, both valuable kinds of knowledge.

When I arrived at Esalen I felt convinced that neither medical nor doctoral training was relevant to encounter group leading except for the parts mentioned. I could see a motive for requiring a doctorate for qualification as a group leader in order to convince the public that these were qualified people. Perhaps as a public relations move that is good, perhaps even the best requirement we have so far, but I did not want to personally help maintain the fiction that these degrees were in fact relevant to good encounter group leading.

When I wanted to train some people to take over my workshops at Esalen, I looked around for the people who seemed to have the greatest potential regardless of academic or any other background, and chose six, the ones who were to become the Flying Circus. I then tried to teach these people by talking to them about theory, referring them to books in the field, and co-leading with them several times. The basic experience for most of them was a very intense six-week-long encounter group as part of the Esalen residential program. This group was intense in the sense that the principles of open encounter as I understood them at that time were used. There was intensive investigation of anger, competition, and power, complete with many wrestling matches and other tests of strength as well as intellectual challenges. Sexual feelings were discussed and acted out, with much intragroup sexual intercourse (outside the group), all of which was discussed at length. The issue of monogamy versus freedom was investigated at length. The issues of loneliness, ingroup-outgroup, scapegoating, and virtually all the other major group phenomena were discussed and experienced thoroughly. In retrospect, this experience turned out to be the most important single training element.

The co-leading was very important, giving me an opportunity to lead with each trainee during five week-long workshops. In addition, we met at lunchtime to discuss the place of each group and the state of each leader with regard to his group. This daily meeting was of central importance, making the self-awareness very specific to the group phenomena. Soon each person was reacting to each of the others and it became a team effort.

The issue of competition among the trainees and of them with me came up early. It became clear that there was a tremendous amount of talent in the group and that the potential for destructive competition was very great. It was important for me to state who threatened me and how, and how I felt I was better and not better than each of them. They responded in kind with respect to me and to each other. We found it very important to keep in touch with that feeling constantly. I think it was and is vitally important. In my view this allowed us to reap the profits of competition, spurring us on to greater accomplishments and allowing us to use and build on each other's ideas, and helped us avoid most of the destructive aspects, such as putting each other down and not hearing each other's ideas. Obviously the need for this exploration continues, as evidenced by the Palmer-Nicklaus anecdote regarding my blockage in writing this book. A threatened feeling has also been expressed lately by several other Circus members. The feeling that one member is excelling dampens the spirit and confidence of another. This is the current issue among us, one that is in the open as always and that I feel can be dealt with profitably.

Clearly, from this description I feel that this training method is by far the most successful. Each of these six has become an outstanding group leader, most of them acquiring their own reputations quite rapidly, each making major creative contributions at a dizzying pace and going on to their own syntheses of methods. This book profits greatly from my interaction with them and the origin and development of many of the ideas here is hard to assign to any one person. A short description of each member of the Flying Circus will illuminate the difficulty of selection and of knowing the best background and training for an encounter group leader.

Steve Stroud is the youngest at 26. He completed one partial year of college, dropped out, and spent two years in the Peace Corps. He then came to Esalen, entered the residential program and then the Flying Circus. He has virtually no academic or psychological background, but is a voracious reader and experimenter, willing to try anything. His risk-taking has been inspirational. He has remarkable openness and self-awareness and intuition about others. He's matured enormously over the past two years in the area of women, forming a very solid relationship with Linda Cross. Steve studied with Bernard Aaronson to learn hypnosis, with which he is very proficient; he has had mystical experiences such as astral projection; he went through a period of trying all the psychedelic drugs available to see what happened. He plays a marvelous guitar, excellent chess—perhaps the best around Esalen—and is exceptionally bright. He and his groups have become increasingly popular and his reputation is growing. He took over the Spring 1970 Esalen residential program but decided it didn't feel right, turned it over to Seymour, and took Linda to Chile where they are being trained by the Sufis, the Moslem mystics. Steve, or Steve and Linda, are among the people I go to first when I have personal troubles. They don't allow any bullshit, are very insightful, and invariably helpful.

Betty Fuller worked on the stage as an actress and director for several years. She received an M.A. in radio and theater direction. She's also extremely bright in a nonthreatening way, and has great empathy and enormous amounts of energy to give her groups. She runs one of the best couples groups anywhere, and has frequently helped me with personal trials. Betty has a host of techniques that she uses very skillfully, especially psychodrama and gestalt, and keeps learning, currently about enriched sexual relations and healing. She has tremendous warmth and humanity. Betty has begun an extended personal body trip, incorporating all the insights and experiences gained from her groups, to lose extra weight she has carried for years. Perhaps the best indication I can give of my confidence in her is that I gave my mother a birthday present of one of my five-day workshops with the Circus, and hoped she would choose Betty's group. She did. Betty, at 43, is especially good with older people.

John Heider, 33, is the closest circus member to having legitimate credentials, for he has a Ph.D. in psychology. But it hardly counts since his dissertation was on meditation. John carries his intellectual flair into his work and will probably write a good deal. He has developed the energy concept a long way and is also very experimental. He has a strong mystical bent that he infuses into his style and is able to take risks and inspire confidence. With his wife Anne he has run couples groups. He did an excellent job leading the Fall 1970 residential program and now feels the need to collect his thoughts and experiences in a year off for writing and integrating. John has developed with Steve the very effective methods of hyperventilation to break through blocks. Incidentally, one valuable feature of the group is successful co-leading, especially among Steve, John, and Seymour. John is particularly good in groups with more Establishment people, having short hair, an air of authority, and the proper degrees.

Seymour Carter, 32, is the most outrageous of the Flying Circus. For many years a mountain hippie, jailed for being a junkie, in the early days of Esalen absconding with funds, he is not the epitome of the well-credentialed encounter group leader. But he's a remarkable man. Seymour is about as self-made a leader as possible. In his dope days he got very interested in Synanon and through that came to Esalen. He wasn't in the residential program but he made his own. He attended most of our meetings and participated in most of the resident activities, learning the various techniques being exposed. When the Flying Circus was being formed, Steve suggested that I include Seymour. Although I liked Seymour very much from the outset, I was very skeptical of this wild man. (At this time he also performed at drum dances by eating fire.) But I took Steve's word for it and tried him. He was the hit of the workshop, obviously a natural. Seymour has a primitive honesty and directness along with the skills he has accumulated. He doesn't have the quick, sharp intelligence of some of the others, but has a slower, very thorough brain. He also has the thirst for newness, with special interest, not unexpectedly, in primitive tribes and rituals. He also learned to be a Rolfer and is incorporating that approach to the body with the others. Seymour's great features are his ability to initiate and his great energy, which he can transmit to others very effectively. He has also gone to the Sufi school in Chile to explore the spiritual dimension.

Stuart Miller is our other Ph.D. (it's in comparative literature). Stuart, 32, has brought a literary element to the Circus along with some erudition and an appropriate degree of intellectual snobbism. His greatest ability is being right there with his feelings, being able to react immediately with the way he feels. He also can express himself with great clarity, style (his favorite word), and humor. He has become director of development for Esalen and his talents have been channelled into money-raising and program directing and his involvement with leading encounter groups has lessened. He has written a marvelous account of his adventures in the residential program that should be published soon (*Hot Springs*, Viking, 1971).

Sukie Unobskey Miller, 29, has an M.A. in education and was specializing in behavior modification when I met her in New York. I was so impressed that I sent for her to join the Flying Circus as it was forming. She's very, very funny. Her energy, wit, and no-nonsense were great assets, and through several training periods she acquired the necessary skills. Then she met Stuart; soon after they were married and her energies were diverted toward helping Stuart program for Esalen and toward being Mrs. Miller. The result is that the Millers do little group leading, except for their brilliant conception of running an encounter group workshop for millionaires, a way of discharging their money-raising function while offering something very significant to people who can contribute financially. Lately Sukie has been exercising her organizational abilities by running the Esalen benefit in New York, which was a great success. She was aided by some of the millionaires. Both the Millers, as well as Betty Fuller, have gotten deeply involved with psychosynthesis, an approach like the Sufis, that integrates the spiritual dimension of man into his other life.

From these brief sketches the irrelevance of formal training of any specific type should be clear.

The problem of licensing is further complicated by the wide variety of situations in which these encounter group leaders function. There are many encounter group leaders who are excellent if all that is required of them is a microlab and a discussion of groups for people who are relatively unacquainted with them. But many of those leaders are not capable of running a weekend workshop alone. Some can do a good job co-leading with a strong leader. Some are very good with high school and college students but not with conservative adults or professionals. Some are the very opposite. Black-white groups offer a different challenge; so do groups of very experienced people. I recommend very few people beyond the Circus for week-long workshops handled alone. In other words, not only are criteria of group leader competence unclear, it's not even certain that there should be one criterion for qualifying leaders without considering the jobs they are to do.

What I have done personally to meet this situation and recognize its complexity is this: When someone asks me to recommend a leader I ask about the situation in which he is to lead. I then offer them as many people as I feel are qualified to do that job well, and describe my impression of how I think each would do it. The rest is up to the employer and employee to work out. No certification or licensing enters since that is an oversimplified dichotomization of the process of recommendation. The same thing applies to workshops for training trainers. I never offer work leading to a degree or certificate of any kind. I simply assume that after the training they are hopefully better encounter group leaders than before. How good they are depends on where they were to begin with and how much they learned.

Obviously this is not a completely satisfactory solution. The consumer of group leaders must take a risk, certainly no more a risk in my opinion than relying on a legal licensing procedure. I have known many wretched psychologists, psychotherapists, psychiatrists, and psychoanalysts, who had all the licenses available. The real problem is not the necessity for licensing, but rather getting to the task of discovering the best selection and training procedures for encounter group leaders.

Toward this end I would offer the following suggestions toward a training program for open encounter group leaders.

1. Selection of trainees should be on the basis of personal qualities, in particular, self-insight, and probably (as it turned out on the basis of the Circus), on very high intelligence. Self-

awareness is crucial. It includes both a person's ability and willingness to be aware of his feelings about himself, and about the members of his group, and the ability and willingness to express these feelings to the group members.

The concept of the leader as completer also provides a basis for selection. Whatever group members are not doing themselves in the direction of becoming an effective group, the leader must cause to be done. This means that if the group is going well, the best the leader can do is nothing, or simply join in as a member. If there is too much defending, he should help the group penetrate it; if they need a model for expressing feeling, he should be able to provide it. These skills require knowledge of groups, perceptiveness, a facility with inductive logic (the ability to go from many small clues to a generalization), and personal freedom.

Too many technically skilled group leaders have never become first-rate because their own personal needs have intruded into the group—perhaps sadism, anger over rejection or lack of respect, passivity due to fear of failure and embarrassment, defensiveness, or a need to be sexually attractive. The importance of intelligence appeared inadvertently as I analyzed the Circus. It seemed to put them all a cut above the average group leader. Inductive reasoning is a central quality because being aware of what is happening in the group requires relating apparently unrelated comments or cues, being alert to small changes in voice, walking, body posture, facial expression, dress, etc., and making hypotheses as to what is happening. Then, too, intuition and sensitivity are essential, but I would feel relatively safe in assuming those if the candidate had self-insight.

2. An important early experience is for the candidate to be a member of at least one intensive encounter group run by a very good leader. Preferably, he should participate in more than one, run by different good leaders. When we were think-

ing of devising a training program, this feature was handled by giving the candidates four weekend group experiences with four of the Circus members, including one co-led by two leaders to give that experience to the trainees, plus an ongoing group over a six-week period.

3. The trainee should have ample opportunity to lead under supervision. One very successful method I have found is to end the trainee's encounter group by turning over the leadership of each meeting to a pair of co-leaders from within the group. The group then has a chance to continue as a group, and the co-leaders can get feedback not only from me but from all group members. Members of the group can tell the co-leaders how their leadership behavior affected them, a unique viewpoint. I usually stay out of the group at this point and just observe so that I can see more, but I'm suspicious of myself here, I think it's just less threatening.

4. From these self-co-leading experiences the candidates go to co-leading with an experienced leader and talk with him at length after each meeting, being sure that the relation between co-leaders is part of the discussion.

5. Running a group of his own under supervision is the trainee's final experience.

6. During these times the candidate should be learning intellectual material from different fields and undergoing experiences as well. The workshops and recommended readings are given in the appendix. They include: psychodrama, fantasy, bioenergetic exercises, Rolf treatments, body movement workshops, breathing, sensory and body awareness, Alexander lessons, theater games, hypnotism, psychomotor therapy, massage, gestalt training, mysticism, meditation, yoga, and tai-chi.

The trainee should also have an intellectual understanding of the major schools of psychotherapy, major personality theories (including Groddeck), group dynamics and group therapy, psychosomatic medicine, anatomy and physiology (including dissection), and inductive logic.

These requirements indicate why I feel that the objections to encounter group leaders by some Eastern Establishment therapists—that they "don't know the (group psychotherapy) literature"—are a bit shortsighted. The literature has gone way beyond group psychotherapy and, indeed, it is more to the point that the group therapists now need to read more.

At this point those are the experiences I would include in an encounter group training program. As far as I know nothing like that is now offered. Even at Esalen we haven't been that complete. It would seem to me that an experimental training program somewhat along these lines and evaluating its success would be a worthwhile step toward a licensing process if that procedure is desirable. But any attempt now to license seems to me not much more than fatuous window dressing with very little relation to protecting the public.

Other Issues

Shouldn't people who come to encounter groups be screened?
Isn't it dangerous to take just anyone?

Some people profit more than others from a group experience. For some, it may even be dangerous, though I feel that they constitute an extremely small number. Some of the strongest objections to encounter groups arise around the issue of screening, especially from professional psychotherapists. The procedures whereby someone enters or doesn't enter, and stays or doesn't stay, in a group are very important, both theoretically and practically.

I think it would be marvelous if people were screened so that those who would profit most would be admitted to encounter groups, and those who would not profit, or who would be damaged, would be excluded. But I have very little idea of how to do this. The early years of my scientific career were spent largely on the topic of group compatibility and I developed several tests, FIRO–B, FIRO–F, and COPE, which are used

from time to time to compose groups to attain certain predictable aims. Several results were published in my early book *FIRO*,
and others were published later, generally finding that these
tests were fairly good instruments for group composition purposes. Later, for a year or two, I participated in the NTL effort
to screen candidates for T-groups, an effort that extended over
about twenty years. My clear impression from these experiences is that the effort expended to screen group members,
whether it be a psychological test, a personal interview, or
personal recommendations, wasn't worth it. Occasionally one
technique would work, but on the whole, it was much more
efficacious to let people who wanted to be in a group come in
unless there was some glaringly obvious reason, like his address
was the back ward of a state mental hospital. Screening, then,
takes place from firsthand contact in the group.

Further, I'm no longer sure I know what I want even if I could
screen. The people that would be most likely to be labeled
prepsychotic often spark the group and send it into valuable
areas that others are afraid to enter. In turn, they often work
very well because they find themselves in a supportive non-
punitive atmosphere. Those that do develop psychotic episodes
are often the most normal-appearing people at the beginning
of the group—a surgeon, a housewife, a business man. Also if a
person is going to go psychotic, many encounter groups, particularly those held at a residential setting with a supporting
community, are among the safest situations in which it can
happen.

Complex psychiatric labeling I find more of a burden to overcome than an aid. I felt this especially when working at a mental
hospital. I would receive patients in my group with the usual
categories—paranoid schizophrenic, depressive, etc.—and find
myself screening out all the behaviors that were contrary to the
diagnosis and noticing every little indication that confirmed it
out of my own anxiety about seeing the patients the way the

senior psychiatrists did. I found it so much in the way that I finally made it a practice not to know their diagnostic classification, but just to meet the patients and experience them myself.

Probably the patients that profit the least and impede the group the most are very uptight, constricted deniers who are often very successful in the world. They either require an inordinate amount of time from the group or else just sit and interfere with the group process because they are on a different level. One such example was reported in the *New York Times Magazine* article on groups by Leo Litwak, where every time he would start to get to very emotional material, another group member called Daniel would try to be helpful by philosophizing, thus bringing Litwak completely out of his feelings. In private life, Daniel is a successful author, wealthy, and to all observations well adjusted. Daniel had no sense of Litwak's feelings; he was able to follow only his words. This type of participant is very draggy on the group.

But even in Daniel's case, a great deal may be learned from him. Often, everyone in the group is, in part, like Daniel, so that when that part is exaggerated in another person, it is easier to see it in oneself.

To the request for screening group members I have two final responses. I'm not sure I'd know what to screen for except in extreme cases, and if I did know, I don't know how to select such people. My suspicion is that there is a bit of righteous arrogance on the part of the established profession.

Isn't it dehumanizing to coerce people into doing things they don't want to do?

The only valid objection I see in this area of group membership has to do with its voluntary character. Much as I despair of a group leader's ability to select people advantageously, I do have confidence in a person's own ability to know when he is ready for a group. Over the years I have decided never to take anyone in a group who is not there voluntarily. I find that involuntary group members are often obstructive and unwilling to participate and I am reluctant to encourage them to do anything they don't want to do since that isn't what we contracted for. I am thereby inhibited and my paranoia takes hold in dampening me from trying to do anything risky because this man might give out a distorted story to the public. Also, if he doesn't want to be in a group, it's very likely that he has a sense somewhere that he isn't ready for such an experience, and that is a sense I usually trust. Similarly, I feel that it is important that anyone have the freedom to leave whenever he wishes.

There are many times that I strongly discourage leaving because it is often detrimental when something has just opened up and not yet had a chance to come to fruition, to play through the energy cycle. And I try to make this clear to participants at the outset. Also, I urge anyone who is leaving to tell it to the group during a regular meeting, not just to sneak out, since this event can turn into an important learning experience for both the leaver and the left. This approach is consistent with the idea of each person being responsible for himself. He must take the responsibility for coming to the group and for either staying or leaving once he's there.

Aren't these groups just instant turn-ons, quick catharses, and emotional orgies that fade when the patient returns to his natural habitat?

As critics are fond of saying, "Where is your follow-up data?" The irony is that it often comes from traditional psychotherapists, psychoanalysts, and psychiatrists. The lamentable state of follow-up research for any type of psychotherapy is well known in the field.

However, we have made some preliminary moves to follow-up by questionnaire what happens to people when they leave open encounter workshops. The early results (about 60 people) seem to parallel those obtained in an earlier, more extensive study (Schutz and Allen), namely, that about 83% think it was essentially a good experience, about 15% feel not much happened to them, and 2% or 3% didn't like it.

Although these results are encouraging, much more persuasive is the later personal contact with participants. Through these contacts I am convinced that good things do happen and that they remain as well as do the results of other therapeutic experiences, perhaps better. Of course, this is a subjective judgment.

Isn't a workshop too short for any lasting effects? Isn't there a lot of emotional catharsis but no working through? Don't people need a continuing long-term relationship, like with a real psychotherapist?

The question of frequency of workshop sessions is very complex. I have experienced everything from a one-day, nine-hour group, to hundreds of hours of five times a week therapy, to a nine-month program, and most situations in between. Many considerations arise that oversimplify the question of time in therapeutic treatment. I feel that the choice of the most valuable experience for a given person in terms of type and the length of time depends upon where a person is in his life flow. I know of many people whose lives were drastically altered for what they and I feel is the better in one weekend, or even in one session. I've known of many others who have been in intensive therapy for up to 23 years and are still unhappy and searching. In one sense no time span is long enough; in another sense, therapeutic experiences must end in order for full growth to occur.

First consider why people come to a workshop, assuming for

a moment that they know their reasons. Many are at a point of crisis in their life. Should they get married or divorced? stay at their job or quit? go to school or drop out? For those people a workshop can help them clarify their feelings about the issue and perhaps help them to reach a decision. And that's all. It may not solve the aberrations in their basic character structure. Another person may come because he's impotent, or depressed, or he can't sing anymore, or he has a bad marriage, or he can't keep a job, or he's successful but unhappy. Some of these problems that were not in awareness get resolved.

I'm finding it hard to say what I want to say and make it more than general and abstract. I'll try a few more approaches. When a patient comes to a doctor for a broken arm we don't usually blame the doctor if the patient comes down with hepatitis three months later. A similar criterion seems fair for a workshop. A person may spend time focusing on one personal issue and not on a second and so will leave the workshop with the second one remaining.

A better way of asking the question of the adequacy of time is to ask whether the time spent in a workshop has been used well. The open encounter techniques are aimed at the best utilization of the time available, attempting to go deeper quicker. ·

Part of the encounter philosophy is to teach self-responsibility, and one of the aspects of responsibility is to know what you need at a given time. Having a place like Esalen, where there is a constantly available menu of different types of experiences, is an alternative to seeing a therapist regularly over a long period. The latter offers only one type of experience with a very small variation in time intervals, with only one person, and with the time intervals determined primarily by the outside person, the therapist. In the Esalen method a person may have a very intense week-long encounter group experience. He then often feels that he wants to go away and let the effects settle for a while, perhaps seeing a therapist once or twice. After a month or so he wants to work on his marital relation so he enters a couples group. When the effects seem to be fading he may choose, perhaps three or four weeks later, to return for a week-end encounter group for reinforcement, or if he needs more intense work he may go to a bioenergetic or gestalt group. Perhaps in a few months he may feel the need to go inside himself to consolidate his changes and choose a massage and meditation workshop. This may awaken him to his body tensions and he may be ready to be Rolfed, or perhaps go to a movement or a yoga workshop. By then the need for another encounter group may be felt, followed by a long period of staying away from workshops while he allows himself to live in the world and integrate his experience. Or, another option at this point is to decide that he needs a deeper immersion in this environment, and he may come to a month-long or four-month residential program, or even come to live and work at Esalen or a similar place.

This outline emphasizes the responsibility for his own growth being in his own hands, including the responsibility for asking advice from other people. It also opens up many possibilities to the person—from total immersion through intensive experiences, through light experiences, to nothing, and from one hour to a whole living style for a protracted period. This method appreciates individual differences as well as differences at various points along a life path requiring appropriate experiences. A disadvantage of the approach is that it is relatively difficult for a workshop participant to work with the same group leader over a long period of time. If a person feels this is what he needs, then he should choose private, individual therapy, another available alternative.

A related problem is the determination of which experiences are required so that the workshop has a lasting effect. My answer lies in the concept of the life flow. Each individual problem may be understood as a blockage of energy impeding the successful completion of a flow cycle; the blockage is physical, emotional, intellectual, and probably spiritual. The job of the workshop is to locate and unblock the blockage, undo the needs that require the block so as to prevent its recurrence, and to allow the person to experience the feeling of functioning with the blockage removed. To the degree that this process is completed in the workshop, the change will be permanent. The completion of the process depends not only on the length of time available, but also on the depth of the problem (strength of the blockage), the effectiveness of the methods used, and the point in his life at which the person enters the group. Some examples should clarify this abstraction.

A former opera singer entered a group with the complaint that she could no longer sing in public. Through feeling support from the group she was able to sing on the first night of the workshop (unblocking through support). Subsequent interaction in the group dealt with her fears surrounding presenting herself in public (dealing with needs to resume blockage), and there were several informal opportunities for her to sing during the week to an audience that requested to hear her (reinforcing the unblocked state).

Often the blockage is more difficult to overcome. Jane was having great difficulty with her man. She was very bright but uneducated compared to his academic erudition. We got nowhere in the group until she was put into a guided daydream fantasy. In the fantasy she saw a long tunnel that she was trying to crawl through. As she got further and further into the tunnel it got smaller and smaller and she became very panicky, fearful that she would be stuck. As her guide, I gave her impetus to continue but minimal support, feeling that the more she did on her own to break through this blockage (represented by the narrowest part of the tunnel), the more lasting the experience would be for her. After her panic and with a great deal of grunting, screaming, and body English, she broke through the opening and got to the other side. She was exhilarated and greatly relieved and continued out the tunnel. But when I asked her to go back to the opening of the tunnel and go through again, she once again got frightened and refused. This meant to me that she had broken through the blockage but the feelings surrounding it were not sufficiently strong for the block not to recur. I therefore urged her to try again using any instruments or people that would make the task easier. She chose a magic pick and set to work making the hole larger. Finally it was big enough to walk through and she walked through it back and forth joyously. Noting that her body also looked very relaxed and satisfied, I took her out of the fantasy at that point. This was another level of retaining the unblocking and experiencing living with the new condition. The meaning of her fantasy symbols was not clear to me. It could have been that the narrow tunnel was her narrow education that would prevent her from progressing beyond a certain point. Realizing that she could go beyond it after all was at first a shaky step, but, with support, she came to accept it and began to express herself fully. But the interpretation did not seem crucial. The work of unblocking was done in the fantasy.

Thus the question of length of time, frequency, and which type of growth experience is most valuable depends on the person, which aspect of life he is in, how deep his blockage is, how effective the tools are, and how appropriate the tools are for the problem. The last one is the reason that people can go to psychoanalysis for years—or yes, even live at Esalen for years —with no significant growth because they are being treated extensively but with the wrong methods. One can learn to be very deft in analysis and learn how to be totally untouched. It is a great art to learn which tools are valuable for which people at what points in their lives. This is the primary reason that open encounter is indeed open; the more techniques that are available, the more likely a person will be affected. Also, the fact that the blockages always occur at all levels means that the tools must deal with all levels in order to achieve the most lasting changes.

Doesn't an encounter group, especially at Esalen, encourage sexual acting out? And don't people come for the wrong reasons, like wanting to get laid, or to release aggression?

It is true that opening people to their body feelings, their sensuality, their longing for touch, for sexual urges, and their desire for intimacy will lead people to be more aware of their sexuality and perhaps more inclined toward sexual intercourse. This drive is enhanced by the intimacy fostered by the groups through the encouragement to reveal deep feelings in the presence of others, a type of intimacy that speeds up relations so that people feel that they have known each other for a long time, though it may be only days or hours. Further, a setting like Esalen is romantic and permissive compared to society, and distant from familiar friends and neighbors. It also features natural hot baths where people see each other nude in this romantic setting, and often there are individual sessions where people take off clothes. All of these factors make sexuality a very real possibility, more so than in most situations.

For some, this setting leads to sexual activity; for others it is paralyzing. It forces each person to face his own sexual feelings. Herein lies the great advantage of the encounter situation. If the encounter rules of openness and honesty are followed, then my attitude as group leader is to allow virtually any behavior to occur, but to insist that it be discussed openly at all points. I will also, if appropriate, contribute my own personal feelings about the situation in general and how I see the present circumstance. The responsibility, as always, is with the group members. This avoids sneaky behind-the-barn, tee-hee sex, and means that each person is responsible for whatever he does. This almost always leads to a valuable outcome. People sometimes learn that they are just using people and have no concern for them as humans, or that they are dishonest in representing their feelings, or that they are very concerned about their potency and (for men) are searching for a woman who can give them a strong erection; or many women learn that they are looking for a man who can give them a full orgasm. Many men learn of their difficulty in being sexually attracted and feeling love for the same woman. Many men find a great hollowness or disgust with their sexual partner when the act is completed, but instead of just leaving as was their habit in the past, they must come to the group, confront their partner, and attempt to understand these feelings. Anything that happens, as long as it remains open, can be the basis for important understanding and growth.

These comments also apply to people who come to workshops with lecherous intentions. One man on the first night of the workshop used the baths to try to fondle women. The next day in the group one girl complained about his lecherous behavior. In quick succession so did three other women, calling him a dirty old man. I asked him to stand in one corner and the four women in the diagonal corner of the room, and for them to approach each other silently and do whatever they wished nonverbally (augmented High Noon). The girls then all walked right by him and left him standing alone in the center of the room, rejected. This stunning experience left him depressed, embarrassed, and abject. It soon led him to get into contact with his desperate loneliness and his alienation from his wife. Even though he came to the workshop for a frivolous reason, the norm of openness allowed his behavior to be used profitably by him and others.

One outcome of this method of dealing with sexuality is that we get a large number of people reporting that their sexual lives are greatly improved after a workshop. They feel freer, less guilt-ridden, more accepting of their body, more aware of the other person involved, and more responsible.

Bulletin: *US–USSR Encounter Group*

January 1984, WASHINGTON, D.C. (Special to *The New York Times*)—In his inauguration speech, the new President reaffirmed his campaign pledge for a prolonged visit to Moscow and described more details of his unusual philosophy of government. "One of the basic sources of most of the world's problems," he said, "is dishonesty and lack of self-awareness. We must replace diplomacy with honesty, we must replace strategy with encounter, we must replace self-righteousness with self-awareness. Only then can we stop fighting interminable little wars, can we stop economically crippling competitions, can we stop supporting the forces of death, instead of the forces of life.

"The heart of our problems lies in the relations among the big powers. I am leaving tomorrow for Moscow to stay as long as necessary until I can work out with the Premier a more satisfactory way of living together in the world. After that, I will go to Peking for the same purpose. By then, hopefully, the world's three major powers will sit down and really talk together.

"I am not concerned whether or not this project takes my

266

entire four-year administration. I have assembled, as you know, an administrative team, headed by the Vice President, whom I feel is fully as capable of being President as I am. The men on this team not only possess the wide range of skills required to run a government, but also have encountered each other, along with myself, for several months, and have developed a close, personal, working relationship. I shall, of course, retain the authority and responsibility for all governmental decisions, but I shall rely heavily on this Presidential team.

"I am going to meet the Russians in Moscow, in the Premier's bathroom if that's his preference, because I have no interest in haggling for months over where to meet. Nor do I want to spend valuable time trying to extract preconference guarantees. The issues before the world are too important for such childish displays of 'you can't push me around.' I have no desire to beat my chest or to try to make my adversaries knuckle down before the world. My only stipulation, one that the Premier has agreed to tentatively and cautiously, is that there be an encounter group leader present, one chosen by both of us. The group leader's job is to help us to be honest and self-aware so that we do not fall into old diplomatic patterns. The Premier and I will each have two advisers; thus our group will consist of six people plus the group leader.

"My fellow Americans, I realize that this is a strange approach to world problems, one probably without precedence in the world's history. I know that it strains your tolerance and asks you to accept, largely on faith, methods that are unfamiliar to most of you. But the science of man must keep up with the physical sciences. For centuries, while physical science developed astonishingly, the science of behavior languished; when it did produce new knowledge, applications to everyday life were very slow in coming. We must now use our new knowledge of behavior because so many of the world's problems are human problems, the difficulties of man working with man. We are

learning more about the importance of honesty and self-awareness in human relations; we are learning about how man is
unified in body, mind, and spirit; we are learning more about
individual responsibility; and we are learning more about how
alike men are below the surface. We must use these important
discoveries, and use them now.

"If this endeavor is successful, perhaps we can stop having
little wars all over the world; we can stop bankrupting each
other with arms races; we can begin full cooperation in science
and research instead of wasteful duplication; we can cooperate
in cleaning up the earth. And perhaps most important of all, we
can elevate the goal of world cooperation from the negative
goal of peace—that is, the absence of war—to a more optimistic
one of individual happiness, joy, and the realization of the nobl-
est potential that is within each person.

"Thank you for giving me your confidence to try this approach. I don't know if I shall succeed. I know I shall make
every effort of which I am capable."

March 1984, MOSCOW—During the first two months of the
US–USSR encounter group, one member from each side left
and was replaced by consent of all. The two replacements have
been well received and interviews with the seven members
indicate general satisfaction with the group as now constituted.
This satisfaction and trust has reached the point that the group
announced tonight that henceforth all of their meetings will be
transcribed verbatim and made available to the world press
unedited and uncensored. In addition, the group agreed to
release transcripts of all meetings held to date.

April 1984, MOSCOW—Following are excerpts from one of
the early meetings of the US–USSR encounter group. (Present
were: Group leader, President, President's advisers Elmer and
Jim, Premier, Premier's advisers Ivan and Boris. All are sitting

on the floor in a bare room with a thick wall-to-wall carpet. There is a mattress in one corner with many pillows on it. All have taken their shoes off and are wearing casual clothes.)

Leader: Gentlemen, in addition to the other encounter group rules I suggested to you, I invite you to speak entirely for yourselves as individuals, not as representatives of your country. Speaking as a representative serves as a way of not taking responsibility for your own personal feelings. If we relate to each other as people, I think the full richness and complexity of our relationships can evolve, and the specific things you must do as representatives can be decided when we are finished. It will probably take us a while to build a group in which there is sufficient openness and trust to do valuable work. I hope you won't be impatient during this period. Now please be honest, talk about and express your feelings, and start in the here and now.

Jim: I feel very nervous, excited, and anxious. I don't know if I'm capable of doing this.

Boris: Do you Americans really believe this will work?

Ldr: Would you please make the statement behind that question?

Boris: What? Oh. I don't think Americans are capable of honesty. Your international behavior over the last few decades is appalling.

Ldr: Would you just sit in front of each American, look him in the eye, and tell him you don't trust him?

Boris: (Slightly irritated) I don't have to. I've just said it.

Ldr: It's sometimes different to say it to a specific person rather than in the abstract.

Boris: All right. (Sits on floor in front of Jim.) I don't trust you. You are not capable of honesty.

Ldr: Would you say he's a liar?

Boris: Yes.

Ldr: Say that to him.

Boris: You're a liar.

Ldr: Louder, scream it!

Boris: (Screams) You're a liar (trails off).

Ldr: What does your body feel like?

Boris: My stomach is fluttering and my hands and arms feel weak. . . . I didn't like saying that.

Ldr: Would you shout "You're a liar" in front of Elmer and the President?

Boris: (Sitting in front of Elmer) You're a liar! (Quickly moves over to the President.) You're a liar! (Moves back to his place in the circle.)

(Long silence)

Ldr: I feel very shaken, almost on the verge of tears.

President: (Looks at leader) So do I. For some reason, I feel closer and more sympathetic to Boris. By the time he . . .

Ldr: Would you speak directly to him?

Pres: (Turns to Boris) By the time you got to me the force had left your voice. You weren't convincing. You looked to me like a nervous little boy.

Boris: Yes, I felt that way. I'm very nervous; my heart is pounding fast. I'm afraid of what Ivan and the Premier are thinking.

Ldr: How are you going to find out?

Boris: (Turns to Ivan and Premier) I think that I made a fool of myself, and I hope you don't.

Premier: I feel very confused. I know the Americans are liars, but now I feel shaken too. There's something very suspicious going on here. This little exercise is making me like the Americans more. I'm getting wary.

Ldr: I feel you don't trust me.

Prem: No, I don't.

Ldr: Would you get behind me and alter ego. I mean, say what you think I'm feeling and not saying? I'll say whether it feels right or not.

Prem: Sounds ridiculous. Another of your little games.

Ldr: It might help.

Prem: All right, this once. (Sits behind leader, talking for him.) I'm a young smart-ass who's learned some clever techniques. In the guise of helping important people, I'm really taking control of the whole situation while acting innocent. Pretty soon they'll all be doing exactly what I want them to do, and they won't even know it. Heh, heh.

Ldr: I think you're right that I would like you to do what I want. But it's your responsibility to agree with me or not. It's not my fault if you do something you don't want to do. It's yours.

Prem: More clever words. I still don't trust you. I want to fight you every step of the way.

Ldr: Let's arm wrestle.

Prem: You're younger than I am and I haven't done this for thirty years.

Ldr: Are you refusing?

Prem: . . . No. Let's go.

(They lie down facing each other, lock hands, look at each other, and start yelling and straining. They struggle on the floor for 10 minutes looking at each other, yelling. The others begin to shout encouragement. Finally, the leader wins. They both collapse, breathing hard for 30 seconds.)

Prem: Let's try the left hands. (Others laugh.)

(Premier gets a quick advantage. They struggle and Premier wins. Both collapse to floor breathing hard. Premier looks pleased. They look up slowly and start to grin. Leader reaches a hand tentatively to the back of Premier's neck, he responds, they laugh.)

Elmer: That scared me. I thought you'd have a heart attack, Premier. I found I was almost rooting for you. I share some of your suspicions of the leader. It shocks me. (Looks bewildered.)

Pres: This is the first time you've talked all day, Elmer.

Elmer: Something strange has been happening to me. It's as if all my clothes have been taken off. I can't use any of the ways I relate to people. They are all called bullshit. I can't ask questions, I can't say I don't know. I have to observe my body and I never paid any attention to it. I feel totally lost.

Ldr: Would you act this out? Close your eyes, get up and walk around lost. Put your hands out in front of you. We'll either try to avoid you or not as we wish.

(Elmer obeys. Everyone gets up and wanders around the room. Ivan isn't sure what to do; leader reassures him. Elmer shuts his eyes, puts his arms out straight and starts to walk; everyone avoids him. He laughs at first, makes a few jokes, then a strained grin, then looks unhappy. He opens his eyes.)

Ldr: Please keep your eyes shut, Elmer.

(He shuts his eyes again and keeps wandering, starts getting panicky, shouts, "Where are you! Don't leave me alone!" All avoid him. He starts sobbing. Opens eyes. All sit on floor and watch Elmer. He has head in hands and is shaking. After about two minutes he raises his head.)

Elmer: My god. That brought me right back to when I was in high school and my friends played a trick on me during hide and seek. They all ran away and I looked for them for hours . . . My mother used to do that too when I was an infant. She wouldn't tell me she was going and then I'd wake up and

there was no one home . . . My heart's beating a thousand
times a minute and I'm all clammy and I can hardly breathe.
Ivan: (Head in hand) I can remember almost the same thing.
Prem: I think I sometimes do that to my children.
Ldr: This reminds me of how I see you in this group. Elmer, you
need structure very badly. You want to make sure everything
is planned and organized and determined beforehand so you
won't be left and not know what to do.
Elmer: Maybe, maybe. God, I'm still shaking.

(Group takes a break. Ivan goes over to Elmer and starts to tell
him about a similar childhood event. Premier smiles fleetingly
at leader, then turns his back and talks to Boris. President and
Jim talk together. Leader is left alone. After a few minutes,
Premier and President walk over and listen to Ivan and Elmer
talking. They look at each other tentatively. Premier reaches
out a hand and touches President's shoulder.)

Applications

The encounter mode of human relating and self-awareness could replace our present hypocritical style. That's a theme of this book, and it is the basis of an encounter culture. I've tried to lay the theoretical basis for such a culture, and to discuss methods and techniques for implementing it. Hypothetical situations in the form of bulletins have indicated some of the ways in which encountering could lead to an encounter culture. Even now, however, there are ways in which it is being and could be used in various aspects of human life.

Psychotherapy is the most obvious area of application. Many psychologists, psychiatrists, and even some psychoanalysts are trying open encounter techniques in their own practice. There is no need to pit one approach to therapy against another, as I in my zealousness sometimes do. I really feel that encounter supplements traditional psychotherapy. As is clear in my debt to Semrad and to my years at a traditional medical school, Albert Einstein, I have learned much from the psychiatric tradition and from Freud. Some basic psychological conceptions underly open encounter, and traditional methods can be enhanced by the open encounter methods. Nonverbal techniques may be added, as well as fantasy and dramatic methods, a heightened awareness of the role of the body, a different conception of the role of the therapist, and some new considerations of the roles of honesty and responsibility. More and more therapists are coming to open encounter workshops to experience this approach for themselves. I foresee an exciting time ahead when therapists begin integrating open encounter methods with their own techniques to devise creative syntheses that apply to populations of psychotics, neurotics, addicts, family groups, adolescents, delinquents, prisoners, and other specialized groups.

Industry. The T-group has long been used in industrial settings, and the open encounter group can increase the value of this experience. Industry's use of encounter implies its acceptance of the values of openness, honesty, and individual responsibility, and its accepting the importance of developing the human potential. Bosses must be willing and able to be open and self-insightful about themselves and their feelings about workers, and the workers likewise about their bosses. Labor-management negotiations should include the personal needs of the negotiators in their dialogue. And the company should accept the possibility that an opening up of an employee may result in his realization that his own best interests will be served by his quitting and going elsewhere.

I feel that this orientation is also highly profitable financially. Finding people who are not happy in an organization and letting them go, establishing closer personal ties between people working together, creating conditions under which people are personally more satisfied, and setting up an organization in which people are placed in the position where they function most effectively, because their personal qualities are considered, are all factors that make for working efficiency, greater personal happiness and fulfillment, and higher profits.

Open encounter can also be applied to all business meetings. Most meetings are a travesty, and the important things often remain unsaid. Open encounter provides means whereby real feelings emerge, and decisions can be made that use the contributions of all members of a meeting. If you are a businessman with some willingness to take risks, try using the rules of open encounter at your next meeting.

If open encounter is used routinely in a business setting, transcendent rewards follow, like seeing work as a meditation. Bitching about your job gives way to seeing the here-and-now pleasure in work and feeling the joy of realizing your human potential. These feelings are within reach if the sham, venality, and hypocrisy of business, labor, and industry are overcome and people come together in the joint effort of accomplishing a civilization's work together.

Theater. For centuries the theater has been a central vehicle for man's expression. Here he portrays his view of life, his feelings, his dreams—three areas where open encounter is pertinent. To the artist, the playwright, a knowledge of self and feeling is crucial. Superficial, sprightly, plastic portrayals of character are always possible if a person is clever enough. But a portrayal with verisimilitude, truth to life, is a wholly different matter. Audiences are absorbed in dramas that reach to human depths with their portrayals of character. And as we've seen, the nearer people are to being penetrated to their essence, the nearer they are to being like everyman. At our deepest we are all one. When an author is opaque, no matter how talented he is, his characters can only glitter like paper in a fire, then die.

The second area of contact between theater and open encounter is the relation between actor and audience. The last decade has seen a great flourishing of different styles of experimental theater: the Open theater, the Guerilla theater, theater of Encounter, *The Concept, Hair,* and many more. Their attempt, in part, was to increase audience involvement. I have nurtured a fantasy of basing a theatrical production on the open encounter, which is, in a profound sense, a type of theater, a communication. In particular, a microlab is a type of theater. Picture a theater with no seats, just a wall-to-wall rug, and a raised platform. The audience is arranged in groups of five or six as in a microlab, and when the play reaches a point where a nonverbal activity is appropriate, the play stops, and each audience group does what the actors do. They actually act out in their groups. This happens periodically so that each audience group is acting in the play, physically, then by identification. Audience involvement is almost total; every spectator is an actor.

A third area of confluence is in actor training. Already Viola Spolin, Stanislavsky, method acting, improvisational theater, and others have used the general concept of seeing the actor as playing a human role, of not acting, in a sense. Nonverbal methods add greatly to the arsenal of techniques to help the actor be in touch with himself and his body, and to understand how his body is integral to his expression of feelings.

Education. A fundamental fact of learning is that the motivation to learn is greatly related to retention. The tragedy of many political-educational leaders is that they don't understand that keeping students in the classroom studying Latin while the world explodes outside doesn't guarantee or even promote learning; further, it fails to capitalize on what could be learned, namely, the fascinating social events of the day. They don't realize that the opportunity to learn about the social phenomena now taking place right on campuses—formation of subgroups, social disobedience, minority problems, development of leadership, problems of democracy, origins of unionism, even the evolution of folk-songs—is unique in our history. That's where the energy is, and that's where important things can be learned and retained. An educator using an open encounter approach would find out where the energy is and support it with people and methods that could best convert the energy into learning.

Several educational innovations in the past few years are based on principles close to open encounter: A. S. Neill's *Summerhill*, Sylvia Ashton-Warner's *Teacher*, and George Leonard's *Education and Ecstasy*, in particular. These have in common the philosophy of starting where the student is and forming the curriculum around him. This follows the encounter concept of making use of where the primary energy is located.

Another important application of encounter to education described in *Joy* is the use of encounter groups in the classroom and in the educational community. These groups have proven extremely profitable. Rightwing opposition to such groups should be respected for children of rightwing parents. As I have often mentioned, I think it is a great mistake to force anyone into an encounter group, including children of parents who object. However, it is outrageous to allow such parents to prevent other children from entering encounter groups. The fear exhibited by the objecting parents is destructive enough to their own children, and certainly should not be allowed to affect the children of others. Educational encounter groups have proven most valuable when group members include a cross section of the educational community: parents, teachers, administrators, school board members, and students. Such groups offer an excellent opportunity for closeness and understanding throughout the entire school system.

In the most successful use of encounter groups in schools that I have participated in, we began by having a general meeting to describe encounter groups and the use we planned to put them to. Then we asked for volunteers and required written consent from both student and parent (this was at the high school level). This practice seems reasonable since encounter groups are relatively new in an educational setting and some parents are justifiably wary. This procedure also allows more cautious parents time to see what the groups do for other children, and time to give their consent when they are ready.

Hopefully, the encounter mode will eventually become a standard type of relating in schools and become an important part of teacher training. Using these groups in school situations is one answer to the question of relevance raised so often today in American education. An encounter group cannot only uncover what is relevant, that is, where the energy is, but can help a student to be more deeply aware of what is relevant to him on a personal level.

Couples. The effect on couples of using encounter has already been described fully. Suffice it to say that open encounter couples generally find a vitality and rejuvenation hard to achieve in other ways. They also must find their own way of being with each other. I'm trying out the results of my personal experience with the remarkable Christie. If it works as well as it seems it will, perhaps we will complete the book on couples I recently abandoned.

Childbirth and Parent-Child Relations. An open encounter approach to childrearing begins prenatally with attention to the mother's emotional well-being, diet, health, and spirit, and her relation to her husband. This care creates an environment in which the fetus can flourish. The delivery is done at home, as we do regularly at Big Sur, with the father delivering or aiding the delivery as much as he feels comfortable doing, with a doctor available in case of emergency. The birth room is filled with close friends. Love fills the atmosphere into which the baby is born. The delivery is by natural childbirth—the Lamaze method seems best—and the child is given to the mother immediately. The child is held and given much physical contact and warmth all over his body so that he experiences total acceptance in a warm, loving world. Sometimes chanting or some caressing sound heightens these feelings. I'm convinced that having the first contact with the outside world be this pleasant has a profound effect on a child in giving him a loving, trusting feeling about life and people.

Treating the infant as a responsible infant continues the communication. The birth situation made clear that the child was included into the social world. Treating him as a responsible person communicates respect for his competence. This means letting the child do all that he's capable of and only taking over when necessary. The communication of affection comes through touch and other nonverbal cues primarily. I find that talking to the part of a child that understands is very heartwarming, and I have the feeling that at some important level he does understand. I don't like baby talk.

My preference is to not force him to be unhappy because it will "get him ready for life" until there is no choice. The longer a child is happy and growing, the stronger and more capable he will be of coping with the world. And he is not a natural enemy, lying in wait to take advantage of the parent. He's just trying to get along like all of us, and we can help him. As he grows up, talking straight to him helps build his self-concept. It seems to be the way children talk to each other; they are natural encounterers.

Religion. Many religious leaders have become involved with open encounter during the last few years. Some feel that the group offers a vehicle for parishioners to experience what the religious service only talks about. A feeling of the brotherhood of man is a common encounter group experience. So is a glimpse of the unity of man, and the sameness of all men. Some basic tenets of the church can be understood better. Should you "love thy neighbor as thyself"? Most of us don't love ourselves very much at all. What happens if you "do unto others as you would have them do unto you"? Many of us are too guilty and seek punishment. Should we then punish others too much? How does a minister really help his parishioners with personal problems? He's not trained in that area. Encounter groups can help that situation, and so more and more clergy are entering groups.

And what about the quest for God? I said earlier that the notion of the God within each man begins to make sense to me as I gain more experience with groups. Isn't that concept very close to developing the human potential? (I see now why I don't like questions in groups. I've lapsed into asking many of them in the last two paragraphs. I find it much easier to write questions. I don't have to commit myself to anything. I'm just doing the time-honored ploy, "raising questions." Clearly I'm doing it because I feel unsure in this area.)

I do think that the encounter group offers a method for feeling and exploring many of these religious abstractions. When the encounter gets more advanced, say, to include meditation, then mystical experiences begin occurring even more frequently. Combining the encounter group with the religious experience has helped me to elevate my aspirations for the encounter group. To look for the God in man and to get in touch with his cosmic energy are becoming meaningful phrases to me and seem to transcend what I had earlier taken as encounter goals. Similarly, looking at interpersonal states in terms of energy exchanges is a religious experience that I can often feel.

Social and Political Mores. This book started with many examples of the nonencounter nature of most of our social mores. Clearly, the dishonest basis on which much of our culture is built should be changed. The phenomena of the government lying to its constituents, administrators lying to students, whites lying to blacks, businessmen lying to tax officers, and governments lying to other governments have led to growing revolt. Open encounter is relevant to this dilemma in several ways.

Several communities have found that they must do something after the confrontation and violence. What happens after a revolt succeeds? What do you do if everyone is willing to sit and talk, have a dialogue, communicate, and listen? In order to make the dialogue most meaningful it must be in an encounter mode. Self-deceptive politeness won't work. Neither does strategy and game-playing. When the people of York, Pennsylvania, got together after much strife and talked for days, one of their chief recommendations was encounter groups for schools. When students went to Washington after Nixon's Cambodia decision and started talking to government officials, one student described the experience as a spontaneous encounter group. Groups are springing up of black-white, police-radical, and occasionally of student-administrator components.

One disagreement I have with the radicals who feel that the system has broken down and needs replacement is that the system has never been tried with honesty as its core way of relating. I'm not ready to give up on the Establishment. There are too many more variations to try. Nor do I feel that it's unrealistic to think that the Establishment can become more honest. Too many "miracles" have occurred in the past two decades to rule out anything. I'd like to see the counterculture evolve into the encounter culture.

Another social application of encounter is the uniting of the revolutions. The social revolutions, the blacks, the students, and the environment need the insight of the personal revolution of encounter groups to keep themselves centered and to separate personal needs from their social goals. The personal revolution needs the social revolutions to keep in touch with the environment and make the personal work relate to the national scene. It is of little value to make a man personally fulfilled and free if he lives in a repressive society. And it is of little value to have a free society if men are prisoners within their own bodies. There are signs of these revolutions coming together.

In politics, the concept of an honest politician, who knows himself and who is candid with his constitutents—even to the point of admitting his own weaknesses—follows from an open encounter orientation. A politician who, like an encounter group leader, can sense the feelings of his constituents, help them get expressed, know his own feelings, use all of these sources of data, and take responsibility for making his own decision is the ideal—an encounter politician. Calls for better communication are usually calls for encounter. I see some politicians going in the direction of honesty and self-awareness, and more, I see the demand for this type of public service becoming a groundswell.

Alongside this model the present manner of political administration seems to be a monstrosity, a horrendous web of intrigue, secrecy, clandestine plots, spies, press secretaries, "no comments," back-room arm-twisting, and power plays. Indeed, the lack of credibility of the government has increased so astonishingly that enormous amounts of governmental energy must be tied up in establishing this false picture. *The New Yorker* of April 18, 1970, had an excellent statement of this phenomenon:

In the days when the [Vietnam] debate was still vigorous, opponents of the war used to find it helpful to expose false claims made by the government, and to point out ironies and contradictions in government policy. They used to say things like "The body count is exaggerated, and anyway a body count is no real measure of success," or, "The pacification program isn't going as well as the government says it is," or, "The South Vietnamese elections are rigged, and the Saigon regime is a dictatorship and doesn't have the support of its own people." And finally they pieced together the ultimate irony—that we seemed actually to be physically destroying the country we were supposed to be saving. In the last year or so, however, opponents of the war have found that it is inadequate to repeat these arguments. Perhaps one reason is that the gap between the official explanations and the realities we are faced with daily on television and in the newspapers has become so staggeringly huge and so obvious that when one persists in making these points one feels almost ludicrously sim-pleminded. Also, pointing out discrepancies between the official ver-sions and the realities seems to presume a rationality in the whole enterprise that is now revealed to be entirely lacking. . . . The disparity between the official policy and the reality is now so great that it ap-pears as though policy is developing in accordance with a set of rules that will be responsive to the political situation in America but that the actual conduct of the war is developing according to a completely separate set of rules, determined by the conditions of unspeakable brutality and confusion in Vietnam itself.

I feel somewhat diffident writing this because I have never run a large organization or been a politician. But I am abso-lutely certain that political behavior can be honest, effective, and successful.

Daily Life. What about the application of open encounter to everyday living? Certainly each one of us can work on self-insight, on getting more in touch with the body, on being more honest with feelings, more sensitive to what is happening to the organism as a whole. Simple things like awareness of breathing and muscle tensions and listening to body pains and illness to see what they are saying are possible to observe. Getting one's self together, having thoughts, feelings, body, and spirit inte-grated, is something that awareness can enhance.

Relating to people more honestly is certainly possible. Find someone you have withheld something from and tell it to him. See what happens. Next time you feel like touching someone, do it. Next time you are hurt or frightened, express it. When you catch yourself trying to project an image, stop, and see if you can be real instead. If you're embarrassed to pay someone a compliment, do it anyway. If you want to know how people respond to you, ask them.

Do this, as Dylan says, at your own chosen speed. But go a little further than you think you can. That's where the growth is. Realize that you are responsible for yourself. You are the primary determiner of your fate. Stop blaming everyone else for your troubles. You can do something about them. Taking responsibility for yourself usually feels marvelous.

In short, find the God that's within you. He's there. You're there. Get in touch. Feel the energy coming from your center and radiating out. That's the power within you. Let it come out, and let it join with other people's energy, and let's do what is within all of us, alone and together.

Here comes everybody.

Appendix: What Next?

This appendix is for those people who are interested in pursuing some of the methods or ideas in this book. There are now over one hundred available growth centers in this country, Canada, Mexico, and England that are more or less modeled after Esalen, and there are many available books if you want to read further about any of these methods. These books also constitute a reading list for the group leader training program referred to above. Along with that reading list is included a group of workshops and workshop leaders I have found valuable. These workshops would be a part of the training program, and would also provide some guidelines for people who simply want a personal experience.

If you want to know anything about Esalen, write to the San Francisco office with the wonderfully patriotic address: Esalen, 1776 Union, San Francisco, California, 94123.

Workshops Recommended for an Open Encounter Group Leader Training Program (as of the writing of this book):

The type of workshop is listed on the left. At least one of each type should be experienced. People listed on the right are those I feel run a very good workshop. There are undoubtedly many more who do. These are simply those I'm familiar with. When there is a criterion for a qualified leader, I've listed the place to write for a copy of that list in the footnote.

EXPERIENCES IN WORKSHOPS

What	Who
Psychodrama	J. L. Moreno, Hannah Weiner (Watching demonstrations is also good.)*1
Fantasy	Robert Gerard, William Swartley, Frank Haronian
Bioenergetics	John Pierrakos, Alex Lowen, Stanley Keleman
Rolf treatments	*2
Body movement	Mary Whitehouse, Judy Aston, Ann Halprin
Breathing	Magda Proskauer
Sensory and Body Awareness	Charlotte Selver, Ed Maupin
Sensory Awakening	Bernard Gunther
Alexander Lessons	Ilana Rubenfeld*3
Theater Games	Viola Spolin, Alan Meyerson
Hypnotism	Steven Stroud
Psychomotor Therapy	Albert Pesso
Gestalt Therapy	Janet Lederman, James Simkin, Claudio Naranjo, Jack Downing, Dick Price
Hatha Yoga	Joel Kramer
Tai-Chi	Don't know it well enough
Group Psychoanalysis	Qualified psychoanalysts
Human Anatomy & Physiology	Standard university course
Inductive Logic	Standard university course
Massage	Esalen masseurs
Meditation and Massage	Seymour Carter, Molly Day Shackman
Meditation	Zen Center, Mike Murphy, John Heider
Synanon Game	Synanon House
Couples' Group	Betty Fuller

1*For qualified psychodramatists, write to:
   J. L. Moreno
   Psychodrama Institute
   Beacon, New York

   Also, the Moreno Institute conducts nightly demonstrations at:
   236 West 78th Street,
   New York, New York 10024

2*For qualified Rolf practitioners, write to:
   Guild for Structural Integration
   1874 Fell Street
   San Francisco, California 94117

3*For qualified Alexander practitioners, write to:
   Ilana Rubenfeld
   c/o American Center for the Alexander Technique
   115 Waverly Place
   New York, New York 10011

Books and Journals

ALEXANDER TECHNIQUE
Alexander, F. Matthais. *Resurrection of the Body.* ed. E. Maisel. New York: University Books, 1969.

BIOENERGETIC EXERCISES
Baker, E. *Man in the Trap.* New York: Macmillan, 1967.
Energy and Character (journal). ed. D. Boadella. Abbotsbury, Dorset, England.
Lowen, A. *Betrayal of the Body.* New York: Macmillan, 1967.
————. *Love and Orgasm.* New York: Macmillan, 1965.
————. *The Physical Dynamics of Character Structure.* New York: Grune, 1958.
————. *Pleasure.* New York: Coward-McCann, 1970.
Reich, W. *Character Analysis.* New York: Orgone Institute Press, 1949.
————. *Function of the Orgasm.* New York: Bantam Books, 1967.

ENERGY

Gallert, M. *New Light on Therapeutic Energies.* London: Clarke & Co., 1966.

FANTASY

Assagioli, R. *Psychosynthesis.* New York: Hobbs, Dorman & Co., 1965.

Publications of Hanscarl Leuner and Robert Desiolle are available from the Psychosynthesis Research Foundation, Room 314, 527 Lexington Avenue, New York, New York 10017.

GESTALT THERAPY

Perls, F. *Ego, Hunger and Aggression.* New York: Vintage Books, 1969.

―――. *Gestalt Therapy Verbatim.* Lafayette, Calif.: Real People Press, 1969.

―――. *In and Out the Garbage Pail.* Lafayette, Calif.: Real People Press, 1969.

Perls, F., Hefferline, R., and Goodman, P. *Gestalt Therapy.* New York: Delta Books, 1951.

MYSTICISM (Selected Titles)

Achad, F. *The Anatomy of the Body of God.* New York: Samuel Weiser, 1969.

Avalon, A. *Serpent Power.* Madras, India: Ganesha, 1964.

Bucke, R. M. *Cosmic Consciousness.* New York: Dutton, 1967.

Fox, O. *Astral Projection.* New York: University Books, 1962.

Kueshana, E. *The Ultimate Frontier.* Chicago: Stelle, 1963.

Leadbeater, C. *The Chakras.* Madras, India: Theosophical Publishing House, 1968.

Mayananda. *The Tarot for Today.* New York: Zeus Press, 1968.

Rele, V. *The Mysterious Kundalini.* Bombay, India: D. B. Taraporevala, 1960.

Rudhyar, Dane. *The Astrology of Personality*. New York: Doubleday, 1970.

Shah, I. *The Sufis*. New York: Doubleday, 1964.

Wilhelm, H. *Eight Lectures on the I Ching*. New York: Harper & Row, 1969.

NONVERBAL ANALYSIS

Darwin, C. *The Expression of the Emotions in Man and Animals*. Chicago: Phoenix, 1965.

PSYCHODRAMA

Moreno, J. L. *Who Shall Survive?* New York: Nervous and Mental Disease Publishing Co., 1934.

ROLFING

Bulletin of Structural Integration, 16756 Marquez Ave. Pacific Palisades, California 90272.

Rolf, Ida. *Structural Integration*. Available from Esalen Books, Big Sur, California 93920.

SENSORY AWARENESS

Gunther, B. *Sense Awakening*. New York: Macmillan, 1968.

TAI-CHI CHUAN

Feng, Gia-Fu. *Tai-Chi, A Way of Centering and I Ching*. New York: Collier Books, 1970.

THEATER GAMES

Spolin, Viola. *Improvisation for the Theater*. Evanston, Ill.: Northwestern University Press, 1963.

YOGA

Vishundevananda, Swami. *The Complete Illustrated Book of Yoga*. New York: Bell, 1960.

ZONE THERAPY
Fitzgerald, W. H. *Zone Therapy*. Health Research, 70 Lafayette St., Mokelninne, California 95245.

OTHER BOOKS
Campbell, J. *The Hero with a Thousand Faces*. New York: Meridian Books, 1967.
———. *The Masks of God* (4 vols.). New York: Viking Press, 1968.
Laing, R. D. *The Politics of Experience*. New York: Ballantine Books, 1967.
And, oh yes:
Schutz, W. C. *FIRO: A Three-Dimensional Theory of Interpersonal Behavior*. Reprinted as *The Interpersonal Underworld*. Palo Alto, Calif.: Science and Behavior Books, 1966.
———. *Joy*. New York: Grove Press, 1967.

For a list of growth centers patterned after Esalen, write to: Association of Humanistic Psychology, 574 Page Street, San Francisco, California 94117.

Index